Collins

A2 Revision**Notes**
Psychology

Mike Cardwell • Cara Flanagan

Series editor: Jayne de Courcy

William Collins' dream of knowledge for all began with the publication of his first book in 1819. A self-educated mill worker, he not only enriched millions of lives, but also founded a flourishing publishing house. Today, staying true to this spirit, Collins books are packed with inspiration, innovation and practical expertise. They place you at the centre of a world of possibility and give you exactly what you need to explore it.

Collins. Do more.

Published by Collins
An imprint of HarperCollins*Publishers*
77 – 85 Fulham Palace Road
Hammersmith
London
W6 8JB

Browse the complete Collins catalogue at
www.collinseducation.com

© HarperCollins*Publishers* Limited 2006

10 9 8 7 6 5 4 3 2 1

ISBN-13 978 0 00 720696 4
ISBN-10 0 00 720696 8

Mike Cardwell and Cara Flanagan assert the moral right to be identified as the authors of this work

British Library Cataloguing in Publication Data
A Catalogue record for this publication is available from the British Library

Edited by Jenny Draine
Production by Katie Butler
Series and book design by Sally Boothroyd
Artwork by Jerry Fowler
Index compiled by Joan Dearnley
Printed and bound by Printing Express, Hong Kong

You might also like to visit
www.harpercollins.co.uk
The book lover's website

CONTENTS

HOW THIS BOOK WILL HELP YOU   vi

1 RELATIONSHIPS

Explanations and research studies of interpersonal attraction	1
Theories and research studies of the formation of relationships	3
Psychological explanations of love	5
Explanations and research studies relating to the breakdown of relationships	7
Relationships in different cultures	9
Understudied relationships	11

2 PRO- AND ANTI-SOCIAL BEHAVIOUR

Social psychological theories of aggression	13
Research on environmental stressors	15
Explanations and research studies of altruism/bystander behaviour	17
Cultural differences in pro-social behaviour	19
Media influences on pro-social behaviour	21
Media influences on anti-social behaviour	23

3 BIOLOGICAL RHYTHMS

Research into circadian, infradian and ultradian rhythms	25
Endogenous pacemakers, exogenous zeitgebers and the consequences of disrupting biological rhythms	27
Ecological theories and research studies relating to the functions of sleep	29
Restoration theories of sleep and research studies relating to the functions of sleep	31
Research relating to the nature of dreams	33
Theories of the function of dreaming	35

4 MOTIVATION AND EMOTION

Role of brain structures in motivational states	37
Physiological, combined and psychological approaches to explaining motivation	39
Emotion	41

5 ATTENTION AND PATTERN RECOGNITION

Explanations of focused attention	43
Explanations of divided attention	45
Controlled and automatic processing	46
Pattern recognition	47
Face recognition	48

6 PERCEPTUAL PROCESSES AND DEVELOPMENT

Structure and functions of the visual system	49
Nature of visual information processing	50
Constructivist theories of visual perception	51
Direct theories of visual perception	52
Explanations of perceptual organisation	53
Infant studies of perceptual development	55
Cross-cultural studies of perceptual development	56
Explanations of perceptual development	57
The nature–nurture debate in perception	58

7 COGNITIVE DEVELOPMENT

Piaget's theory   59
Vygotsky's theory   61
Applications of Piaget's and Vygotsky's theories   63
Development of intelligence test performance   65
Theories of moral understanding/pro-social reasoning   67
Influences on moral understanding   69

8 SOCIAL AND PERSONAL DEVELOPMENT

Psychodynamic explanations of personality development   71
Social learning explanations of personality development   73
Explanations of gender development   75
Social development and formation of identity in adolescence   77
Adolescent relationships and cultural differences in behaviour   79

9 DETERMINANTS OF ANIMAL BEHAVIOUR

Evolutionary explanations of the behaviour of non-human animals   81
Classical conditioning and its role in the behaviour of non-human animals   83
Operant conditioning and its role in the behaviour of non-human animals   85
Explanations and research studies of social learning   87
Intelligence in non-human animals   88

IO EVOLUTIONARY EXPLANATIONS OF HUMAN BEHAVIOUR

Sexual selection and human reproductive behaviour   89
Evolutionary explanations of parental investment   90
Evolutionary explanations of mental disorders   91
Evolution of intelligence   93

II PSYCHOPATHOLOGY

Psychopathology – clinical characteristics of schizophrenia, depression
    and anxiety disorders   95
Schizophrenia   97
Depression   99
Anxiety disorders   101

I2 TREATING MENTAL DISORDERS

Biological therapies   105
Behavioural therapies   107
Alternatives to biological and behavioural therapies   109

I3 ISSUES

Gender bias in psychological theories and studies   113
Cultural bias in psychological theories and studies   115
Ethical issues and socially sensitive research   117
    Non-human animals in psychological research   119

14 DEBATES IN PSYCHOLOGY

Free will and determinism   121
Reductionism   123
Psychology as a science   125
Nature–nurture   127

15 APPROACHES IN PSYCHOLOGY

The behavioural approach   129
The psychodynamic approach   131
The biological approach   133

INDEX   135

HOW THIS BOOK WILL HELP YOU

This book has been designed to make your revision as easy and effective as possible.

Here's how:

SHORT, ACCESSIBLE NOTES THAT YOU CAN INTEGRATE INTO YOUR REVISION FILE

Collins Revision Notes A2 Psychology have been prepared by top examiners who know exactly what you need to revise in order to be successful.

You can *either* base your revision on this book *or* you can tear off the notes and integrate them into your own revision file. This will ensure that you have the best possible notes to revise from.

STUDENT-FRIENDLY PRESENTATION

The notes use visual aids – flowcharts, tables, boxes, etc. – so the content is easier to remember.

There is also systematic use of colour to help you revise:

MUST KNOW...
Green panels summarise what you need to revise.

MUST REMEMBER ...
Red panels draw attention to key aspects.

MUST TAKE CARE...
Purple panels highlight tricky areas.

Dark blue outline and tint panels contain research studies.

Orange outline and tint panels indicate AO2 commentary and evaluation.

Green outline *panels contain short hints for using the information in exam questions.*

Yellow highlighting or bold emphasise important words and phrases.

CONTENT MATCHED TO YOUR SPECIFICATION

This book has primarily been designed to cover the AQA A2 Psychology specification. If you are following the OCR A2 Psychology specification, you will still find it useful to revise from this book and its companion, *Collins Revision Notes AS Psychology*.

GUIDANCE ON EXAM TECHNIQUE

This book concentrates on providing you with the best possible revision notes.

At the end of each unit there are also some typical questions, with hints, so that you can see how you will need to apply your knowledge. If you want more guidance on exam technique, then use *Collins Do Brilliantly A2 Psychology* in conjunction with these Revision Notes.

Using both these books will help you to achieve a high grade in your A2 Psychology exams.

EXPLANATIONS AND RESEARCH STUDIES OF INTERPERSONAL ATTRACTION

THE FILTER MODEL OF ATTRACTION

The 'filter model' theory in a nutshell
People rely on a number of social and personal factors to filter potential friends and romantic partners from the 'field of eligibles'.

Similarity
People are drawn to individuals who have perceived similarity in important characteristics (e.g. beliefs, interests, attitudes, personality). These can help us to become attracted to others who match.

Complementarity of needs
We are attracted to those with personality traits different from our own, i.e. qualities that fulfil our needs. This brings together people who complement each other, e.g. dominant/submissive, extrovert/introvert.

THE FILTER MODEL OF ATTRACTION (KERCKHOFF AND DAVIS, 1962)

Proximity
Most people form relationships with other people who live close by. People get to know each others' characteristics more easily, and frequent interaction increases non-verbal feedback which may reaffirm attraction.

Physical attractiveness
When one person is physically attracted to another, there is an increased desire to interact with them. Research has shown that men are more influenced by the physical attractiveness of women than are women by the attractiveness of men.

Competence
People are more attracted to others who appear intelligent and competent than those who are less so. Some people appear to be 'too perfect', therefore Aronson (1976) suggests we are more attracted to people who have at least one glaring fault.

THE MATCHING HYPOTHESIS

The matching hypothesis in a nutshell
People are attracted to those who are perceived as having a similar level of physical attractiveness to their own.

The nature of matching
Although we are attracted to, and desire people with a higher level of physical attractiveness than our own, we tend to form relationships with those we perceive to be about as attractive as we perceive ourselves to be.

Consequences of mismatching
In relationships which are mismatched, the less attractive partner may feel insecure and jealous of the attention given to their more attractive partner. This may place strains on the relationship and threaten its long-term success.

THE MATCHING HYPOTHESIS (WALSTER ET AL., 1966)

Attraction and rejection
There are benefits of having an attractive partner (e.g. it boosts our self-esteem), but there are possible costs involved. These include possible rejection if they do not see us as attractive, and other related costs (e.g. jealousy).

Matching over time
With the passing of time, any effects that might diminish the perceived attractiveness of our partner (e.g. boredom) appear to be balanced by others which tend to increase it (e.g. familiarity) (Yela and Sangrador, 2001).

Partner perception
Research (e.g. Yela and Sangrador, 2001) suggests that despite the matching effect, we tend to have a biased perception of our partner as being a little more attractive than ourselves.

RESEARCH SUPPORT FOR THE FILTER MODEL

SIMILARITY (NEWCOMB, 1961)
- Offered free accommodation to students who were initially strangers to each other. Each student was randomly allocated a room mate.

FINDINGS
- The most stable friendships developed between room mates from the same type of background and those with the same attitudes and interests.

One reason why...
Similarity is important because it leads to validation of our beliefs. If others express similar attitudes and beliefs, then we can feel more confident that we are right. As a result, we find those people more attractive.

PROXIMITY (FESTINGER ET AL., 1950)
- Studied patterns of attraction and friendship formation in a student apartment block in US university residences.

FINDINGS
- People were more likely to become friends with those who lived close by, e.g. 44% lived next door to each other, 22% two doors away, etc.

This suggests that...
Psychological distance is more important than physical distance. Some people were more likely to form relationships because of mere 'exposure'.

PHYSICAL ATTRACTIVENESS (WALSTER ET AL., 1966)
- After taking part in a 'computer dance' where they had been randomly matched with a partner, students were asked how much they liked their 'date' and how much they wanted to go out with them again.

FINDINGS
- Physical attractiveness of the partner was the biggest single factor for males in determining how much they liked their date and whether they wanted to see her again. This was irrespective of the attractiveness of the male.

Criticism
This study has been criticised as it bears very little relationship to real-life. In Western cultures, people are rarely assigned dating partners. This limits the relevance of this study to an understanding of real-life relationships.

RESEARCH SUPPORT FOR THE MATCHING HYPOTHESIS

WALSTER AND WALSTER (1969)
- As an extension to the 'computer dance' study, students were allowed to state what kind of dating partner (i.e. how attractive) they wanted, in advance.

FINDINGS
- This time students did not just choose the most attractive people as potential dating partners, but chose someone of comparable physical attractiveness to themselves.

This suggests that...
Because students now had the opportunity to think more about what they wanted in a potential partner, they were more realistic in their choices. This supports the claim in the matching hypothesis that people tend to form relationships with those perceived to be of a similar level of attractiveness.

MURSTEIN (1972)
- Photographs of couples who were 'going steady' or engaged were compared with the faces of random couples in terms of physical attractiveness.

FINDINGS
- The real couples were judged as being more similar to each other in terms of physical attractiveness than were the randomly pairs of males and females.

This shows that...
People are more likely to initiate a relationship with someone with a similar market value, thus supporting the matching hypothesis.

TYPICAL QUESTIONS...

1 Outline and evaluate two or more explanations of interpersonal attraction. (24 marks)

2 (a) Outline two or more explanations of interpersonal attraction. (12 marks)

(b) Evaluate the two or more explanations of interpersonal attraction that you outlined in (a) in terms of relevant research studies. (12 marks)

3 Describe and evaluate research studies of interpersonal attraction. (24 marks)

4 Discuss research (explanations and/or studies) of interpersonal attraction. (24 marks)

THEORIES AND RESEARCH STUDIES OF THE FORMATION OF RELATIONSHIPS

MUST KNOW...
- Two theories of the formation of relationships.

REINFORCEMENT-AFFECT THEORY

Reinforcement-affect theory in a nutshell

We like people who satisfy our needs, e.g. we like people who make us feel good about ourselves.

Operant conditioning
People may reward us directly, perhaps by meeting our psychological needs (such as the need for friendship, love or sex). This type of reinforcement is explained by the theory of operant conditioning.

Attractive people
Argyle (1992) claims that individuals who are rewarding (e.g. they are friendly, helpful and cheerful) tend to be liked most. As a result, they are the people who tend to be chosen for relationships, rather than those who are less rewarding, or are associated with an unhappy event or negative state of mind.

REINFORCEMENT-AFFECT THEORY (BYRNE AND CLORE, 1970)

Classical conditioning
People may also reward us *indirectly*, in that they are associated with pleasant circumstances. This type of reinforcement is explained by the theory of classical conditioning.

Affect
If we meet someone when we are in a good mood, we may associate that person with our good mood. As a result, we like them more and are more likely to enter into a relationship with them.

Reinforcement
Because some people are directly associated with reinforcement (i.e. they provide it), we like them more and so are more likely to enter into a relationship with them.

HUMAN NEEDS AFFECTING SOCIAL BEHAVIOUR

Needs/Motives	How relationships help meet needs
Biological needs	e.g. Collective eating and drinking behaviours.
Dependency	e.g. Being comforted or nurtured.
Affiliation	e.g. Seeking the company and approval of others.
Dominance	e.g. Making decisions for other people, being 'bossy'.
Sex	e.g. Flirting, making love.
Aggression	e.g. Engaging in football violence.
Self-esteem and ego identity	e.g. Being valued by others.

MUST REMEMBER...
That exam questions **can** ask for just **one** theory, but more usually ask for an outline of **two** theories.

Source: adapted from Argyle (1994)

COMMENTARY ON REINFORCEMENT-AFFECT THEORY

Limitations
- In non-Western collectivist cultures, reinforcement does not appear to play a significant part in the formation of social relationships.
- For example, Hill (1970) found that kinship bonds are far more important than satisfaction of individual needs.
- This suggests that this theory may only apply to relationships in Western, individualist cultures, where personal goals are more important.

Giving and receiving reward
- In a study of student friendships, Hays (1985) found that as much value was given to rewarding others as was given to receiving rewards ourselves.
- The key factor for successful relationships appears to be having a balance between both giving and receiving.
- The fact that *equity* in a relationship is more important than the maximisation of personal benefits undermines any theory based purely on reinforcement alone.

Gender differences
- There are gender differences in the application of reinforcement-affect theory.
- Research has shown that in many cultures, women are socialised into being more attentive to the needs of others rather than the gratification of their personal needs (Lott, 1994).
- However, it may be argued that for many, the gratification of others' needs may itself be reinforcing.

SOCIAL EXCHANGE THEORY

Social exchange theory in a nutshell

All human relationships are developed on the basis of a subjective cost-benefit analysis and the comparison of alternatives to the current relationship.

Rewards and costs
- People exchange resources with the expectation that the rewards will exceed the costs incurred.
- Rewards from a relationship include being cared for, companionship and sex.
- Costs include effort, financial investment and missed opportunities with others.

MUST TAKE CARE...
To elaborate critical points to make them **effective**.

Profit and loss
- A relationship produces a profit if the calculation of rewards minus costs produces a positive outcome.
- Social exchange theory predicts that any commitment to a relationship is dependent on the profitability (or not) of this outcome.

Stages in a relationship
- Sampling: a person considers potential costs and rewards of a new relationship and compares it to other available relationships.
- Bargaining: partners give and receive rewards which test whether a deeper relationship is worthwhile.
- Commitment: partners know how to elicit rewards from each other and costs are lowered.
- Institutionalisation: norms are developed which establish the pattern of rewards and costs for each partner.

SOCIAL EXCHANGE THEORY (THIBAUT AND KELLEY, 1959)

Comparison level for alternatives (CLa)
- A person may also weigh up any potential increase in rewards from a different partner, *less* any costs associated with ending the current relationship.
- If the profit level is significantly higher in a new relationship, this may lead to them ending their current relationship in favour of the new one.

Comparison level (CL)
- Our CL helps us to judge whether a new relationship is likely to be worthwhile.
- The CL is a product of our experiences in other relationships plus general views of what we might expect from this particular exchange.
- If the potential profit in a new relationship exceeds our CL, the relationship is judged as worthwhile.

COMMENTARY ON SOCIAL EXCHANGE THEORY

Limitations
- The theory sees people motivated only by selfish concerns, therefore may only apply to relationships in individualist rather than collectivist cultures.
- Research has suggested that people are more motivated by the need for a balance in rewards and costs rather than simply trying to maximise their profits. This led to the development of equity theory to take this into account.

Profit and loss
- Social exchange theory has been used to explain why some women stay in abusive relationships.
- Rusbult and Martz (1995) argue that if investments are high (e.g. young children) and alternatives are low (e.g. divorce would lead to a significant reduction in living standards) this makes ending the relationship less profitable than staying.

Strengths
- The theory can be used to explain individual differences in the way people respond to relationships.
- People perceive the profits and losses of relationships differently and what is acceptable for one person may not be acceptable for another.
- Over time, alternatives may change and this changes the person's comparison level accordingly.

TYPICAL QUESTIONS...

1 Outline and evaluate two or more theories of the formation of relationships. (24 marks)

2 Discuss research (theories and/or studies) into the formation of relationships. (24 marks)

3 Describe and evaluate one or more theories of the formation of relationships. (24 marks)

PSYCHOLOGICAL EXPLANATIONS OF LOVE

THREE-FACTOR THEORY

Three-factor theory in a nutshell
In a **love-oriented culture**, the presence of a **love object** plus the presence of **physiological arousal** = **LOVE**.

Physiological arousal
• In certain circumstances, our emotional experience is determined by a general arousal state, which the individual then interprets by referring to external factors or cues.
• If we are in the presence of a desired lover, we may become sexually aroused, and so interpret this state of arousal as 'love'.

Appropriate love object
• In order to fall in love, we need a recipient for our desires.
• Appropriate criteria would include gender, age, attractiveness, and any other factors that may be determined by our culture or our personal preferences.
• Some people may be inappropriate because they are not sufficiently attractive or they are committed to someone else.

THREE-FACTOR THEORY (HATFIELD AND WALSTER, 1981)

Cultural exposure
• Our culture provides a model of love so we can make sense of our experience.
• This points our attention in certain directions, e.g. research has shown that the more we think about love, the more likely we are to fall in love, and the more we believe in 'love at first sight', the more likely it will happen to us.

TRIANGULAR THEORY OF LOVE

Triangular theory in a nutshell
Different types of love can be explained as different combinations of **intimacy, passion** and **commitment**, which change over time as the relationship develops.

Components of love
• Intimacy: a feeling of closeness between two people, characterised by mutual dependence, supporting and sharing.
• Passion: the drive that leads to intense feelings, physical attraction and sexual involvement.
• Commitment: making a deliberate choice to stay with someone and to forego similar relationships with others.

TRIANGULAR THEORY OF LOVE (STERNBERG, 1986)

Types of love
• Different types of love determined by the presence or absence of the three components of love or the relative importance of one over the others.
• If love only has passion it is 'infatuation', if it has only intimacy, it is 'liking', if it has only commitment, it is 'contractual' love. If all three are present, it is consummate love.

These are three points of a triangle, with all types of relationship being bounded within that triangle.

PASSION / INTIMACY / COMMITMENT

EVALUATION OF THE THREE-FACTOR THEORY

MUST REMEMBER...
Not just to **describe** an alternative explanation but to **use** it as part of a critical commentary on the theory being evaluated.

APPROPRIATE LOVE OBJECT

- Sternberg (2000) challenges the view that love can be analysed purely in terms of different constituent factors.

- He suggests instead that love between two people follows a story which begins in childhood, as people form stories about what they believe love should be.

- The key to romantic compatibility with a partner is whether our stories match (e.g. the 'fairytale story' – of prince and princess, or the 'gardening story' – that love must be nurtured to survive).

- This is in direct contrast to Hatfield and Walster's claim that physiological arousal is a necessary component of love.

ROMANTIC OR SEXUAL LOVE?

- Huang (2003) suggests that it is possible to experience romantic love without physiological arousal.

- He tested the impact of romantic love and passionate (sexual) love on consumers' attitude to advertisements based on these themes.

- The impact of the two sub-types of love demonstrated distinctive paths of attitude change following the different advertisements.

- This suggests that not all types of romantic love are sexual, i.e. there is an undervaluation of romantic love as an independent theme in advertisements.

EVALUATION OF THE TRIANGULAR THEORY OF LOVE

RESEARCH SUPPORT

- Sternberg (1998) has provided research evidence to support this theory.

- He found that couples with compatible triangles tended to be more satisfied in their relationships than were couples with less compatible triangles.

- All three components of love (passion, intimacy and commitment) were found to be predictive of satisfaction in close relationships.

RELIABILITY AND VALIDITY

- The validity and reliability of Sternberg's Triangular Love Scale was tested by Hale and Lemieux (1999).

- They tested undergraduate students to see if the three components were present in any of their relationships.

- The results showed that although the scale was valid (i.e. it did measure different types of love), it was not reliable (i.e. it failed to give consistent results over time).

CULTURAL DIFFERENCES IN LOVE

Is romantic love universal?

- It is commonly believed that love is an important prerequisite for marriage in individualistic societies but is less important in collectivistic societies (Dion and Dion, 1996), where arranged marriages are common.

- However, passionate love has been found even in societies that do not approve of it, suggesting that the Western version of romantic love exists in all societies but is expressed in differing forms.

If romantic love is not found in all cultures, it would challenge the view that this is a universal aspect of human behaviour and would limit the value of these theories.

For practice in answering A2 Psychology questions, why not use *Collins Do Brilliantly A2 Psychology*?

TYPICAL QUESTIONS...

1 Outline and evaluate two psychological explanations of love. (24 marks)

2 Describe and evaluate one or more psychological explanations of love. (24 marks)

EXPLANATIONS AND RESEARCH STUDIES RELATING TO THE BREAKDOWN OF RELATIONSHIPS

DUCK'S MODEL OF RELATIONSHIP DISSOLUTION (DUCK, 1988)

Intra-psychic phase
One of the partners becomes increasingly dissatisfied with the relationship. If this dissatisfaction is sufficiently great, there is progression to the next phase.

Dyadic phase
The other partner now becomes involved. If the dissatisfaction is not acceptably resolved, there is progression to the next phase.

Social phase
The break-up is now made public to friends and family. The social implications (e.g. division of the home or care of the children) are negotiated. If the relationship is not saved here, it progresses to the final phase.

Grave-dressing phase
Each partner begins the organisation of their post-relationship lives and 'publicise' their own accounts of the breakdown. These tend to absolve the person from blame so that they may still be seen as a suitable new partner for others.

These commentary points are general and so can be used for either explanation.

REASONS FOR THE BREAKDOWN OF RELATIONSHIPS (DUCK, 1999)

Lack of skills
Some people find relationships difficult because they lack the necessary social skills to make the relationship satisfying for themselves and for their partner. Because of this lack of skills, others may perceive them as not being interested in maintaining the relationship and so it tends to break down.

Lack of stimulation
Duck claims that lack of stimulation (i.e. boredom) is a common reason for breaking off a relationship. As people expect relationships to develop, when they do not, this is seen as a reason to end the relationship or begin a new one.

Maintenance difficulties
In some circumstances relationships become strained simply because partners cannot maintain close contact. This means that the relationship cannot be properly maintained, and so there is pressure for its dissolution.

EVIDENCE FOR DUCK'S REASONS FOR RELATIONSHIP BREAKDOWN

- Some relationships do survive despite the maintenance difficulties associated with long distance relationships. Rohlfing (1995) found that 70% of students had experienced at least one long-distance romantic relationship. Holt and Stone (1988) claim that relationship satisfaction can be maintained provided partners/lovers are able to see each other on a regular basis.

- It is possible that these factors only apply to certain groups of people. For example, the processes involved in the *formation* of relationships in non-Western cultures are known to be different, therefore it is likely that there will be different pressures operating during their dissolution.

Is the model universal?
There is some evidence (Masuda, 2001) that this model applies to Japan as well as Western cultures, but there are differences. For example, in Japan, as in other collectivist cultures, the social network plays a more prominent part in helping the couple work through problems before they get out of hand.

Does research support the model?
Research has not really supported the whole model, although there are aspects of the model that have support. For example, in the dyadic phase, partners not only spend more time talking to their partner about the relationship, but the amount of time spent with people outside the couple appears to decline sharply.

COMMENTARY ON DUCK'S EXPLANATIONS OF RELATIONSHIP BREAKDOWN

Are there sex differences?
Men and women tend to focus differently on relationships, with women paying more attention to the details of the relationship, and are more sensitive to the ways in which it is failing to live up to expectations. Despite this, the reasons given for breaking up relationships are the same for both sexes.

RESEARCH STUDIES INTO THE BREAKDOWN OF RELATIONSHIPS

LEE (1984)

- Analysed the results of a survey of 112 break-ups of pre-marital relationships and found evidence of five distinct stages.

FINDINGS

- Exposure (**E**) and negotiation (**N**) were experienced as the most intense and negative stages.
- In some cases, individuals missed out these stages and went straight from **D** (dissatisfaction) to **T** (termination).

This shows that...

- There are individual differences in the route people take through this process:
  - those who went, reported having felt less intimate with their partner during the relationship
  - whereas those who had a long journey from **D** to **T** had more attraction for their former partner, and experienced the most loneliness following the break-up.
- This was confirmed by Akert (1992) who found that those who did not initiate the break-up were more likely to report high levels of loneliness and depression compared with those who did initiate the break-up of the relationship.

An implication of this research is that...

The early stages of the dissolution process tend to be more important than the later stages, particularly the painful stages of exposure and negotiation.

ARGYLE AND HENDERSON (1984)

- They asked people to think of a friendship that had broken down (for reasons attributable to the relationship itself) and then asked them to rate the extent to which the breakdown had been caused by a failure to keep friendship rules.

FINDINGS

- They found the rule violations that were most critical in relationship breakdown included:
  1. jealousy
  2. lack of tolerance for a relationship with a third party
  3. disclosing confidences to others
  4. not volunteering help when needed
  5. criticising the other person publicly.

MUST TAKE CARE...

To balance the AO1 and AO2 material in answers to any questions in this area.

MUST REMEMBER...

That some of these studies can be used as research support (AO2) for the explanations overleaf.

INDIVIDUAL DIFFERENCES

- Argyle and Henderson's research discovered some important individual differences regarding tolerance to these rule violations:
  - women identified 'lack of emotional support' as a critical factor in the breakdown of relationships, whereas men thought 'absence of fun' was of greater importance
  - younger participants identified 'being criticised in public' as a critical factor, whereas older participants thought 'lack of respect' more important.

MAINTENANCE DIFFICULTIES
(SHAVER ET AL., 1985)

- Surveyed 400 first year students at the University of Denver, asking them about current relationships, social skills, strategies for dealing with loneliness, etc.

FINDINGS

- Found that the move away to university for one of the partners was responsible for the decline of nearly half (46%) of pre-university romances in the students interviewed.

This suggests that...

The opportunity to be in new relationships is too distracting and the pressures to develop (potentially exciting) new relationships too great compared to the difficulties and inconvenience of maintaining existing ones.

TYPICAL QUESTIONS...

1. Describe and evaluate research (explanations and/or studies) into the breakdown of relationships. (24 marks)

2. Outline and evaluate two or more explanations of the breakdown of relationships. (24 marks)

3. Discuss research studies into the breakdown of relationships. (24 marks)

RELATIONSHIPS IN DIFFERENT CULTURES

EXPLANATIONS OF RELATIONSHIPS IN DIFFERENT CULTURES

CULTURAL NORMS

- Norms are descriptions of what is considered appropriate behaviour within a relationship, e.g. the norm of reciprocity, i.e. for every benefit received, one should be returned.

- Although this norm appears to be universal, it takes different forms in different cultures.

- In individualist cultures voluntary reciprocity is the norm, but in collectivist cultures reciprocity in relationships is more obligatory (Ting-Toomey, 1986).

- The USA is often cited as an example of an individualist culture, and Japan as an example of a collectivist culture, but the assumption that they do possess these characteristics has not been tested.
- Takano and Osaka (1999) reviewed studies that compared the US and Japan in terms of individualism/collectivism. These studies did not support the view that such a difference existed between these cultures.

SUBCULTURAL DIFFERENCES IN RELATIONSHIPS

These are differences (e.g. social class) that exist based on group classifications *within* cultures (based on research by Argyle, 1994).

MUST KNOW...

- How relationships differ across different types of cultures, and be able to comment on these differences.

In individualist cultures, the emphasis is on 'I' rather than 'we', with individual rights, goals being seen as more important than group goals. People strive for autonomy, and dependence is not seen as desirable. ←→ In collectivist cultures, the group is valued more than the individual, and responsibilities to the group are seen as more important than individual desires. Interdependence is valued.

RULES OF RELATIONSHIPS

- Rules define the responsibilities of each partner in a relationship. These may be explicit (in a formal relationship) or implicit (e.g. amongst friends). These serve to maintain relationships so that the goals of those relationships can be achieved.

- Argyle et al. (1986) examined relationship rules in the UK, Italy, Hong Kong and Japan, and found that different rules applied to different forms of relationship in these four cultures. There were also similarities (e.g. showing courtesy and respect).

- Argyle's findings are consistent with the differences that might be predicted based on the individualism/collectivism distinction.
- In Japan (a collectivist culture) they found more evidence of rules which stressed obedience to superiors and the maintenance of group harmony.

Friendship
- Friendship is more important to the middle classes than the working classes, for whom there is more emphasis on kin.

Nature of friendships
- Middle-class (M/C) friends are selected on the basis of shared interests and attitudes. Working-class (W/C) friendships tend to be based on location, leading to the formation of tight knit neighbourhood groups.

Husbands and wives
- M/C marriages tend to be more symmetrical than W/C marriages, i.e. husbands and wives tend to share the same friends and leisure activities, and are more likely to make joint decisions.

Fathers and their children
- M/C families tend to be more child-centred, and fathers play a more significant role in family life than in W/C families.

This is supported by...
- Shucksmith et al. (1993) who found evidence that young people from M/C backgrounds spend longer in mixed sex groups.
- This may be due to the fact that they anticipate a longer period before they 'settle down', as M/C children are more likely to go to university.

However...
There are gender differences, with boys placing more value on looking and behaving like their friends, whereas girls are more likely to value qualities in the personality of their friends (Shucksmith et al., 1993).

However...
- Marcussen and Piatt (2005) argue that little attention has been paid to differences in how husbands and wives experience their roles within different ethnic groups.
- This limits the extent to which this claim can be applied to all cultures.

RESEARCH STUDIES INTO CULTURAL DIFFERENCES IN RELATIONSHIPS

VOLUNTARY AND INVOLUNTARY RELATIONSHIPS

- Rosenblatt and Anderson (1981) claim that few societies are characterised by the extremes where partners have no choice who they marry (i.e. totally involuntary) or total freedom of choice.

- In Western cultures, love is seen as important when marrying. However, Simpson et al. (1986) report that the importance of love as a necessity for marriage had increased over the last 30 years.

- The most common form of marriage partner selection worldwide is by arrangement, with parents having the most significant say (Ingoldsby, 1995).

How common are arranged marriages?
- Goodwin et al. (1997) found that only 8% of 70 Hindu Gujarati couples had 'arranged' marriages. This might be explained in terms of the greater mobility of UK Asians compared to those still living in non-Western cultures.

Is love *universally* important?
- As cultures become more industrialised and individualistic, so the percentage of people believing love is necessary for marriage increases. However, in a study by Levine et al. (1995), people from collectivist societies were more likely to say they were willing to marry without love compared to those from individualist societies.

PERMANENT AND IMPERMANENT RELATIONSHIPS

- Nearly all cultures have some provision for divorce, but there is greater stigma attached to divorce in cultures with traditional arranged marriages.

- In China (a collectivist culture), the divorce rate is very low, as divorce carries shame for both partners and their families.

- Simmel (1971) argues that individualism is associated with higher divorce rates because individuals are constantly encouraged to search for their 'ideal' partner.

Why are divorce rates higher in individualist cultures?
- Individualism creates barriers to healthy relationships because of the difficulties of maintaining individuality and autonomy (valued characteristics in individualist societies) at the same time as fulfilling marital role requirements and obligations.

Historical changes
- The shift to non-permanent relationships in Western cultures has been fairly recent. With greater urbanisation and mobility over the last 50 years, the impermanence of relationships has become a feature of urban societies.

CULTURAL DIFFERENCES IN LOVE

- Because family ties are relatively more important in collectivist rather than individualist cultures, collectivist societies might be expected to place tighter controls on love.

- Medora et al. (2002) compared romanticism scores for people from the US (individualist), India (collectivist) and Turkey (between the two). The US sample scored higher than the other samples, while the Indian sample scored the lowest.

Limitations of cross-cultural research
- In research where members of different cultural groups are studied, it is assumed that direct comparisons can be made which are meaningful. However, the validity of cross-cultural research on relationships is limited because a direct comparison of behaviour in different cultures is not straightforward. For example, participants may have quite different social backgrounds.

MUST TAKE CARE...
To include both AO1 **and** AO2 material in answers to questions on this topic.

TYPICAL QUESTIONS...

1 Discuss research (explanations and/or studies) into cultural differences in relationships. (24 marks)

2 (a) Outline and evaluate two or more explanations of cultural differences in relationships.
   (12 marks)

(b) Outline and evaluate two or more studies of cultural differences in relationships.
   (12 marks)

UNDERSTUDIED RELATIONSHIPS

GAY AND LESBIAN RELATIONSHIPS

- Research suggests that gay men desire specific physical attributes in a partner (e.g. attractive face, athletic body) and they also value many of the 'status symbols' (e.g. a professional career) that go with the male role in Western cultures (Davidson, 1991).
- Lesbians are more likely to emphasise personality characteristics than physical appearance, and appear to value self-sufficiency and strength in a long-term partner (Huston and Schwartz, 1995).

◀ **FORMATION** ▶

Women face an additional problem when trying to form a same-sex relationship. Most women have been socialised into being more *reactive* than *proactive* in relationships. As a result, neither woman may feel comfortable making the first move and asking the other out.

- For lesbian couples, strategies used to maintain a healthy relationship include:
  - a high degree of emotional intimacy
  - an equitable balance of power (Eldridge and Gilbert, 1990).
- For gay couples these include:
  - minimal conflict
  - high appreciation of the partner (Jones and Bates, 1978).

◀ **MAINTENANCE OF RELATIONSHIPS** ▶

- Conversation as a maintenance strategy tends to be used differently by gay and lesbian partners:
  - for lesbian couples, it is used to establish and maintain intimacy between the two partners
  - for gay couples, conversational arguments are frequently used as a way in which one person might get their own way over their less powerful partner (Huston and Schwartz, 1995).

Differences between heterosexual and non-heterosexual relationships (gay and lesbian) can be used as AO2 commentary.

Emotional intimacy
- Nardi and Sherrod (1994) found that the avoidance of emotional intimacy tends to be a characteristic of heterosexual rather than homosexual males.
- They found no differences in levels of openness and self-disclosure in same-sex relationships of lesbians and gay men.

After the relationship
- Unlike heterosexual couples, lesbians and gay men are more likely to remain friends after a relationship has finished (Nardi, 1992).
- For heterosexual couples, sexual intimacy is likely to *end* a friendship, whereas for lesbians and gay men, it is more likely to lead to continuing friendship (Nardi, 1992).

DIFFERENCES BETWEEN HETEROSEXUAL AND NON-HETEROSEXUAL RELATIONSHIPS

Partner preferences
- Dunbar and Waynforth's analysis of personal ads found that gay men offered resources half as often as heterosexual men, and lesbians offered cues of physical attractiveness about one quarter as much as heterosexual women.
- This explains *why* homosexuals have different partner preferences – because reproduction is not an issue.

Durability
- Gay and lesbian relationships do not last as long as heterosexual ones. Blumstein and Schwartz (1983) found that 48% of lesbians and 36% of gays broke up within two years of being interviewed, compared to 14% of married couples.
- Barriers to dissolution are largely absent in non-heterosexual relationships as families rarely support the relationship and there tend to be no children involved.

MEDIATED RELATIONSHIPS

COMPUTER MEDIATED COMMUNICATION (CMC)

CMC = Relationships conducted over the Internet.

- CMC is seen as inferior to face-to-face (F2F) communication because it offers partners less cues to work with when developing a relationship.
- Reduced cues theory (Culnan and Markus, 1987) claims that CMC filters out important aspects of F2F communication (e.g. intensity and body language), stripping it of much of its meaning.

- The reduced cues available to each partner in the communication may lead to deindividuation (lack of individual identity) which in turn may lead to anti-social behaviour.
- Because CMC lacks the norms and standards that regulate F2F behaviour, users can become more aggressive and impulsive when communicating with others.

- Because bodily and contextual information are removed in CMC, text assumes a much higher importance.
- CMC relationships are described as 'asynchronous', in that they do not have to be tied to one specific time or place, but can be carried on at the convenience of either partner.

SMS-BASED RELATIONSHIPS (AO1)
- SMS ('texting') has an important role in the **formation and maintenance** of relationships.
- Ling and Yttri (2002) found that adolescents frequently exchange texts following an initial meeting, thus showing their interest in forming a relationship.
- Once a relationship has developed, texting allows partners to manage it in the most efficient way. The immediacy of text messaging (compared to e-mail) means that the mobile phone is more useful in this context.

- Sprecher and McKinney (1987) claimed that some common obstacles to beginning a F2F relationship are shyness and lack of confidence in one's physical appearance.
- In CMC, because self-representation is entirely within the person's own control, some of these barriers are removed or diminished.

SMS-BASED RELATIONSHIPS (AO2)
- An **advantage** of SMS messaging is that once someone comes into our circle of friends, we are always available (through text). This means that maintenance of friendships is more convenient.
- Although SMS messaging can maintain relationships, even when we are some distance apart, a **disadvantage** is that it can also *weaken* F2F ties, as it becomes easier to 'send a text' than to make the effort to visit someone.

Mediated relationship = one that isn't primarily face to face, but is conducted through some medium, e.g. by letter, over the phone or through the internet.

Advantages of CMC
- Internet relationships are good for people who are shy, lack access to suitable others, lack sufficient time, or have physical handicaps that hinder the formation of F2F relationships (Duck, 1999).
- The 'ACE' model of CMC emphasises positive characteristics of anonymity, convenience and escape (Young, 1999).

The SIDE model (Lea and Spears, 1991)
- This offers an alternative to the reduced cues theory claim that CMC will always lead to antisocial behaviour. Instead, it is claimed, CMC *reinforces* existing social norms.
- Anonymous individuals in CMC are inclined to accept 'in-group' norms (e.g. a chat-room) and reject 'out-group' norms. This increases in-group favouritism, and increases bias toward out-group members.

COMMENTARY ON CMC

Disadvantages of CMC
- Individuals may become overly reliant upon CMC for initiating relationships. As a result, they will have less incentive to develop their F2F social skills or to overcome shyness.
- Because individuals can control their self-representation, this can lead to deception and abuse, making it much more difficult to develop trust between individuals.

Research support
- Psychological research concerning the success (or otherwise) of on-line relationships is relatively sparse.
- Most of the information in this area comes from anecdotal articles in magazines rather than from properly controlled scientific studies.

MUST TAKE CARE...
Not to include **technical** details about e-mail or other forms of CMC.

TYPICAL QUESTION...

Discuss research (theories and/or studies) into two or more types of understudied relationship. (24 marks)

For practice in answering A2 Psychology questions, why not use *Collins Do Brilliantly A2 Psychology*?

SOCIAL PSYCHOLOGICAL THEORIES OF AGGRESSION

MUST KNOW...
- Two social psychological theories of aggression and research studies related to these theories.

SOCIAL LEARNING THEORY (SLT)

Social learning theory in a nutshell
Human aggression is learned either through direct experience or by observing aggressive behaviour in other people.

ASSUMPTIONS OF SLT

1 If a child acts aggressively against another child and as a result gets what they want, their aggressive behaviour has been reinforced. This is an example of learning by direct experience, derived from the principles of operant conditioning.

2 If a child observes a role model behaving in an aggressive manner, they may imitate that behaviour themselves, particularly if they see the model reinforced for behaving in that way. This is an example of learning by vicarious experience.

MUST TAKE CARE...
Not just to describe Bobo doll studies instead of social learning **theory**.

REINFORCEMENT

The likelihood of a person behaving aggressively in a particular situation is determined by:
- their previous experiences of aggressive behaviour
- the degree to which their behaviour has been successful in the past
- the likelihood of their aggressive behaviour being successful in the current situation
- any other factors that might be operating at the time (such as fear of retaliation, high levels of heat or noise, etc.).

THE ROLE OF THE MEDIA

- Aggression observed in films and on TV is more likely to be imitated if:
  - the observed violence appears to be 'real' behaviour, i.e. it occurs in a realistic setting, such as domestic violence, rather than a fantasy setting
  - the viewer identifies with the aggressive model in some way (e.g. heroes are more powerful models than villains).
- If the observed aggression is *unsuccessful* (e.g. the model is punished for their aggressive behaviour), then imitation is less likely.

MUST REMEMBER...
That questions tend to ask for an outline of **two** theories, so must be able to provide a précis of each of these.

DEINDIVIDUATION THEORY

Deindividuation theory in a nutshell
People temporarily lose their socialised individual identity (e.g. when in a large crowd), and so become more likely to engage in anti-social, unsocialised behaviour.

ASSUMPTIONS OF DEINDIVIDUATION THEORY

1 People don't normally act aggressively because they are easily identifiable in societies that have strong norms against aggressive behaviour.

2 In certain situations (such as in large crowds), people are less easily identifiable and so these restraints may become relaxed. As a result, they may be more inclined to act in a more selfish and anti-social manner.

INDIVIDUATED AND DEINDIVIDUATED BEHAVIOUR

- Individual behaviour is rational and conforms to social norms, but deindividuated behaviour is based more on primitive urges and does not conform to societal norms.
- Being part of a crowd can diminish a person's awareness of their individuality, making them anonymous. The larger the crowd, the greater the anonymity.
- Conditions that increase anonymity also decrease fear of evaluation and feelings of guilt.

PUBLIC AND PRIVATE SELF-AWARENESS

- Being a part of a large crowd can make us relatively anonymous to others (reduced public self-awareness).
- Being swept along with a crowd can also cause us to lose focus on our own actions (reduced private self-awareness).
- Aggressive behaviour is more associated with reduced private self-awareness rather than being anonymous to others.

RESEARCH SUPPORT FOR SOCIAL LEARNING THEORY

BANDURA ET AL. (1961)

- Nursery school children watched a film where an adult model behaved aggressively or non-aggressively towards a Bobo doll.

MUST TAKE CARE...

To make the findings from each of these studies into AO2 by using a phrase such as 'SLT is supported by the finding that...'.

BANDURA AND WALTERS (1963)

- Children watched an adult behaving aggressively towards the Bobo doll, and were either rewarded or punished for their aggressive behaviour.

FINDINGS

- Children in the aggressive condition reproduced the physical and verbal behaviours modelled by the adult.
- Children in the non-aggressive condition showed very little aggression towards the doll.

FINDINGS

- When allowed to play with the Bobo doll:
  – children who saw the adult rewarded for their aggression behaved most aggressively
  – children who saw the adult rewarded for non-aggression behaved least aggressively.
- When rewards offered for performing aggressive acts, became evident that all children had learned the aggressive acts modelled by adult.

This shows that...

Children acquire aggressive behaviours from watching the actions of others.

However...

- Some methodological problems with these studies (e.g. unrealistic as no risk of retaliation from doll) which undermine its support for SLT.
- In another study (Johnston et al., 1977), children who behaved most aggressively to doll were rated by teachers as most violent generally.

This shows that...

- Behaviour that is *learned* from watching others may not always be *performed*.
- Only behaviour that is likely to be rewarded is reproduced, i.e. children adjust their behaviour on the basis of the likely consequences.

OTHER COMMENTARY ON SOCIAL LEARNING THEORY

EXPLAINING INCONSISTENCIES IN AGGRESSIVE BEHAVIOUR

- SLT can account for the fact that a person's aggressive behaviour may not be consistent across different situations. It may be reinforced in some situations, but punished in others.

ALTERNATIVE EXPLANATIONS

- Biological explanations (e.g. levels of testosterone are linked to aggressive behaviour) challenge the view that social learning is the primary causal factor in aggression.
- However, cultural explanations support view that aggression is primarily a learned behaviour (e.g. study of the non-aggressive Amish in the USA).

COMMENTARY ON DEINDIVIDUATION THEORY

RESEARCH SUPPORT

- Mann (1981) found evidence of deindividuation in the 'baiting crowd' – crowds frequently baited a potential suicide victim to jump. Baiting was increased under conditions which increased the anonymity of the crowd (e.g. numbers, darkness and distance from victim). This therefore supports the claim that deindividuation increases aggressive behaviour.

SOCIAL NORMS AND BEHAVIOUR

- According to deindividuation theory, being a member of a large crowd undermines the influence of social norms and so makes it more likely that a person will act anti-socially.
- However, research suggests that being in a crowd makes it more likely that people will act according to group norms. These may sometimes be anti-social but at other times may be *pro*-social.

FOOTBALL CROWD VIOLENCE

- This theory fails to provide a convincing explanation for football crowd violence, despite many of the conditions of deindividuation being present.
- Marsh et al. (1978) found that football violence was frequently highly organised and ritualised rather than a product of 'primitive urges' arising as a result of deindividuation.

TYPICAL QUESTIONS...

1 Describe and evaluate one social psychological theory of aggression. (24 marks)

2 Outline and evaluate two social psychological theories of aggression. (24 marks)

MUST REMEMBER...

That questions which ask for 'two theories' do not require the same amount of material for each theory, but both must be detailed.

RESEARCH ON ENVIRONMENTAL STRESSORS

TEMPERATURE AS AN ENVIRONMENTAL STRESSOR

Laboratory studies
Halpern (1995)
• In a review of studies, Halpern found evidence of an inverted-U relationship between heat and aggression, with maximum aggression being elicited by moderate heat levels.
• As temperature rises, so does aggression, but after a certain point, aggression begins to decline, as the need to aggress gives way to the need to escape from the heat.

RESEARCH SUGGESTS THAT HIGHER TEMPERATURES LEAD TO AGGRESSIVE BEHAVIOUR

Explaining the relationship
• Negative affect escape theory (Bell and Baron, 1976): aggression is a direct consequence of high temperatures, i.e. high temperatures → increase in anger → increase in desire to escape → aggression if escape impossible.
• Routine activity theory (Cohen and Felson, 1979): opportunities for interpersonal aggression increase during hot weather as people are more likely to be outdoors (increased contact with others) and more likely to drink alcohol.

Violent crime statistics
• Baron and Ransberger (1978) found that the number of riots in the US increased up to a temperature of 85°C, and decreased after that.
• Anderson (1987) examined violent crime statistics and found there was a relationship between heat and violent crimes (such as murder, rape and assault). These tended to rise in the hotter months and in hotter years. Non-violent crime statistics did not follow the same trends.

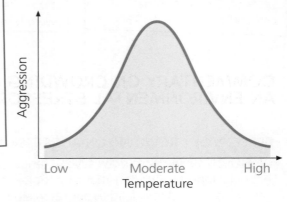

COMMENTARY ON TEMPERATURE AS AN ENVIRONMENTAL STRESSOR

*These 'extensions' increase the **effectiveness** of the AO2 commentary points.*

HOTTER CLIMATES AND AGGRESSIVE BEHAVIOUR
• Early research (e.g. Lombroso, 1911 and Brearley, 1932) supports the view that high temperatures lead to aggressive behaviour, with higher murder rates found in more southerly parts of Italy and the USA than in the northern regions of these countries.

However...
Moghaddam (1998) suggests that these trends may be due to other differences between the North and South (e.g. levels of wealth) that might better explain murder rates in these regions.

HEAT AND VIOLENT CRIME
• Routine activity theory suggests that aggression increases when people are more likely to come into contact with each other (during hot weather), thus suggesting that high temperatures alone may not be responsible for the rise in aggressive behaviour.

This is supported by...
American crime statistics show that murder rates show two peak periods (late summer and around Christmas) when people are more likely to be socially active (Moghaddam, 1998).

LABORATORY STUDIES
• Some studies have found an increase in aggression with increasing temperature, but others have found a decrease. Baron and Bell (1976) found that people who are cold and angry display more aggressive behaviour than those who are hot and angry.

This shows that...
Studies have failed to establish a clear-cut relationship between temperature and aggression, and that other variables (e.g. anger) may interact with temperature to produce aggressive behaviour.

CROWDING AS AN ENVIRONMENTAL STRESSOR

CROWDING OCCURS IF OUR PERSONAL SPACE IS VIOLATED BY OTHERS. THIS PRODUCES DISCOMFORT WHICH MAY THEN LEAD TO AGGRESSIVE BEHAVIOUR.

The effects of crowding
- Early research using animals found that as the population density of rats increased, so did their aggressive behaviour (Calhoun, 1962).
- If an increase in social density is seen as undesirable, the outcomes for an individual tend to be negative. As a result, they show more aggression and less cooperation with those around them (Horn, 1994).

Crowding in nightclubs
Macintyre and Homel (1997) studied six Australian nightclubs and found that more aggressive incidents were observed in the more crowded venues. This was the case even when other factors (e.g. drunkenness) were taken into account.

Explaining the relationship
Stokols (1976) identifies three explanations for the relationship between crowding and aggression:
- **Stimulus overload:** high density may cause us to be overwhelmed by sensory input. If this exceeds our ability to cope, aggression may occur.
- **Behavioural constraint:** high density reduces behavioural freedom. This may produce aggression if it prevents us from doing something we want to do.
- **Ecological model:** high density leads to insufficient resources so aggression becomes a way of dealing with this insufficiency.

These all have a feature in common – **loss of control** is likely to lead to negative consequences.

COMMENTARY ON CROWDING AS AN ENVIRONMENTAL STRESSOR

EFFECTS OF CROWDING ON AGGRESSION
- Research allows us to draw several tentative conclusions. Higher densities of people can be unpleasant and may lead to aggressive behaviour and/or greater withdrawal.

However…
These effects may be different for males and females. Stokols et al. (1973) found that increased density was related to increased levels of aggression in males but not in females.

SOCIAL VERSUS SPATIAL DENSITY
- It is important to recognise the difference between *social* density (number of people in a space) and *spatial* density (the amount of space available). High levels of social density appear to produce more negative consequences than high levels of spatial density.

Therefore…
Although social density manipulation nearly always produces negative consequences, spatial density manipulations only appear to produce negative consequences among males in same-sex groups (Paulus, 1977).

CROWDING IN CITIES
- Some studies (e.g. **Milgram, 1970**) have shown that living in cities is considerably more stressful than living in more rural surroundings, and more likely to produce aggressive behaviour in individuals.

This supports the view…
That crowding is related to increases in aggression as urban environments have higher levels of social density, *but* they also have higher levels of noise and inconvenience.

TYPICAL QUESTION…

1 Outline and evaluate research into the effects of two or more environmental stressors on aggressive behaviour. (24 marks)

For practice in answering A2 Psychology questions, why not use *Collins Do Brilliantly A2 Psychology*?

EXPLANATIONS AND RESEARCH STUDIES OF ALTRUISM/BYSTANDER BEHAVIOUR

MUST KNOW...
- Two explanations of altruism and/or bystander behaviour and research studies related to these.

THE EMPATHY–ALTRUISM MODEL

Batson's empathy–altruism model in a nutshell

Altruistic behaviour is a consequence of 'empathy', an emotional response consistent with the emotional state of another person. As a result, witnessing another person in distress motivates us to help them.

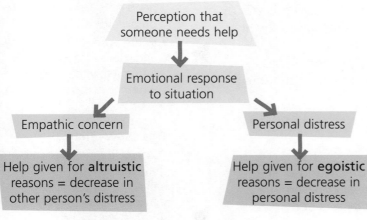

Perception that someone needs help
↓
Emotional response to situation
↓ ↓
Empathic concern — Personal distress
↓ ↓
Help given for **altruistic** reasons = decrease in other person's distress — Help given for **egoistic** reasons = decrease in personal distress

MUST REMEMBER...
Can choose two theories of altruism, two of bystander behaviour, or one of each.

EMPATHY INVOLVES A NUMBER OF COMPONENTS, INCLUDING:

Perspective taking
- This is the ability to take another person's point of view.
- Without this, we would experience only personal distress rather than empathic concern.

Empathic concern
- We feel compassion for the welfare of the person in distress.
- Help is then given for altruistic reasons – i.e. to decrease that person's distress.

Personal distress
- This is an emotional reaction experienced when we see someone else suffering.
- If our motivation to help is due more to the need to reduce our own distress (e.g. guilt or sadness), then help is given for egoistic (selfish) reasons rather than altruistic ones.

THE COGNITIVE MODEL OF BYSTANDER BEHAVIOUR

Latané and Darley's cognitive model of bystander behaviour in a nutshell

This is a five-stage model of the decision-making process people go through when deciding whether to help in an emergency. Helping behaviour can be inhibited at each stage if a 'no' decision is made.

Latané and Darley (1970) claimed that two psychological processes made it less likely that people would help another person in an emergency.

DIFFUSION OF RESPONSIBILITY

- If one person is present at an emergency, they have 100% responsibility to help.
- As the number of bystanders *increases*, so the individual responsibility for each individual *decreases*.
- People are therefore slower to react to emergencies when there are lots of other bystanders who witness the event.

PLURALISTIC IGNORANCE

- When we have to make a decision whether or not to help, we look to see what other bystanders are doing.
- If others appear to define the event as an emergency, we act accordingly.
- If others are not acting, we assume that it is not an emergency and so do not give any help.

THE FIVE STAGES

Notice the event: the person may or may not notice that someone needs help.
↓
Interpret as an emergency: the situation may be ambiguous, in which case the person looks to the behaviour of other bystanders for guidance.
↓
Assume responsibility: the person may avoid taking responsibility for helping by assuming that others will (diffusion of responsibility).
↓
Know what to do: a person may decide to help if they feel competent to do so, or not help if they lack appropriate skills.
↓
Implement decision: the person may still decide not to help if they decide it is against their interests to do so.

RESEARCH SUPPORT FOR EMPATHY–ALTRUISM THEORY

BATSON ET AL. (1981)
- Manipulated levels of empathy to see if it made any difference to whether participants helped another person in need (showing empathetic concern) or simply left (showing personal distress).

FINDINGS
- Participants in the high empathy condition were more likely to take the place of someone in distress.
- Those in the low empathy condition were more likely to take the easy way out and leave.

This shows that...
People help for reasons other than just the reduction of their own personal distress, although it is possible that other factors (e.g. demand characteristics) might be responsible for the difference between conditions.

FULTZ ET AL. (1986)
- Investigated the possibility that it is the expectation of negative social evaluation for not helping that causes people to give help.

FINDINGS
- The possibility of social evaluation did not increase helping in the high empathy condition.
- In low empathy condition, less helping if no possibility of evaluation.

This suggests that...
- When empathy is aroused, people are likely to help for purely altruistic reasons.
- In the absence of empathy, egoistic reasons are more influential in determining whether help will be given.

KRUGER (2003)
- Compared the influence of altruistic factors (e.g. empathy) and egoistic factors (e.g. genetic relatedness) on a person's intention to perform a risky rescue behaviour.

FINDINGS
- Reciprocal altruism and kinship (genetic relatedness) were the strongest predictors of helping.
- Empathy made a small but significant contribution in predicting intention to help.

This shows that...
Some of the mechanisms that lead to altruistic behaviour (e.g. empathy) may operate within a more selfish system where the need for reciprocity and genetic relatedness are more important.

RESEARCH SUPPORT FOR LATANÉ AND DARLEY'S COGNITIVE MODEL

DARLEY AND LATANÉ (1968)
- Participants were led to believe they were either alone with another participant or part of a group. They then heard their companion apparently having an epileptic seizure.

FINDINGS
- Help was less likely and slower when participants believed that other potential helpers were present, whereas *all* responded if they believed they were on their own.

This supports...
The idea of diffusion of responsibility. As the number of bystanders increases, so does the time taken to respond to an emergency, and the probability that help will be given decreases.

BRYAN AND TEST (1967)
- Investigated whether people would be more likely to help a motorist if they had already witnessed an example of helping behaviour.

FINDINGS
- They found that people were more likely to help if they had earlier witnessed an act of helping, particularly if it was the same behaviour.

This might be explained by...
- The process of conformity to social norms, i.e. people use the actions of others as cues to decide what are appropriate responses.

TYPICAL QUESTIONS...

1 Describe and evaluate two or more explanations of altruism/bystander behaviour. (24 marks)

2 Discuss research (explanations and/or studies) into altruism/bystander behaviour. (24 marks)

3 Describe and evaluate two or more studies of altruism/bystander behaviour. (24 marks)

4 (a) Outline two explanations of altruism/bystander behaviour. (12 marks)

(b) Evaluate the two explanations of altruism/bystander behaviour that you outlined in (a) in terms of relevant research studies. (12 marks)

CULTURAL DIFFERENCES IN PRO-SOCIAL BEHAVIOUR

DIFFERENCES BETWEEN CULTURES

INDIVIDUALISM AND COLLECTIVISM
Individual societies stress the need for *independence* whilst collectivist societies stress *interdependence*.

NADLER (1986, 1993)
• Compared people in Israel brought up communally (on a kibbutz) with those raised in a city, and found the former (kibbutz) were more likely to help and seek help than the latter (city).

MILLER (1994)
• Compared Hindu culture of India (collectivist) with US (individualist) and found Hindus felt an obligation to respond to others' needs, whereas Americans felt no such obligation.

TOWER ET AL. (1997)
• Compared British (individualist) and Russian (collectivist) students and found British tended to share resources in a way that benefited them, whereas Russians shared more in a way that benefited others.

THE REGULATION OF SOCIAL RELATIONSHIPS
Differences may exist because of the different ways that cultures enact their interpersonal relationships.

MOGHADDAM (1998)
• Some Chinese still practice *guanxixue* – a link between people who have a mutually dependent relationship. This creates obligations and indebtedness.
• Americans generally avoid relationships of mutual dependence rather than seeing such relationships as essential to daily life.

BOND AND LEUNG (1988)
• Found that while Chinese and Japanese participants offered more help than did Americans to others whom they perceived to be from an **in-group**, they were less likely than Americans to help those perceived to be from an **out-group**.

In-group = those similar to us and with whom we identify.
Out-group = those dissimilar to us.

Guanxixue and networking
Although in the West we do not have the equivalent of *guanxixue*, we do have the notion of 'networking' which involves more limited obligations. Networking entails becoming acquainted with people who may be in a position to give assistance in areas that are personally important to us.

Laboratory and field studies
Much of the research on human altruism carried out in the West takes place in laboratories, whereas much of the research in non-Western cultures is field research. Laboratory studies lack the social context of helping, where people actively help and seek out help to extend their social relationships.

The imposed etic
A problem with carrying out comparative research in two different cultures is that psychologists tend to use research methodologies imposed in one culture (e.g. the US) to measure behaviour in another (the imposed etic). These may have different meanings in the second culture, and lead them to draw unjustifiable conclusions about people from that culture.

COMMENTARY ON CULTURAL DIFFERENCES

DIFFERENCES **WITHIN** CULTURES

GENDER DIFFERENCES

- Research has shown that girls tend to be more helpful in a variety of different tests of pro-social behaviour.

GENDER ROLES

- In Western cultures the gender role for women emphasises the importance of helping others, therefore women tend to show more social responsibility.
- However, the gender role for men emphasises achievement and risk-taking, therefore they would be more likely to help in some situations.

SEEKING HELP

- Cultural rules governing gender relations may account for the fact that in most cultures women seek help more than men. These rules allow women to present themselves as being 'in need', whereas male concerns with being 'tough and independent' may prevent them from seeking help from others.

URBAN–RURAL DIFFERENCES

- Early research found that people living in rural areas were more likely to offer help than those living in urban areas.
- Later research suggests that population density is a better predictor of helping than population size.

INFORMATION OVERLOAD

- Milgram (1970) suggested that people in cities are so familiar with emergency situations that they treat them as everyday occurrences. They are therefore less likely to attract interest and so people are less likely to offer help.

DIFFUSION OF RESPONSIBILITY

- Latané and Darley (1970) suggest that higher populations create greater diffusion of responsibility, therefore leading to less individual responsibility for helping. Increased population density has also been shown to lead to increases in aggressive behaviour.

Defying stereotypes
- Although girls tend to be more helpful in tests of pro-social reasoning, research findings tend to be inconsistent. In a meta-analysis of 99 different studies, Eagly and Crowley (1986) found that in 62% of these studies men were actually more helpful than women. This disconfirms the popular stereotype of women being more helpful than men.

COMMENTARY ON CULTURAL DIFFERENCES

Explaining contradictory research
- Although some psychological studies support the claim that people in rural areas are more helpful, others find no difference. An explanation for these apparently contradictory results is that when the stimulus input is high (e.g. noisy, crowded streets), people tend to be less helpful in both urban and rural areas.

TYPICAL QUESTIONS...

1 Discuss cultural differences in pro-social behaviour. (24 marks)

2 (a) Outline research (explanations and/or studies) of altruism/bystander behaviour. (12 marks)

(b) To what extent are there cultural differences in such behaviour? (12 marks)

For practice in answering A2 Psychology questions, why not use *Collins Do Brilliantly A2 Psychology*?

MEDIA INFLUENCES ON PRO-SOCIAL BEHAVIOUR

EXPLANATIONS OF THE RELATIONSHIP BETWEEN PRO-SOCIAL MEDIA AND BEHAVIOUR

MUST KNOW...
- Explanations **and** research studies into the relationship between pro-social media and pro-social behaviour.

MUST TAKE CARE...
Not to confuse **explanations** with **research studies** when answering questions.

EXPLANATIONS OF MEDIA INFLUENCES ON PRO-SOCIAL BEHAVIOUR

Exposure to pro-social messages
- Studies (e.g. Liebert and Poulos, 1975) have shown that pro-social content is as evident on television as is anti-social content.
- However, these pro-social acts frequently appear alongside acts of anti-social behaviour (Greenberg et al., 1980) which may explain why their influence is overshadowed.

Social learning theory
- Bandura (1965) claims that children learn by observing behaviour, imitating those behaviours that are likely to bring rewards.
- Unlike the media portrayal of anti-social acts, pro-social acts are more likely to match social norms.
- As a result, they are more likely to be associated with reinforcement and so child is motivated to repeat them.

Developmental trends
- Pro-social reasoning (such as perspective-taking and empathy) continues to develop throughout childhood and adolescence.
- Research suggests that young children have more difficulty understanding abstract pro-social messages and so may be less affected by them (Mares, 1996).

May need to expand each of these three points.

Social learning theory
- Exposure to filmed models has less effect than exposure to real models.
- Any effect of pro-social programming tends to be relatively short-lived and may not generalise to new settings.
- However, prolonged viewing of pro-social programming can result in substantial increases in children's pro-social reasoning (Eisenberg, 1983).

Exposure to pro-social messages
- A number of studies have supported the claim that pro-social messages in the media are getting through to children (e.g. Mares, 1996).
- However, studies have also found that children fail to generalise from the specific act modelled to more general pro-social behaviour in their own lives.
- Some specially-made pro-social material is criticised for not having the same production quality (and so less impact) as broadcast programmes.

COMMENTARY ON EXPLANATIONS

Developmental trends
- Research has shown that, contrary to what we might expect, pro-social messages have a greater effect on young children than adolescents.
- However, this may be because young children and adolescents have different motives.
- Young children may imitate pro-social acts if they believe this will bring them a reward, whereas adolescents may act for more altruistic reasons.

MUST REMEMBER...
That some questions will require both AO1 and AO2, but in others only AO1 will be required for these explanations. This AO2 material can then be adapted to provide expansion for the AO1 points.

RESEARCH STUDIES OF THE RELATIONSHIP BETWEEN PRO-SOCIAL MEDIA AND BEHAVIOUR

DIFFERENT PROGRAMME TYPES

Pro-social only (only pro-social behaviours modelled)

- Several studies (e.g. **Sprafkin et al., 1975**) have shown the positive effects of pro-social models on TV on children's helping behaviour.

- The measures of pro-social behaviour tend to be taken in an artificial and contrived environment which **limits their application** to children's behaviour in real-life settings.

Pro-social conflict resolution (pro-social behaviours presented alongside anti-social)

- **Paulson (1974)** found programmes designed to teach pro-social means of resolving conflicts produced increases in specific pro-social behaviours in viewers.
- In this study there was no increase in the *general* level of children's pro-social behaviour after viewing.

- A limitation of this approach is that children **might adopt the anti-social behaviours** that are modelled alongside the pro-social behaviours in these programmes.
- If both pro- *and* anti-social behaviours are presented, characters frequently demonstrate **justification for their aggression**, and so legitimise it for those watching.

Conflict without resolution (problems presented that suggest pro-social solutions)

- **Rockman (1980)** found that children do generate pro-social solutions to the problems portrayed in programmes rather than anti-social solutions.
- Other research has suggested limited potential for pro-social change after exposure to this type of programme (**Johnston et al., 1983**).

- Such programmes have a **therapeutic value**, but may result in frustration on the part of the viewer who may not be able to work out how to resolve the issue(s).
- However, caution should be used when very young children are the intended audience as children younger than 7 or 8 **might not benefit** from this modelling strategy as effectively as older children (**Lovelace and Huston, 1983**).

META-ANALYSES OF MEDIA INFLUENCES

HEAROLD (1986)

Carried out a meta-analysis of 230 studies of the effects of television and found:

- Pro-social themes had a greater effect on pro-social behaviour than anti-social themes had on anti-social behaviour.
- These were consistently higher for both boys *and* girls.

MARES (1996)

Carried out a meta-analysis of 39 studies of pro-social media effects and found:

- A moderate effect size for programmes showing positive interaction (modelling of friendly interactions, expressions of affection, etc.) and altruism (e.g. sharing and offering help).
- A moderate effect size for programmes modelling self-control (e.g. resistance to temptation) and anti-stereotyping (e.g. the portrayal of counter-stereotypical attitudes).

- **Comstock (1989)** has explained Hearold's findings as being due to the fact that pro-social programmes are generally *designed* to give pro-social messages whereas anti-social programmes are not designed to give anti-social messages.
- Hearold reported gender differences in the effects of pro-social messages, which appear to have a stronger effect on girls than on boys.

- Mares also found significant gender differences, with more positive effects evident for girls.
- However, in many studies, any pro-social effects were limited to situations that were similar to the specific pro-social act modelled in the programme.
- Contrasts with finding that viewers can generalise *anti-social* acts from one context to another.

TYPICAL QUESTIONS...

1 Critically consider research (explanations and/or studies) into the pro-social effects of the media. (12 marks)

2 (a) Outline and evaluate two or more explanations of the pro-social effects of the media. (12 marks)

(b) Outline and evaluate two or more studies of the pro-social effects of the media. (12 marks)

3 Describe and evaluate two or more studies of the pro-social effects of the media. (24 marks)

MEDIA INFLUENCES ON ANTI-SOCIAL BEHAVIOUR

EXPLANATIONS OF THE RELATIONSHIP BETWEEN ANTI-SOCIAL MEDIA AND BEHAVIOUR

This is the AO1 bit!

COGNITIVE PRIMING

• Aggressive ideas in violent media activate aggressive thoughts in viewers because they are associated in memory.
• After watching a violent film, the viewer is primed to act violently because a network of memories associated with violence has been activated.
• Exposure to violent media may lead children to store scripts for aggressive behaviour that are recalled later if any aspect of the original situation is present.

• A series of studies show that the observation of aggression evokes aggression-related thoughts and ideas (e.g. Berkowitz, 1970, Hansen and Hansen, 1990).
• The concept of cognitive priming is useful in explaining why the observation of aggression in the media is often followed by aggressive acts that differ from the original behaviour, e.g. violent themes in audio tracks may be linked to aggressive behaviour later on (Huesmann, 2001).

OBSERVATIONAL LEARNING

• Bandura (1986) has argued that television can teach skills that may be useful for committing acts of violence.
• Through the processes of imitation and vicarious reinforcement, children learn forms of behaviour that appear relatively resistant to extinction.
• If an actor is reinforced for a specific behaviour, the likelihood of the child imitating that behaviour increases.
• If the actor is seen as possessing desirable characteristics (e.g. the hero), imitation is more likely.

• Felson (1996) lends support to this idea, providing research evidence that exposure to television violence has an effect on violent behaviour for some viewers through the process of social learning.
• He suggests that this is possibly because violent media directs viewers' attention to novel forms of violent behaviour that they would not otherwise consider.

DESENSITISATION

• Under normal conditions, anxiety about violence (which is unpleasant) inhibits its use.
• Frequent viewing of television violence causes viewers to be less anxious about actual violence, seeing it as 'normal'.
• They may also show less empathy for the victims of violence.
• In the absence of this anxiety, violence is no longer inhibited and aggressive behaviour portrayed on television may be imitated.

• This explanation has received research support from field and laboratory studies.
• For example, Cline et al. (1973) found that boys who watched a steady diet of violent television showed less physiological arousal to new scenes of violence than did participants in a control group.
• Freedman (2002) argues that although exposure to media violence causes people to become less excited by subsequent *media* violence, it does not produce a reduced responsiveness to *real* violence.

JUSTIFICATION

• Under normal circumstances, aggressive behaviour should produce feelings of guilt in the individual who behaves that way.
• Violent individuals may enjoy violent behaviour in the media because it justifies their own aggressive actions as being normal and acceptable.
• As a result of this justification, violent children may feel less inhibited about behaving aggressively in the future.

• Evidence that justification is an important mediator in the link between media violence and violent behaviour is limited, and it is more relevant to aggression than to violence.
• For example, studies of responses to violent video games have found that people who were initially more aggressive were more affected by playing these games in terms of subsequent aggressive behaviour, thoughts and emotions (Anderson and Dill, 2000).

RESEARCH STUDIES OF THE RELATIONSHIP BETWEEN ANTI-SOCIAL MEDIA AND BEHAVIOUR

MUST REMEMBER...
That a research **finding** can be used as either AO1 or AO2, but it would be used differently in each context.

BELSON (1978)

- Carried out a **longitudinal study** of over 1,500 adolescent boys. He interviewed them on several occasions concerning their exposure to violent TV programmes and their aggressive behaviour.

FINDINGS

- He found that serious interpersonal violence was increased by long-term exposure to:
1 programmes about violent **personal relationships**
2 **gratuitous** violence
3 realistic **fictional** violence
4 violence portrayed as being in a **good cause**.

However...
The conclusion that TV *caused* high levels of aggression is undermined by the research findings that problem behaviours are already well established by pre-school age (Cumberbatch, 2003).

ST. HELENA STUDY (CHARLTON ET AL., 2000)

- This was a **natural experiment**, carried out when St. Helena received television for the first time. The researchers have monitored children's behaviour since 1995.

FINDINGS

- Two years after television was introduced, there has been no increase in anti-social behaviour among the children. The high levels of good behaviour before TV have been maintained.

This is contrary to...
The claim that exposure to violent television encourages children to behave violently, and despite the fact that levels of violence in programmes are similar to those found in the UK.

PAIK AND COMSTOCK (1994)

- Carried out a **meta-analysis** of 217 studies of media violence carried out between 1957 and 1990.

FINDINGS

- They found an overall correlation of .31 between exposure to violent media and violent behaviour. The size of the correlations varied depending on age of participant and genre of programming.

However...
Critics argue that these correlations are relatively small. However, Bushman and Anderson (2001) point out that this effect was second in size only to the association between smoking and lung cancer.

ANDERSON AND BUSHMAN (2001)

- Carried out a **meta-analysis** of 33 studies of the relationship between violent video games and aggressive behaviour.

FINDINGS

- They found a correlation of 0.19 between exposure to violence during game play and subsequent aggressive behaviour.

However...
Despite the fact that their correlations are even smaller than Paik and Comstock's, they are still larger than many other well-established relationships, e.g. exposure to lead and low IQ.

YES (Huesmann and Moise, 1996)

1 Relationship between exposure to media violence and aggression has been supported in many different studies and in different countries.
2 Because heroes in the media are admired, children are likely to learn that aggressive behaviour is a good thing.
3 Children under the age of 11 are less able to make the distinction between fiction and reality, and so are vulnerable to all forms of violent media.

These arguments can be used as AO1.

DOES MEDIA VIOLENCE PROMOTE AGGRESSION?

These counter-arguments can be used as AO2.

NO (Freedman, 1996)

1 Studies of the relationship between violent media and aggressive behaviour have yielded inconsistent results, and many have methodological flaws.
2 What children tend to learn from the media is that good tends to overcome evil, and that aggression frequently does not pay.
3 Children *are* able to recognise fiction as early as age 5, and children as young as 7 can talk intelligently about the media.

TYPICAL QUESTIONS...

1 Critically consider research (explanations and/or studies) into the anti-social effects of the media. (12 marks)

2 (a) Outline and evaluate two or more explanations of the anti-social effects of the media. (12 marks)

(b) Outline and evaluate two or more studies of the anti-social effects of the media. (12 marks)

3 Describe and evaluate two or more studies of the anti-social effects of the media.

RESEARCH INTO CIRCADIAN, INFRADIAN AND ULTRADIAN RHYTHMS

CIRCADIAN RHYTHMS

- Circadian rhythms occur once every 24 hours, e.g. the human sleep/waking cycle.

- Important because they synchronise an organism's behaviour and body states to changes in the environment (e.g. the cycle of light and dark).

THE SLEEP–WAKE CYCLE

- Siffre (1972) spent six months in a cave, separated from light and dark cues. His sleep/waking cycle settled down to a regular pattern of between 25 and 30 hours, i.e. longer than a 24-hour cycle.
- Aschoff and Wever (1976) placed student participants in an underground WWII bunker without any cues to light or dark. Most displayed circadian rhythms between 25 and 27 hours.

TEMPERATURE

- Core body temperature is subject to a circadian rhythm determined by changes in heat production and loss over a 24-hour period.
- Research has shown that some abilities (e.g. memory) vary with this temperature-related circadian rhythm. Folkard et al. (1977) read stories to children at either 9 a.m. or 3 p.m. After one week, the 3 p.m. group showed superior recall and comprehension → recall from LTM best when body temperature highest.
- In contrast, Monk and Embrey (1981) found alertness best when body temperature lowest (early morning and early evening).

THE HUMAN MENSTRUAL CYCLE

- The human menstrual cycle = approximately 29.5 days between ages of 15 and 40 (Binkley, 1997).
- Although variation in period length between individual women, possible that use of artificial light and blocking out of the moon by curtains and blinds in modern life affects the timing of the cycle – returns to 29.5 days without these artificial cues.

INFRADIAN RHYTHMS

- Infradian rhythms occur less than once a day.

- Some are synchronised to the waxing and waning of the moon that forms a lunar month (29.5 days). These are known as circalunal rhythms. Many cycles are coordinated with the lunar month (e.g. the human menstruation cycle).

- Some infradian rhythms occur once a year and so are known as circannual rhythms (e.g. hibernation in squirrels).

CIRCANNUAL RHYTHMS IN HUMANS

- Research has revealed circannual changes including white blood cell function, blood pressure, the secretion of cortisol (a stress hormone) and levels of serotonin (Egrise et al., 1986).
- Men have circannual rhythms in testosterone production, and mental health also has a seasonal component – seasonal affective disorder (Blehar and Rosenthal, 1989).

The sleep/waking cycle is circadian and the stages within sleep are ultradian.

SLEEP STAGES

- There are several ultradian sleep cycles each night, each lasting about 90 minutes.
- Two main types of sleep within this cycle: non-REM sleep (stages 2 to 4) and REM sleep.
- The sleeper progresses through the four stages of non-REM sleep, then moves into REM sleep.
- This cycle is repeated every 70–90 minutes throughout the night with the REM stage getting longer as the night progresses.
- Disturbance of these sleep cycles interferes with mood regulation and can lead to depression (Armitage et al., 1999).

ULTRADIAN RHYTHMS

- Ultradian rhythms are rhythms that have more than one complete cycle every 24 hours, e.g. eye blinks (24 per minute in humans) and sleep patterns in mammals.

- Also seen in other behaviours such as food-seeking in non-human animals.

THE BASIC REST ACTIVITY CYCLE (BRAC)

- Research has shown that humans are genetically programmed to operate on a rest–activity cycle, known as the BRAC.
- This is a 90-minute cycle of waxing and waning alertness controlled by a biological clock in the brain stem.

COMMENTARY ON BIOLOGICAL RHYTHMS

CIRCADIAN RHYTHMS

THE SLEEP–WAKE CYCLE

- Czeisler et al. (1999) found that the circadian rhythm can be affected by artificial light. Participants' circadian rhythms were manipulated down to 22 hours and up to 28 hours using just ordinary room lighting.

This challenges the belief that...
Circadian rhythms are **endogenous** and therefore cannot be changed by artificial light alone.

TEMPERATURE

- Hawkins and Armstrong-Esther (1978) found that nurses on shift duty were able to adjust relatively quickly to changes in their sleep–wake cycle, but it took at least a week for their temperature cycle to change.

This suggests that...
- There are different biological clocks involved in the regulation of the sleep-wake cycle and the temperature cycle.

IMPORTANCE OF CIRCADIAN RHYTHMS (CR)

- Research on CR has influenced the design of spacecraft environments, as systems which mimic the light/dark cycle have been found to be highly beneficial to astronauts.
- Disruption to CR usually has a negative effect with long-distance travellers suffering from 'jet-lag' and shift workers suffering from 'shift-lag' (i.e. showing symptoms of fatigue, disorientation and insomnia).

INFRADIAN RHYTHMS

SEASONAL AFFECTIVE DISORDER (SAD)

- Some studies have suggested that SAD shows an infradian cycle, being reported more in the winter months, but a study in Iceland (Magnusson and Stefansson, 1993), did not find a higher incidence of SAD in the winter months despite the prolonged winter darkness associated with countries at this latitude.

However...
Relatively few published studies are available for this area, as hospital admissions for SAD are rare. Takei et al. (1992) claim that firm conclusions are inappropriate as most studies fail to consider the different diagnostic subtypes, gender or age at onset when looking at seasonality in SAD.

THE MENSTRUAL CYCLE

- Russell et al. (1980) supported the claim that the menstrual cycle has an infradian rhythm. He collected daily samples of sweat from one group of women and rubbed them onto women in a second group. Despite the fact that the groups were kept physically separate, their menstrual cycles became synchronised with their odour donor.

However...
- As with other similar studies there are a number of methodological flaws (e.g. the use of scientists directly involved in the research as 'sweat donors').
- Despite the implication that a pheromone is involved in this process, scientists have yet to isolate it.

ULTRADIAN RHYTHMS

THE BASIC REST ACTIVITY CYCLE

- Grau et al. (1995) confirmed the existence of an ultradian rhythm in the motor activity in humans. By recording the mobility of 13 adults who remained alone and isolated for five hours in a monotonous environment with nothing to do, they found that 12 out of the 13 participants showed a stable cycle of activity of between 30 and 150 minutes.

This suggests that...
- Despite the presence of individual differences in the length of each cycle, there exists an innate mechanism in adult humans that organises motor activity in ultradian rhythms.

IMPORTANCE OF ULTRADIAN RHYTHMS (UR)

- UR can be **disrupted by stress**, which can lead to serious stress-related illness. These disruptions prevent the body from functioning normally, and make it less resistant to infection.

TYPICAL QUESTIONS...

1 Discuss research (theories and/or studies) into two or more biological rhythms. (24 marks)

2 Discuss research (theories and/or studies) into circadian and infradian rhythms. (24 marks)

ENDOGENOUS PACEMAKERS, EXOGENOUS ZEITGEBERS AND THE CONSEQUENCES OF DISRUPTING BIOLOGICAL RHYTHMS

THE ROLE OF ENDOGENOUS PACEMAKERS

- Research suggests that the production of melatonin is not influenced solely by the link from retina to SCN, but can also be influenced by light to the back of the knees. This could shift the circadian rhythm in body temperature and melatonin secretion (Campbell and Murphy, 1998).

- This is supported by research which shows that chickens wake and become active as dawn breaks (i.e. external light levels rise) and melatonin levels fall (Binkley, 1979).

The pineal gland
- In birds and reptiles, this contains light receptors which respond to external light and in turn influence the activity of neurons in this gland.
- These neurons convert serotonin into melatonin which is responsible for the rhythmic nature of many activities.

The suprachiasmatic nucleus (SCN)
- A neural pathway connects the retina to the SCN, which allows light falling on the retina to influence neurons in the SCN.
- These neurons have an inbuilt circadian firing pattern, and through their connection with the pineal gland, they regulate the manufacture and secretion of melatonin in that gland.

- Morgan (1995) found that if hamsters were bred to a circadian rhythm of 20 hours rather than 24 hours, and had their SCNs transplanted into a normal hamster, it will then also display a 20-hour circadian rhythm.

ENDOGENOUS PACEMAKERS
- Endogenous pacemakers **regulate other neural structures** so that they maintain set rhythms.
- Must also **respond to exogenous zeitgebers** so that the organism is fully coordinated with the external world.

Advantages and disadvantages of endogenous pacemakers
- Advantages: without a biological clock, an animal's behaviour would be totally determined by environmental cues. This could be life-threatening as there would be no regularity to their behaviour.
- Disadvantages: having inbuilt biological rhythms can be problematic because they won't change when we want them to. Circadian rhythms evolved before the days of air travel and shift work, therefore can create problems in those circumstances.

THE ROLE OF EXOGENOUS ZEITGEBERS

Light as a zeitgeber
- Daylight is considered to be the main zeitgeber. Avery et al. (1993) found that exposure to bright light suppresses melatonin production (terminating sleep and promoting wakefulness).
- Daylight re-sets the pacemaker to compensate for slight changes in the hours of light and darkness.

EXOGENOUS ZEITGEBERS
- Because light levels change over the year, the pacemaker needs to be re-set daily using external cues (zeitgebers).
- The most important of these external cues are the light cues of sunrise and sunset.

Social cues as zeitgebers
- Social cues (e.g. meal-times, etc.) may act as zeitgebers.
- These may be more important in determining our daily rhythms, i.e. behaviour is governed more by social convention than internal biology.

- The importance of daylight as a zeitgeber is demonstrated in studies of blind people. In one study, a man blind from birth displayed a circadian rhythm of 24.9 hours. Despite being exposed to various other zeitgebers such as clocks and social cues, he had great difficulty reducing this to a 24-hour cycle (Miles et al., 1977).

- However, a study of men on US nuclear submarines found that despite numerous social cues operating to suggest an 18-hour day (three 6-hour shifts) when on a long undersea tour of duty, this was insufficient to shift the rhythm of melatonin secretion in these men from its 24-hour cycle (Kelly et al., 1999).

THE CONSEQUENCES OF DISRUPTING BIOLOGICAL RHYTHMS

JET LAG

- Caused by a sudden disruption of the body's circadian rhythm as a result of travelling across time zones.
- Body clock is thrown out of 'sync' if it experiences daylight and darkness at the wrong times in a new time zone.
- A person's body is still working to the original rhythm, e.g. they will be ready for sleep in daytime.
- Symptoms of jet lag persist for a few days while the body clock adjusts to the new time zone.
- Jet lag more severe from West to East than from East to West – traveller must adjust to *losing* hours (phase advance).

THE ROLE OF MELATONIN

- Because melatonin has a controlling role in the onset of sleep, it has been studied as a possible treatment for jet lag.
- Some researchers have found that administration of melatonin speeds up the resynchronisation of body rhythms after a long flight, and helps to reduce the symptoms of jet lag (Takahashi et al., 2002).

However...

Spitzer et al. (1999) studied doctors who travelled from Norway to New York for five days, and who took melatonin or a placebo. Melatonin was no better than a placebo at preventing symptoms of jet lag.

EFFECTS OF JET LAG

- A meta-analysis of studies of the effects of jet lag (BRE, 2001) showed the main effects of jet lag were:
  - desynchronisation of circadian rhythms, and difficulties getting to sleep
  - reduced alertness and concentration.

However...

Findings on *mental* performance were inconsistent, varying across studies. This is possibly due to differences in motivation or some other confounding variable.

However...

Studies have looked at the effects of jet lag on athletes, but findings have been inconclusive, suggesting that performance is not adversely affected provided motivation is high.

SHIFT WORK

- In shift work, employees required to work when would normally be sleeping and sleep when normally awake.
- Switching between day and night shifts disrupts links between external zeitgebers (day/night) and biological rhythms.
- Many shift patterns require a change every week (short rotation pattern).
- This results in a permanent state of 'shift lag', impairing performance and increasing stress levels.

THE EFFECTS OF SHIFT WORK

- Research by Czeisler et al. (1982) found evidence of health problems, sleep difficulties and work-related stress in staff employed in short rotation shifts.
- In a study of the Philadelphia Police, which had been using the short rotation shift pattern, half had sleeping difficulties and 25% had had an accident the preceding year (Czeisler et al., 1982).

An implication of this is that...

- Changing to a longer shift rotation (3 weeks) should reduce the ill effects of shift work.
- Czeisler introduced this for two years – found that productivity increased by 20%; marked improvement in job satisfaction and less sick time.

Similarly...

After a year of a longer shift rotation, accidents decreased by 40%, use of alcohol to combat stress dropped by 50%, and sleep disturbances decreased.

THE ROLE OF MELATONIN

- Arendt et al. (2005) studied shift workers on oil rigs – for men working a split-shift pattern, their levels of melatonin did not become synchronised to new sleep times after shift changes.

An application of this is...

Sharkey (2001) found that the use of melatonin could speed up adjustment to shift patterns.

However...

In 1997, US guidelines concluded that research on melatonin was insufficient to recommend it as an aid for shift workers.

TYPICAL QUESTIONS...

1 Discuss research (theories and/or studies) into the role of endogenous pacemakers **and** exogenous zeitgebers in the regulation of biological rhythms. (24 marks)

2 Discuss the consequences of disrupting biological rhythms. (24 marks)

3 (a) Outline research (theories and/or studies) into circadian rhythms. (12 marks)

   (b) Assess the consequences of disrupting biological rhythms. (12 marks)

ECOLOGICAL THEORIES AND RESEARCH STUDIES RELATING TO THE FUNCTIONS OF SLEEP

ECOLOGICAL THEORIES

PREDATOR AVOIDANCE (MEDDIS, 1979)

- Sleep evolved to keep animals inconspicuous and safe from predators at times of the day when they are most vulnerable.
- This is evidence from the observation that predator species (e.g. lions) sleep a great deal more than prey species (e.g. gazelles).
- Logically, prey animals should not sleep at all as this makes them vulnerable, but if sleep serves a vital function then they should sleep when they are least vulnerable.
- According to Meddis, sleep is what animals do when they have nothing better to do with their time, or when they might be at risk of predation.
- Some species specialise in being nocturnal and foraging while other species are asleep, but the principle is the same, as they have adapted to foraging at night and sleeping during the day.

IS SLEEP THE MOST ADAPTIVE APPROACH?

- Not clear why a complex physiological mechanism such as sleep would evolve simply to keep vulnerable animals out of harm's way.
- A state of behavioural inactivity would serve the same purpose, as well as making animals less vulnerable.
- The fact that many animals 'freeze' when threatened by predators supports the view that the safest state would be to remain inconspicuous but alert.

THE DISADVANTAGES OF SLEEP

- Sleep is a costly behaviour – while animals are asleep, cannot be vigilant against predators, forage or take care of their young.
- For aquatic mammals, sleep underwater can be dangerous because they need to breathe. The bottlenose dolphin solves this problem by 'switching off' one cerebral hemisphere at a time.

REM AND NREM SLEEP

- The energy consumption of the brain drops only in NREM sleep, whereas during REM sleep the brain is still relatively active and using energy.
- This suggests that it is only NREM sleep that has evolved for energy conservation.

ENERGY CONSERVATION (WEBB, 1982)

- Warm-blooded animals need to expend a great deal of energy to maintain a constant body temperature.
- Small animals have a higher metabolic rate and so use more energy when foraging, escaping from predators, etc.
- Sleep provides a period of enforced inactivity where the animal is able to conserve energy.
- The energy consumption of the brain drops considerably during NREM sleep, although not during REM sleep.
- This is evident from the observation that the amount of time spent sleeping varies according to the size and metabolic rate of a species.
- Also varies with other factors such as foraging needs and predator avoidance.

SLEEP VERSUS REST

- Compared to resting, sleep reduces energy rates by only 10%, suggesting that rest would be almost as effective as a way of conserving energy.
- The greater risks associated with sleeping (rather than simply resting) would outweigh any small advantage gained.

UNILATERAL SLEEP

- The fact that some animals engage in unilateral sleep shows that whatever the function of sleep, it can be satisfied while an animal is partially active.
- This suggests that conservation of energy cannot be the sole function of sleep.

RESEARCH SUPPORT FOR MEDDIS' THEORY (SLEEP AND PREDATOR AVOIDANCE)

ALLISON AND CICCHETTI (1976)

- Studied 39 species of mammal to see if there was any relationship between the amount of sleep taken by each species and the degree of danger experienced in their natural habitat.

FINDINGS

- They discovered that the amount of sleep taken by an animal correlated negatively with the amount of danger typically experienced. In particular, they found that **REM sleep was associated with predatory danger.**

This supports the claim that...

The evolution of sleep has been associated with the need to remain safe from predators, and suggests that large amounts of REM sleep are disadvantageous in prey species.

MUKHAMETOV (1984)

- Studied how marine mammals have dealt with the need to sleep at the same time as avoiding the dangers in their environment.

FINDINGS

- The bottlenose dolphin and porpoise 'switch off' one hemisphere at a time (unihemispheric sleep). During sleep, they are still able to come up to the surface to breathe, as their sleep is not accompanied by motor paralysis.

This shows that...

- One hemisphere remains alert (against potential danger) while the other is able to catch up on sleep.

RATTENBORG ET AL. (1999)

- When mallard ducks sleep, the two at the end of the line should display unihemispheric sleep because of greater vulnerability to predators.

FINDINGS

- They found that these birds were more likely to sleep with one eye open than birds elsewhere in the line. They kept their outward facing eye directed towards any potential danger.

However...

When Boerema et al. (2003) deprived chickens of sleep, they found that the fraction of monocular sleep (one eye shut) decreased in favour of binocular sleep (both eyes shut). This suggests that chickens abandon unihemispheric sleep when sleep deprived, at the cost of reduced alertness.

RESEARCH SUPPORT FOR WEBB'S THEORY (SLEEP AND ENERGY CONSERVATION)

ZEPELIN AND RECHTSCHAFFEN (1974)

- Studied species of mammals to investigate relationship between metabolic rate and how long each species spent sleeping.

FINDINGS

- Found a negative correlation between the body size of a species and the amount of time it spent sleeping. Small animals spent more hours asleep; larger animals relatively little.

This supports the claim that...

Animals with higher metabolic rates must conserve energy by sleeping for longer periods.

ENDOTHERMY AND NREM SLEEP

- Evidence in favour of the energy conservation theory is the universal presence of NREM sleep in endothermic (warm-blooded) mammals and birds, and its absence in ectotherms (cold-blooded).

This suggests that...

NREM sleep evolved as a way of offsetting the increased energy consumption required for endothermy.

However...

Kavanau (2004) claims that as endothermy evolved and the energy demands necessary to maintain higher body temperatures increased, the loss of muscle tone associated with NREM may have become insufficient to prevent muscle contractions during sleep. This would have created adaptive pressure which led to the inhibition of muscle tone associated with REM sleep.

TYPICAL QUESTIONS...

1 Critically consider one or more ecological theories of sleep. (24 marks)

2 Discuss research (theories and/or studies) related to the ecological account of sleep. (24 marks)

3 Describe and evaluate two or more research studies related to the ecological account of sleep. (24 marks)

4 (a) Describe one or more ecological theories of sleep. (12 marks)

(b) Evaluate the one or more ecological theories of sleep that you described in (a) in terms of research evidence. (12 marks)

RESTORATION THEORIES OF SLEEP AND RESEARCH STUDIES RELATING TO THE FUNCTIONS OF SLEEP

OSWALD'S RESTORATION THEORY

REM sleep and brain restoration
- High levels of brain activity seen during REM sleep indicate brain recovery.
- During REM sleep, the brain engages in protein synthesis – in a six-week period over half the total protein in the brain is replaced.
- This is consistent with the increases in REM sleep time that occur after brain insults such as drug overdose or intensive ECT.
- Sleeping also helps to conserve neurotransmitters, levels of which fall over the course of a day.
- During REM sleep, neurons that have been active during the day cease firing, but they continue to synthesise new neurotransmitters for release during the next day.

MUST KNOW...
- Two restoration theories of the functions of sleep and research studies relating to those theories.

SWS and bodily restoration
- An increase in the body's hormone activities during SWS reflects restoration and recovery in the body.
- The secretion of growth hormone (important in protein synthesis) at night is dependent on uninterrupted Stage 4 sleep.
- Berger and Oswald (1962) showed that on the first night after sleep deprivation a marked increase in NREM sleep was observed whilst REM remained the same. On subsequent nights REM sleep was higher, showing that NREM sleep has priority in the recovery process.

Challenges for Oswald's theory
- Effect of energy expenditure: intense energy expenditure during the day should increase the duration of sleep in order to restore the resources used. However, intense exercise does not cause people to sleep for longer (Rosenzweig et al., 1999).
- SWS and protein synthesis: Horne (1988) points out that as amino acids (the constituents of proteins) are only freely available for five hours after a meal, and most people eat several hours before going to bed, this suggests that not much protein synthesis goes on during sleep.

OSWALD (1980)

Support for Oswald's theory
- Animal studies: prolonged sleep deprivation in rats causes them to increase their metabolic rate, lose weight and die (Everson et al., 1989). Allowing these animals to sleep prevents their death. However, difficult to separate the effects of sleep deprivation and the methods used to keep the animals asleep (i.e. constant stress).
- Studies of newborns: the view that REM sleep is essential for brain restoration is supported by the high proportion of REM sleep observed in the newborn baby (50–60% of sleep time compared to 25% in adults).

HORNE'S CORE SLEEP THEORY

CORE SLEEP
- Horne (1988) claimed that sleep deprivation in normal participants produced only mild effects (e.g. the case of Randy Gardner).
- Sleep recovery following deprivation was mainly Stage 4 SWS and REM sleep.
- Horne proposed that Stage 4 sleep and REM constitutes core sleep, which is essential for normal brain functioning in humans.
- He claimed that the lighter stages of NREM sleep are not essential and so are referred to as optional sleep.
- Bodily restoration takes place during periods of relaxed wakefulness leaving core sleep to provide for the restoration of brain systems.

MUST REMEMBER...
That questions may just ask for 'the restoration' approach, in which case either or both of these theories would be relevant.

HORNE (1988)

- In support of this theory, Horne (1988) reviewed 50 studies in which people had been deprived of sleep – very few reported that sleep deprivation interfered with the ability to perform physical exercise.
- To challenge the idea that sleep is necessary for bodily restoration, Horne and Minard (1985) gave participants exhausting tasks to see if this increased the duration of their sleep. Participants went to sleep faster than usual, but not for longer.
- However, although REM sleep is part of core sleep, humans can do without it for months at a time without any ill effects. This suggests that much of REM sleep is dispensable.

RESEARCH SUPPORT FOR OSWALD'S THEORY

OSWALD (1969)
- Observed patients recovering from drug overdoses or other brain insults (such as those occurring as a result of intensive ECT).

FINDINGS
- He found that all these brain insults were followed by a significant increase in the quantity of REM sleep.

This suggests that...
This was indicative of recovery processes going on in the brain.

MOLDOFSKY ET AL. (1975)
- Deprived healthy volunteers of Stage 4 sleep. In adulthood, a chronic lack of this type of sleep is found in sufferers of fibrositis.

FINDINGS
- The disturbance of Stage 4 sleep in these volunteers caused the symptoms of fibrositis to appear.

This supports the view that...
SWS (Stage 4) promotes bodily growth and repair, as disruption of this type of sleep leaves patients deriving little benefit from sleep.

DEMENT (1978)
- Studied the case of a 17-year old schoolboy (Randy Gardner) who stayed awake for a total of 264 hours.

FINDINGS
- His sleep deprivation resulted in consequences, including blurred vision and incoherent speech.
- Effects were mild – recovered quickly when he eventually slept.
- Recovery was mainly restricted to Stage 4 SWS and REM sleep.

This challenges the view that...
All stages of sleep are important in bodily restoration, as very little of stages 1–3 was recovered during the days after deprivation.

MUST REMEMBER...
These studies can be used to evaluate the two theories covered overleaf (as AO2).

RESEARCH SUPPORT FOR HORNE'S THEORY

BERGER AND WALKER (1972)
- Studied the effects of sleep loss on subsequent sleep recovery.

FINDINGS
- First night after deprivation – large increase in the relative amount of Stage 3 and 4 sleep at the expense of the lighter stages of sleep.
- Second and third nights after deprivation – a relative increase in the amount of REM sleep.

This supports the view that...
Stage 4 sleep and REM sleep constitute 'core' sleep, as following sleep deprivation, they are almost completely recovered. The remainder (optional sleep), must therefore have no physiological function.

STERN AND MORGANE (1974)
- Studied whether patients on anti-depressant drugs would show increased levels of REM sleep following a period of sleep deprivation. REM sleep is important because it usually replenishes neurotransmitters used up during the previous day.

FINDINGS
- No increase in REM sleep (i.e. no REM rebound) when patients slept normally after their sleep deprivation.

This means that...
Because these drugs increase the levels of serotonin and dopamine in the brain, this reduces the need for REM sleep rebound.

TYPICAL QUESTIONS...

1 Critically consider one or more restoration theories of sleep. (24 marks)

2 Discuss research (theories and/or studies) related to the restoration account of sleep. (24 marks)

3 Describe and evaluate two or more research studies related to the restoration account of sleep. (24 marks)

4 (a) Describe one or more restoration theories of sleep. (12 marks)
  (b) Evaluate the one or more restoration theories of sleep that you described in (a) in terms of research evidence. (12 marks)

RESEARCH RELATING TO THE NATURE OF DREAMS

RESEARCH INTO THE CONTENT OF DREAMS

MUST KNOW...
• Description of and commentary on research into the nature of dreams (e.g. content, duration or type).

This is supported by...
• Watson (2003) – found evidence that personality characteristics were the most significant factor in dream recall.
• Those prone to imagination and fantasy much more likely than others to remember dreams and report them with vivid imagery.

Who do we dream about?
• Dreams usually involve other people, although the dreamer is nearly always involved in their own dream. Kahn et al. (2000) analysed hundreds of dream reports, and found that half the people appearing in dreams were known personally by the dreamer, with fewer than one in six being completely unknown.

Nightmares
Gibson (2005) argues that the content of nightmares revolves around the **threat of imminent harm** to the individual. This would explain why many people involved in the September 11th terrorist attack in New York have since experienced nightmares involving terrorists, people jumping from buildings, etc.

Dreams and creativity
• The dream experience is believed to be the most creative form of consciousness for some people, e.g. Coleridge's epic poem *Kubla Khan* was written moments after rising from a deep sleep. The symbols, images and experiences of dreams are believed to represent what is going on at the deeper levels of the psyche.

RESEARCH INTO THE CONTENT OF DREAMS

Emotional content
• Dreams frequently have a strong emotional content.
• PET scans taken during REM sleep show that brain regions associated with emotions tend to be very active during REM sleep, but thinking and decision-making areas are less active.

This is supported by...
Strauch and Meier (1996) – found little evidence of the dreamer being emotionally involved in events in their NREM dreams, but plenty of evidence of this in REM dreams.

REM and NREM differences
• Research suggests that there are content differences between REM and NREM dreaming.
• REM dreams are reported as being more emotional than NREM dreams.
• NREM dreams tend to be less vivid and more thought-like than REM dreams.

This is supported by...
Physiological observations of increased blood flow to the amygdala (which plays a role in the formation and consolidation of memories of emotional experiences) during REM dreaming (Maquet et al., 1996).

Lucid dreaming means dreaming while knowing that you are dreaming.

DREAMS AND REAL TIME
• Dement and Wolpert (1958) attempted to mark a point in the passage of dreaming time by spraying water over their sleeping participants.
• They then compared the length of time elapsed between this stimulation and the waking of participants with the length of the reported dreams.
• The results indicated that the events reported in the dream corresponded approximately to the actual passage of time.

RESEARCH INTO THE DURATION OF DREAMS

This is supported by...
• Research by LaBerge et al. (1981) – asked **lucid dreamers** to estimate various intervals of time while dreaming.
• The dreamers were able to mark the beginning and end of estimated dream time intervals with eye movement signals.
• Comparison of these estimates with actual time showed that the intervals of time estimated during the lucid dreams were very close to the actual elapsed time.

DIFFERENT TYPES OF DREAM

MUST REMEMBER...

That an answer to the question below can use any combination of the research on these two pages.

Evaluation

- Martin (2002) claims that although many of the features of REM dreams are present in hynopompic and hypnagogic dreams, there are fewer of these in any one dream, suggesting that they are a 'reduced' version of normal dreaming.

Hypnopompic dreams

- Prior to a person waking up, a state similar to the hypnagogic state may occur.
- The most common bodily sensation during the hypnopompic state is sleep paralysis.

Hypnagogic dreams

- These are a type of dream state a person can go through when falling asleep.
- When experiencing hypnagogia, the individual is still conscious of their surroundings, and so is effectively dreaming while still awake.
- When in this state, a person can experience lifelike auditory, visual, or tactile hallucinations, yet be unable to react to them.

Evidence for hypnagogic dreams

- In one study, participants were required to play the computer game *Tetris* for several hours.
- Many of these participants later reported vivid dreams about *Tetris* as they fell asleep (Stickgold et al., 2000).

Gender and cultural differences in nightmares

- Women report having nightmares more often than men, although unclear whether women *experience* different rates of nightmares, or are simply more likely to report them.
- Some cultures view nightmares as indicative of mental health problems, whereas others view them as related to supernatural phenomena.

Nightmares

- Nightmares refer to elaborate dreams that cause high levels of anxiety or terror.
- They occur almost exclusively during REM sleep. As REM sleep periods become longer in the second half of the night, nightmares become more intense during this time.
- Nightmares are common in the early phases after a traumatic experience.

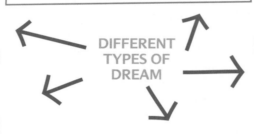

DIFFERENT TYPES OF DREAM

Precognitive dreams

- These are dreams that appear to predict the future. The future can be revealed in a dream by the dreamer directly seeing a future event taking place, or through some form of symbolism which must then be interpreted to give it meaning.

Evidence for precognitive dreams

- Stowell (1997) interviewed five people who claimed to have precognitive dreams.
- Of the 51 presumed precognitive dreams, she was able to demonstrate that 37 had come true.
- In addition, all five dreamers had precognitive experiences while awake – many of these confirmed.

Applications of lucid dreaming research

- LaBerge (1998) argues that lucid dreaming offers potential for a variety of practical applications.
- These include enhancing self-confidence, overcoming nightmares, improving mental health, and helping creative problem-solving.

Lucid dreaming

- Lucid dreamers develop a frame of mind that allows them to recognise when they are dreaming.
- Some researchers believe that in order for the state of a dreaming person to be classified as lucid, that person must have control over their 'dreamscape'.

MUST TAKE CARE...

To elaborate any AO2 commentary in order to make it **effective**.

TYPICAL QUESTION...

1 Discuss research (theories and/or studies) into the nature of dreams. (24 marks)

For practice in answering A2 Psychology questions, why not use *Collins Do Brilliantly A2 Psychology*?

THEORIES OF THE FUNCTION OF DREAMING

NEUROBIOLOGICAL THEORIES

MUST KNOW...
- Two neurobiological and two psychological theories of the functions of dreaming.

Reverse learning

- The cortex cannot cope with the vast amount of information gathered during the day without developing 'parasitic' thoughts.
- These unwanted connections in the cortex would disrupt the efficiency of memory if not removed.
- During REM sleep, these connections are wiped out by impulses coming from subcortical areas.
- The strength of the individual synapses associated with these connections is modified during reverse learning so that they are less likely to be activated in the future.
- As a result, other adaptive memories are made more significant, since there is no longer as much irrelevant information to check through.
- The content of dreams is a consequence of these parasitic thoughts as they are erased from memory.

Reverse learning: 'we dream to forget'.

Reverse learning in a nutshell

The brain is 'off-line' during dreaming, which enables it to sift through all the information gathered during the previous day, and discard anything that isn't needed.

THE REVERSE-LEARNING MODEL (CRICK AND MITCHISON, 1983)

MUST TAKE CARE...
Not to mix up neurobiological and psychological theories when answering exam questions.

Research support

- Studies of the spiny anteater have shown that it has no REM sleep, but has an enlarged frontal cortex.
- Crick and Mitchison argue that this excessive cortical development is necessary in order to store both adaptive *and* parasitic memories, which in humans would be disposed of during dreaming.

Problems for this model

- Dreams are often organised into clear narrative (i.e. stories). The model fails to explain why this should happen if they consist simply of disposable, parasitic thoughts.
- Crick and Mitchison later restricted the reverse learning model to apply only to dreams with bizarre imagery and no clear narrative.

Activation

- Evidence from EEG measurements shows that the cortex is highly active during REM sleep.
- During REM sleep, motor output (bodily movement) and sensory input are inhibited, so that we experience sleep paralysis, and external stimuli are prevented from entering our brain.
- Pathways ascending from the brainstem carry random signals to higher areas of the brain, producing rapid eye movements and spreading activation over the association cortex, where memory traces are stored.

Activation-synthesis in a nutshell

During REM sleep, all sensory input and motor output are blocked, yet the neurons in the cerebral cortex are still activated by random sensory impulses. The forebrain attempts to make sense out of this internally generated information, and a dream is created.

THE ACTIVATION-SYNTHESIS MODEL (HOBSON AND MCCARLEY, 1977)

Research support

- Braun et al. (1997) used PET scans to show that the brainstem is active during REM sleep. This gives support to the *activation* part of the activation-synthesis model.

Synthesis

- When this activation reaches the areas of the brain that normally process external sensations, these areas essentially do the same job that they do during wakefulness, i.e. they try to make sense of the stimuli being received.
- The sometimes bizarre nature of dreams is due to the mixing of the random stimuli received from the brainstem with stored images in memory and the brain's efforts to make sense of this mix.

Research challenge

- The activation-synthesis model has been challenged by the following findings:
  - Vogel (1978) has shown that dreams indistinguishable from the dreams of REM sleep can occur in the absence of REM sleep → dreams can arise *without* the brainstem activation produced during REM sleep.
  - Likewise REM sleep can occur in the absence of dreaming (Frank, 1950), i.e. synthesis does not take place.
  - Solms (2000) studied case histories of brain-damaged patients – when people incur injuries to their brain stem, REM activity almost invariably ceases but dreaming continues.

PSYCHOLOGICAL THEORIES

MUST TAKE CARE ...
Not to write about Freud's theory of personality development.

FREUDIAN THEORY OF DREAMING
Dreams represented the disguised fulfilment of desires repressed into the unconscious mind.

Function of dreams
Dreams protect the sleeper from urges that would be unacceptable to them when awake, but at the same time allow some expression of them.

Manifest and latent content
The *real* meaning of a dream (latent content) is transformed into a more innocuous form (manifest content) which can be interpreted by an analyst.

Dream work
The transformation of repressed desires into symbols in the dream is through dream work, e.g. 'representability' (hidden thoughts are translated into visual images).

Dream symbols
Some parts of manifest content typically correspond with certain latent content, and so have constant meaning.

RESEARCH SUPPORT
- Kohler and Borchers (1996) tested Freud's assumption that the content of dreams would reflect the **repressed unconscious** and that interpretation based on this content should produce resistance from the individual.
- The resulting feelings of uneasiness were more pronounced during associations to the person's own dreams than to those of another individual.

PROBLEMS WITH THE THEORY
- Hobson and McCarley (1977) argue that dreams are simply an artifact of brain activity during sleep, and therefore **have no real meaning or emotional content**.
- This view is markedly different from Freud's view that dreams represented the fulfilment of unconscious desires.

- The primary function of dreams is the organisation of a new emotional experience, relating it to what we have learned from past experience, i.e. dreams serve an important mood regulation function.
- We don't dream about everyday experiences, but those that are novel and have produced an emotional response.

Conflicting evidence
- Several studies (e.g. Cartwright, 1986) have found that dream recall is increased during times of emotional stress (e.g. women undergoing divorce).
- However, research with combat veterans and trauma survivors (e.g. Lavie and Kaminer, 1991) has found very low dream recall among individuals exposed to extreme stress.
- This finding appears to be at odds with the mood regulation role of dreams.

MOOD REGULATION HYPOTHESIS (CARTWRIGHT, 1984)

- Cartwright's research has shown that people who are more worried or unhappy than usual will start the night with a short dream with some negative feelings. The next dream is more complicated but still has negative feeling.
- By the third dream there is a change in feeling to be more positive and the last dream produces a better solution to the emotional problem.

Subjectivity of dreams
- To interpret dreams, psychologists must rely on the subjective report of the dreamer.
- Goes against the scientific requirement that behaviour should be observable and objective.
- May limit the validity of any conclusions as researchers must trust the accounts given by participants.

TYPICAL QUESTIONS...

1 Describe and evaluate one or more neurobiological theories of the function of dreaming. (24 marks)

2 Outline and evaluate two psychological theories of the function of dreaming. (24 marks)

3 (a) Outline and evaluate one neurobiological theory of the function of dreaming. (12 marks)

(b) Outline and evaluate one neurobiological theory of the function of dreaming. (12 marks)

ROLE OF BRAIN STRUCTURES IN MOTIVATIONAL STATES

HUNGER

OUTLINE OF THEORY
• Hypothalamus – operates on principle of homeostatic drive reduction.
• Ventromedial hypothalamus (VMH) – satiety centre.
• Lateral hypothalamus (LH) – feeding centre.

◄ **DUAL-CENTRE HYPOTHALMIC MODEL** ►

RESEARCH STUDIES
• Hetherington and Ranson (1942): lesions of VMH caused overeating in rats.
• Anand and Brobeck (1951): lesions of LH inhibited eating; rats lost weight.

In essays on theories, can use research studies as AO1 or AO2. In essays on research studies, can use theories as AO2 (implications).

• Limitations – not a complete explanation because it needs information about body's energy reserves, e.g. glucose – but still not clear how these are signalled.
• Abnormal function may cause eating disorders (AS studies).

OUTLINE OF THEORY
• Hypothalamus triggered by blood glucose levels.
• Glucoreceptors in blood vessels, liver and brain (hypothalamus).

◄ **GLUCOSTAT HYPOTHESIS** ►

RESEARCH STUDIES
• Tordoff et al. (1982): injected glucose → decreased food intake.
• LeMagnen (1981): higher insulin levels during day → lower blood glucose → increase appetite.

Challenged by...
• Wickens, 2000:
  – High levels of glucose (in diabetics) lead to coma but not increased appetite.
  – Injections of glucose into hypothalamic glucoreceptors do not inhibit eating.

• Not full explanation – blood glucose levels vary little even after starvation because:
  – homeostasis ensures that when less is eaten, stored fat is converted to glucose
  – intake of excess sugar converted to fat by insulin.

OUTLINE OF THEORY
• Hypothalamus monitors fat levels and maintains at a set-point.
• Set-point fixed by inherited factors and early nutritional experience.

◄ **BODY WEIGHT SET-POINT** ►

RESEARCH STUDY
• Nisbett (1972): VMH lesions caused overeating in rats until weight reached set-point.

Challenged by...
• Weindruch et al. (1986): reduced intake of calories → improved health but not weight loss.
• Kagawa (1978): human studies of Japanese – low calorie diet → high life span.

• Support for theory – body weight regulated in most people.
• Implications – lack of weight loss due to having high set-point.
• It isn't good for your health to follow hypothalamic urges, e.g. Kagawa found that Japanese have low calorie intake but long lifespan.

OUTLINE OF THEORY
• Leptin (protein) produced by fat tissue.
• Acts as a hormone and decreases appetite.

◄ **GLUCOSTAT HYPOTHESIS** ►

RESEARCH STUDIES
• Zhang et al. (1994): mice with genetic mutation were extremely obese; not producing leptin.
• Halaas et al. (1995): demonstrated cause by injecting leptin into mutant mice → weight loss.

THIRST

OSMOTIC THIRST

1 Loss of water (e.g. sweating, urination) raises osmotic pressure of extracellular compartments.

2 Causes water from intercellular to pass through semi-permeable membrane to equalise pressure.

3 Happens in all cells including pre-optic area (hypothalamus).

4 Osmoreceptors stimulate drinking and release of ADH (anti-diuretic hormone) from pituitary which promotes water recovery in kidneys.

HYPOVOLEMIC THIRST

1 Sudden water loss, e.g. bleeding.

2 Low blood volume stimulates baroreceptors (in walls of blood vessels).

3 Sends message to hypothalamus to stimulate drinking and release ADH.

4 Stimulates kidneys directly to release renin (hormone).

5 Renin converts angiotensin into angiotensin I → angiotensin II – constricts blood vessels and thus raises blood pressure.

6 Angiotensin II also effects release of ADH.

7 Falling salt levels lead to release of aldosterone (hormone) – reduces water and salt loss from kidneys.

RESEARCH STUDY

• Injecting salt solution into pre-optic area stimulates drinking and release of ADH.

• Injecting water decreases in both.

• More complex than osmotic thirst.
• Desire for salty food may be increased by aldosterone.

• Other brain circuits involved, e.g. acetylcholine (neurotransmitter) and the limbic system = cholinergic theory of drinking.
• Simpler system for thirst than hunger and system understood better.
• Non-human animals – may not be totally reasonable to generalise from such studies to humans.

RESEARCH STUDIES

• Epstein et al., 1970: injection of angiotensin II into rats' pre-optic area stimulated drinking even if not deprived of water.

MUST REMEMBER...
Research studies can be AO1 or AO2 depending on hour they are presented.

PLEASURE

PLEASURE CENTRES

1 Animals and people motivated by rewards.

2 Stimulation of MFB (median forebrain bundle) creates feelings of pleasure.

3 Satisfying hunger/thirst stimulates MFB, but stimulation stops when satiated.

4 MFB may also be involved in addictive behaviour – drugs increase neurotransmitter activity in MFB.

RESEARCH STUDIES
Olds and Milner (1954)

• Found rats in Skinner box sought ESB (electrical stimulation of the brain) applied to septal area (limbic system), i.e. it was rewarding.

• ESB to amygdala and hypothalamus rewarding too, and especially the MFB.

• Rewarding – hungry/thirsty rats preferred ESB to eating/drinking.

• Didn't stop with satiation – they kept on pressing.

• Drugs of abuse (e.g. ecstasy and cocaine) stimulate noradrenaline and dopamine, neurotransmitters involved in reward pathways.

• ESB is artificial – not naturally motivated behaviour, thus findings should be interpreted cautiously.
• Non-human animals used in most experimental studies.

TYPICAL QUESTIONS...

1 (a) Describe the role of brain structures relating to **one** motivational state. (12 marks)
  (b) Evaluate the role of brain structures described in part (a) with reference to research studies. (12 marks)

2 Discuss theories of the role of brain structures relating to **two** motivational states. (24 marks)

3 Critically consider research studies relating to **one or more** motivational states. (24 marks)

PHYSIOLOGICAL, COMBINED AND PSYCHOLOGICAL APPROACHES TO EXPLAINING MOTIVATION

MUST KNOW...
- Physiological and combined physiological/psychological approaches to explaining motivation.
- Psychological approaches to explaining motivation.

PHYSIOLOGICAL APPROACH

HOMEOSTATIC DRIVES

LONG TERM
- e.g. Eating reduces **hunger** drive.
- Eating → calories → increase body weight.
- Long-term – body weight **maintained** within narrow limits (i.e. homestasis).

- Over-simple – based on tissue needs; human behaviour more complex.
- Psychological factors, e.g. social customs (see psychological theories overleaf).
- Sensory factors, e.g. children eat more different-coloured *Smarties* than if they were all the same (Rolls et al., 1982).
- Obesity – shows that food intake not simply homeostatic.
- Non-human animals used in most experimental studies.

*Must use other theories **effectively**.*

SHORT TERM
- Homeostasis regulated in:
  - **mouth** (taste)
  - **stomach** (signals satiety via vagus nerve)
  - **small intestine** (CCK released after meal).

- Spiegel (1973): liquid food passed to stomach through tube, body weight maintained through food intake but meals unsatisfying – craved taste.
  - Shows taste important but not necessary to regulate hunger.

- Antin et al. (1975): tube inserted in rats so food didn't reach stomach → ate more.
  - Shows taste not sufficient to regulate hunger.

- Cannon and Washburn (1912): hunger pangs correlated with stomach contractions using swallowed balloon.
  - Shows stomach signals fullness and sensitive to quality as well as quantity.
- Deutsch et al. (1978): rats with intestine block ate smaller amounts of high-calorie food.

Must be clear whether research studies are used as AO1 or AO2.

- People with parts of stomach removed have problems with food intake.
  - Shows stomach not only source of feedback.

- Injections of cholecystokinin (CCK) reduce meal size.
  - Could be satiety hormone; no direct evidence.

COMBINED APPROACH

DRIVE-REDUCTION THEORY

OUTLINE OF THEORY (HULL, 1943)
- Drives for e.g. food, warmth.
- Homeostasis → **drive-reduction**.
- Rewarding and reinforces behaviour.
- Thus behaviour **learned**.
- **Secondary reinforcers**, e.g. baby's mother associated with food and thus a link learned between the reward and mother.

- Testable theory.
- Complexity of human behaviour explained with secondary reinforcers, but not convincing, e.g. Alexander the Great motivated by seeking mother's approval.
- Absence of rewards – rats did learn in maze (Tolman, 1948).
- Behaviour that isn't drive-reducing can't be explained, e.g. spatial learning.
- Circular explanation – drive exists because animal does it; long list of drives.
- Cognitive processes – e.g. expectation, not included. Ideal model would combine Hull with Maslow (see overleaf).

Can use drive-reduction as a physiological approach.

PSYCHOLOGICAL APPROACHES

OPTIMAL AROUSAL THEORY

OUTLINE OF THEORY
- Under-aroused – seek stimulation, e.g. puzzles.
- Over-aroused – avoid stimulation.
- Applied to personality – **sensation seekers** (people who seek thrills), **Zuckerman, 1994.**

- Improvement on homeostatic model but still homeostatic, e.g. reduction of boredom.
- Can explain behaviour with no purpose, e.g. play – though explained as skill practice.
- Too simple – explaining exploration as due to boredom overlooks main purpose, i.e. for survival.
- Arousal involves many pathways and not one single system.

EXPECTANCY THEORY

OUTLINE OF THEORY
- Emphasis on **pull** rather than push.
- **Incentives** – we go to work because we expect to get rewards.
- **Persistence** – once reward pathways activated, then response not extinguished even if need not satisfied.

- Explains children and rats preferring chocolate to muesli (Valenstein, 1967).
- Can't explain 'pointless' behaviour, e.g. computer games.
- Complexity of human behaviour not explained, e.g. long-term incentives.

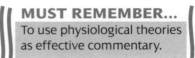

MUST REMEMBER...
To use physiological theories as effective commentary.

MASLOW'S HIERARCHY OF NEEDS

OUTLINE OF THEORY
- Basic needs satisfied first (**prepotent**).
- Higher needs less easy to satisfy.
- Higher needs more long-term.
- **Self-actualisation** difficult to reach and often transitory (e.g. sport, childbirth).

- Human emphasis – psychological (higher) needs.
- Humanistic approach emphasises capacity of each person to be self-determining.
- Useful framework for discussing complexity of human motivation.
- Hierarchy – questionable, e.g. great artists paint rather than eat; people pursue dangerous sports.
- Self-actualisation – vague concept; may be culture-specific.
- Lack of research evidence – difficult to collect.

Self-actualisation, e.g. peak experience

Aesthetic, e.g. love of art and nature

Cognitive, i.e. knowledge

Esteem, e.g. respect and self-respect

Love and belonging – individual and group

Safety – physical and psychological

Physiological, e.g. hunger, thirst, sex, sleep

For practice in answering A2 Psychology questions, why not use *Collins Do Brilliantly A2 Psychology*?

TYPICAL QUESTIONS...

1 Describe and evaluate physiological approaches to explaining motivation. (24 marks)

2 (a) Discuss **one** physiological approach to explaining motivation. (12 marks)
(b) Discuss **one** combined psychological and physiological approach to explaining motivation. (12 marks)

3 Critically consider **one or more** psychological approaches to explaining motivation. (24 marks)

4 (a) Discuss **one** physiological approach to explaining motivation. (12 marks)
(b) Discuss **one** psychological approach to explaining motivation. (12 marks)

EMOTION

THE ROLE OF BRAIN STRUCTURES

THE LIMBIC SYSTEM

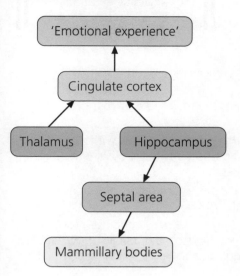

OUTLINE OF ROLE OF BRAIN STRUCTURES
- Cerebral cortex – removal led to decorticate rage if animal angered.
- Temporal lobes and amygdala – Kluver-Bucy syndrome (placid, over-sexual and orality).
- Papez circuit (1937): hypothalamus (emotional expression) and the limbic system (emotional experience).
- Papez-Maclean model (1949): limbic brain (emotional feeling and behaviour), 'new mammalian cortex' (higher cognitive emotional functions), brainstem (physiological functions).

- Kluver and Bucy (1939) removed temporal lobes in Rhesus monkeys.

- Papez (1937) observed heightened emotional behaviour of people with rabies, which affects hippocampus.

- Morris et al. (1996): PET scan showed increased amygdala activity with fearful faces in humans.

- Mitchell and Blair (2000): some mental disorders may be linked to abnormal amygdala.

Must emphasise brain structures if James-Lange theory used in question on brain structures.

- Research evidence – as above right.
- Non-human animals used in research; focused on expression not experience.
- Limited range of emotions – model applies to dramatic emotions, e.g. rage, fear.
- Generalising to humans may be difficult.
- Applications: psychosurgery to treat emotional disorders, e.g. frontal lobe lesions.

PHYSIOLOGICAL APPROACHES

JAMES-LANGE THEORY

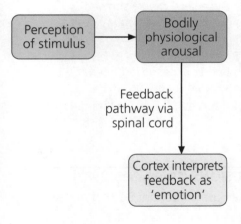

OUTLINE OF THEORY
- Emotion-arousing stimulus (e.g. hungry bear) → behavioural response (e.g. running away).
- Physiological changes interpreted by brain as fear.
- Emphasises the role of feedback to the brain from peripheral physiological arousal.

- Limited patterns of arousal – should have a different pattern of arousal for each emotion. True for extreme emotions (e.g. fear) but not others.
- Physiological change slow – emotions are almost instantaneous.
- Over-reliance on feedback – patient with spinal damage experienced emotion (Dana, 1921) *but* other patients do experience reduced feelings (Hohmann, 1966).
- Exercise should produce emotion, e.g. running up stairs.
- Drugs may produce emotion, e.g. Marañon (1924) – 'as if' experiences from injected adrenaline.

CANNON-BARD THEORY

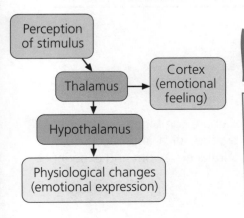

OUTLINE OF THEORY
- Perception of stimulus triggers conscious emotional experience.
- Simultaneously triggers bodily arousal and muscular activity.

Can use Cannon-Bard as AO1 or AO2.

COMBINED APPROACHES

COGNITIVE LABELLING THEORY (CLT) (SCHACHTER AND SINGER, 1962)

MUST KNOW...
• Combined physiological/ psychological approaches to explaining emotional behaviour and experience.

OUTLINE OF THEORY

1 Emotion is combination of peripheral and central factors:
  • Perception of stimulus triggers bodily arousal.
  • Cognitive appraisal determines particular emotion.
2 Like James-Lange theory:
  • Arousal → emotion.
  • But CLT says same pattern of arousal in different emotional states.
3 Like Cannon-Bard theory:
  • Brain (cognitive appraisal) → emotional experience.
  • But CLT adds role of the environment.

• Conclusion – arousal is a necessary but not sufficient condition.
• Strength – demonstrates the major role of cognitive processes.
• Arousal without emotion – sadness occurs without arousal. Valins (1966) showed participants felt arousal when told their heart rate increased.
• Different physiological states – for primary emotions such as fear (Schwarz et al., 1981).
• **Alternative theory:** Zajonc (1984) – cognitive processes and emotion can be independent, e.g. babies show fear with no high-level cognitive abilities.

RESEARCH STUDY

Schachter and Singer, 1962

• Theory predicts that an individual who experiences a state of unexplained bodily arousal seeks an explanation from the environment.
• Procedure:
  1 Uninformed and informed participants: some had 'unexplained arousal' – given vitamin (Suproxin), actually adrenaline; other participants knew what expected effects would be.
  2 Environment – confederate acting euphorically or angry during questionnaire session.
• Findings: uninformed group reacted more euphorically or angrily than the informed group.

Remember that the participants in Marañon's study were an informed group – no need to 'seek explanation'.

• Control group – participants' emotional state not assessed beforehand.
• Internal validity – some participants worked out that the injection led to arousal.
• Representativeness – unexplained bodily arousal is not a 'normal' state.
• Emotion or imitation? Observers' report showed emotional differences but not the participants' self-reports. Adrenaline may facilitate imitation.
• Supported by: e.g. **Dutton and Aron (1974)** – participants on a high bridge experienced intensified physical attraction; two-factor theory of love.
• Attempts to replicate unsuccessful – e.g. Marshall and Zimbardo (1979).

CONCLUSIONS (Strongman, 1987)

• Bodily arousal important but not necessary.
• Cognitive processes necessary.
• Vast range of human emotions means that a simple model linking emotion, arousal and cognition is unrealistic.

TYPICAL QUESTIONS...

1 Critically consider the role of brain structures in emotional behaviour and experience. (24 marks)

2 Describe and evaluate physiological approaches to explaining emotional behaviour and experience. (24 marks)

3 Describe and evaluate combined physiological/psychological approaches to explaining emotional behaviour and experience. (24 marks)

EXPLANATIONS AND STUDIES OF FOCUSED ATTENTION

EXPLANATIONS

BROADBENT'S FILTER MODEL OF SELECTIVE ATTENTION

Early-selection models propose a filtering mechanism that selects some inputs and rejects others early on in the attentional process, before analysis for meaning occurs.

TRIESMAN'S ATTENUATOR THEORY

OUTLINE OF THEORY
- Flow diagram represents attentional processes.
- Human brain (computer) handles large amounts of information which may exceed capacity.
- Each ear represents a separate channel.
- Inputs selected at filter stage on physical properties.

OUTLINE OF THEORY
- Filter selects one channel on basis of physical properties.
- Unattended channels continue in attenuated form.
- Semantic analysis stage involves dictionary units.
- Different recognition thresholds.

EXPANSION
- Computer is analogy for human thinking (information processing approach).
- Inputs processed selectively to avoid overload.
- Only one channel attended to.
- Can follow conversation in a noisy room by focusing on, e.g. sound of another person's voice, location of sound.

EXPANSION
- Passed on for semantic analysis.
- 'Breakthroughs' from unattended channel occasional and under certain circumstances.
- Allows all inputs to receive semantic analysis.
- Some permanently low firing thresholds; others fluctuate depending on current relevance.

- Supported by: Cherry (1953) and Broadbent (1954)'s research – showed selection on basis of physical properties.
- Challenged by: semantic processing, e.g. Moray (1959; practice effects (e.g. Underwood, 1974) found target detection improved from 8 to 67% – difficult to accommodate in Broadbent's model.
- What is a channel? → No precise definition, may not apply to real-life settings, e.g. listening to radio.

- Model is flexible – means that research findings explained, e.g. Moray (1959).
- Supported by: Treisman (1960, 1964), see overleaf.
- Attenuation and dictionary units – these parts of model not clearly specified.

DEUTSCH AND DEUTSCH'S MODEL OF SELECTIVE ATTENTION

OUTLINE OF THEORY
- Both attended and unattended inputs fully analysed for meaning.
- Only one input reaches conscious awareness.
- Late selection on basis of salience (relevance to person).

Late-selection models claim that both attended and unattended inputs are analysed for meaning before one input is selected.

- Supported by: Lewis (1970) – found longer processing times when non-shadowed words semantically-related. See also Corteen and Wood (1972).
- Challenged by: Treisman and Geffen (1967) – found detection rates higher (87%) on attended channel than unattended channel (8%) in shadowing tasks.
- Inefficient system – Johnston and Heinz (1978) – suggest selection occurs as early as possible but related to task demands, supported by their study (1979).

EXPANSION
- Explains breakthrough of information from unattended channel.
- Bottleneck occurs late in the system.

STUDIES OF FOCUSED ATTENTION

OUTLINE OF STUDIES

Study 1: Cherry (1953)

- Investigated the cocktail party effect using dichotic listening task.
- Unattended ear – can't recall if isolated words or prose, or switched from English to German, or if played backwards.
- Did notice if gender of speaker, volume or pitch changed.

Study 2: Broadbent (1954)

- Digits presented using split-span procedure.
- Ear-by-ear recall easier than pair-by-pair.

Study 3: Treisman (1960)

- Bilingual participants shadowed message in English; non-shadowed message in French.
- 50% of participants realised both messages were the same.

Study 4: Treisman (1964)

- Ability of participants to shadow message (passage from a novel) worse when non-shadowed message same novel and read in same female voice.
- Task easier when passage different and speaker different.

Study 5: Corteen and Wood (1972)

- Participants conditioned: electric shocks given for words from list related to cities.
- Raised GSR (galvanic skin response) when words from list played to non-attended ear but no conscious awareness.
- Raised GSR when related words played to non-attended ear.

Study 6: Johnston and Heinz (1979)

- High sensory-discriminability (HSD) condition – male and female voice for each channel.
- Low sensory-discriminability (LSD) condition – same voice.
- More successful at shadowing HSD condition.
- Unexpected recall better in LSD condition.

> Six studies would be OK for depth and breadth.

MUST TAKE CARE...
To elaborate commentary.

- Shows: selection on physical properties.
- Challenged by: Moray (1959) – found 35% of participants responded to own name in unattended channel, therefore some semantic processing.

- Shows: ears act as separate channels; pair-by-pair requires channel switching.
- Challenged by: Gray and Wedderburn (1960) – found no ear-by-ear if words semantically related (words to be recalled presented to alternate ears: 'Dear Aunt Jane').

- Shows: semantic processing of unattended channel, challenging Broadbent's filter model.
- Challenged by: Treisman (1960) – participants switched ears to follow a story that switched to non-attended ear, i.e. difficult to ignore non-attended ear if meaningful content.

- Shows: physical aspects important but semantic content important too.
- Inconsistent with Broadbent's filter model which operates solely on physical aspect.

- Shows: semantic content of non-attended channel is processed unconsciously, as predicted by the late selection model.
- Supported by: Lewis (1970) – longer processing times when non-attended words semantically-related.

- Shows: non-target words processed more thoroughly in LSD because selected out later. In HSD condition could be selected early on physical characteristics.
- Shows: support for late-selection model.

GENERAL COMMENTARY

- Ecological validity – tasks used in experiments may not generalise to real-life settings.
- Difficult to demonstrate unconscious processing.

TYPICAL QUESTIONS...

1 Outline and evaluate **two or more** explanations relating to focused attention. (24 marks)

2 Discuss research studies related to focused attention. (24 marks)

3 (a) Describe **one or more** explanations relating to focused attention. (12 marks)

  (b) Evaluate the explanations you described in part (a) using research studies. (12 marks)

EXPLANATIONS OF DIVIDED ATTENTION

EXPLANATION 1: KAHNEMAN'S (1973) CAPACITY/RESOURCE ALLOCATION MODEL (A CAPACITY MODEL)

OUTLINE OF THEORY

• Central processor controls and allocates limited pool of processing resources.

• Resources allocated according to task demands and environmental factors.

• Interference occurs when one or more tasks exceed attentional capacity.

• Central processor determines which tasks take precedence.

EXPANSION

• Amount of attentional capacity varies, e.g. arousal.

• Task demands – mental effort causes increase; practice causes decrease.

• Environmental factors, e.g. heat, noise, anxiety.

• Interference can occur at any stage, not just at a 'bottleneck'.

• CP decision affected by momentary intentions and personality characteristics ('enduring dispositions').

• Flexibility – improvement on single channel models (people can do two or more tasks at one time). Can explain dichotic listening tasks – shadowing may use available resources but enduring dispositions can explain breakthroughs from non-shadowed message.

• Dual task – e.g. Allport et al. (1972) – participants could do shadowing and recognition task equally well singly or together.

• Practice effect – e.g. Spelke et al. (1976) – participants read short stories and simultaneously wrote down unrelated words and word category. After six weeks' practice, no interference. Shows that practice can change ability to divide attention. *However*, only two motivated students took part and may be due to attention switching.

• Task similarity – Segal and Fusella (1970) – showed that auditory and visual imaging tasks were equivalent, yet auditory (not visual) imaging impaired an auditory detection task but was less disruptive on visual detection task. Capacity model doesn't account for task similarity.

• Circularity – central processing capacity not independently defined (Allport, 1980) – capacity defined only in terms of whether tasks can or cannot be performed concurrently.

• Arousal – can't explain Yerkes-Dodson Law (reduced performance when arousal too low or too high).

Dual task performance technique – participants are given tasks singly or together to see how performance is affected.

Don't forget to use explanations of focused attention as commentary.

EXPLANATION 2: MODULAR THEORIES

OUTLINE OF THEORY

• Several different processing mechanisms (modules).

• Each module specialised for handling particular tasks.

• Each module has limited capacity.

• No overriding central processor.

• Shows: why dissimilar tasks can be combined with no decrement in performance, but not true for similar tasks.

• Vagueness – can explain anything by adding another module – post hoc explanation, i.e. after the fact.

• Coordination – no explanation of how the modules are coordinated.

TYPICAL QUESTIONS...

1 Critically consider **one or more** explanations of divided attention. (24 marks)

For practice in answering A2 Psychology questions, why not use *Collins Do Brilliantly A2 Psychology*?

CONTROLLED AND AUTOMATIC PROCESSING

MUST KNOW...
- Research into controlled and automatic processing including slips associated with automatic processing (performance deficits).

RESEARCH INTO CONTROLLED AND AUTOMATIC PROCESSING

THE TWO PROCESS MODEL (SHIFFRIN AND SCHNEIDER, 1977)

OUTLINE OF THEORY
- Two modes of information processing:
  - controlled: conscious, slow, easily interrupted
  - automatic: no conscious awareness, rapid, doesn't interfere with other mental activities.
- Tasks done under controlled processing learned quickly and modified easily.
- Automatic processing is result of practice; it is unavoidable (e.g. reading words).

RESEARCH STUDIES
Healy (1976)
Participants more likely to detect 't' in uncommon words because reading of common words is automatic.

Stroop (1935)
Reading colour words in conflicting colours is slower than in black.

Shiffrin and Schneider (1977)
Search times slower when more distractors (letters in digit list) but speed improves with practice (moves from conscious to automatic processing).

Poltrock et al. (1982)
Similar effects for auditory detection task.

- Supported by: studies of focused and divided attention.
- Lack of explanatory power – practice doesn't explain automaticity; may just speed things up; Cheng (1985) suggests that new, more efficient strategies developed.
- Lack of clear distinction – some tasks involve both (e.g. preparing a meal), therefore not discrete entities.

SLIPS ASSOCIATED WITH AUTOMATIC PROCESSING

THEORY OF ACTION SLIPS (REASON)

OUTLINE OF EXPLANATION
1 Superficial level – automatic.
2 Deeper level – more attention required if routine is wrong.
3 Even deeper – focus all conscious control (though anxiety at this stage may block clear thinking).

- Individual differences – some people more prone to slips (habit intrusions).

DIARY STUDIES (REASON, 1979)
- 35 participants kept diaries for two weeks.
- 400 errors.
- Five types of failures:
  1 Storage (40%) – e.g. putting sugar in tea twice
  2 Test (20%) – e.g. making coffee instead of tea
  3 Sub-routine (18%) – e.g. putting water in teapot but no tea
  4 Discrimination (11%) – e.g. stirring tea with fork
  5 Programme assembly (5%) – e.g. putting tea in bin and packet in pot.

- Accuracy – may not record every slip (e.g. embarrassed); some more noticeable.
- Classification – may be different underlying mechanisms for superficially similar slips.

LAB STUDIES (REASON, 1992)
- Questions – e.g. participants told that a funny story is a joke; then asked 'what is the white of an egg called?' – 85% said 'yolk' (answer should be 'albumen').

- Lacks representativeness of everyday situations.

SCHEMA THEORY MODEL OF ATTENTIONAL SLIPS AND LAPSES (NORMAN, 1981)

OUTLINE OF EXPLANATION
1 Action sequences controlled by schemas linked together.
2 The goal = a **parent** schema.
3 Component schemas = **child**/sub-schemas.
4 **Slips:** faulty specification or faulty triggering.

RESEARCH STUDY
- French and Richards (1993): participants asked to draw clock face; clocks use IIII, but participants drew IV because memory affected by schematic knowledge.

- Validity – predicts that slips occur in everyday, highly practised acts; may not record every slip (e.g. embarrassed); some more noticeable.
- Classification – different underlying mechanisms for superficially similar slips.
- Automatic versus controlled processing – circus performers don't have slips.

TYPICAL QUESTIONS...

1 Discuss research into controlled and automatic processing. (24 marks)

2 Describe and evaluate research into slips associated with automatic processing. (24 marks)

PATTERN RECOGNITION

EXPLANATIONS OF PATTERN RECOGNITION

TEMPLATE THEORY

- Simplest.
- Incoming info matched against LTM templates.
- Needs **exactly right** match.

- Application: computer recognition, barcode scanning.
- Inefficient – huge set of templates not feasible.
- Orientation – can't account for letters at other angles.
- Inadequacy – can't account for complex visual scenes.

CONTEXT

- **Bottom-up** – e.g. pattern recognition theories above and right.
- **Top-down** – (conceptually-driven): explains effects of expectation.
- Likelihood principle – von Helmholtz, 19th C.
- Hypothesis testing – **Gregory, 1973**.

- Supported by: **Palmer (1975)** – loaf of bread recognised in kitchen scene faster than, e.g. letterbox.
- Visual illusions demonstrate mistaken hypotheses, e.g. Ponzo lines.
- Can account for complex pattern recognition, e.g. reading.

PROTOTYPE THEORY

- **More** flexible.
- Prototype stores most typical features.
- Incoming information matched against LTM prototype.
- **Reasonably close** match.

- More flexible/economical – can account for recognition of different pictorial representations of same object.
- Supported by: e.g. **Solso and McCarthy (1981)** – prototypes in identikit recognition.
- How are they stored?
- What about partially obscured images?

BIOLOGICAL MECHANISMS (HUBEL AND WIESEL, 1962, 1979)

- Microelectrodes in visual cortex of cats and monkeys.
- Cortical neurons responded to oriented lines.
- Simple cells – lines, bars, slits of specific orientation.
- Complex – moving lines.
- Hypercomplex – specific length, moving corners.

FEATURE DETECTION THEORY

- **Most** flexible.
- Images processed in terms of constituent parts.
- Features of a pattern, **not the whole**.
- e.g. Pandemonium model (Selfridge, 1959): hierarchy of feature demons. **Decision demon** at the top identifies pattern.

- Supported by:
  - **Neisser (1964)** – 'Z' found faster in curved letters.
  - **Gibson (1969)** – P/R distinction slower than G/M.
  - biological evidence (e.g. **Hubel and Wiesel, 1962**).
- Descriptive model – relationship between features overlooked.
- Ignores effect of context – would predict that complex patterns take longer but **Pomerantz (1981)** found odd-one-out task not affected by complexity.
- Lacks complexity – appropriate for simple patterns.

- Influential research – won Nobel prize.
- Supported by: feature detection theory.
- Research studies used animals; ignored role of context.

TYPICAL QUESTIONS...

1 Discuss **two or more** explanations of pattern recognition. (24 marks)

2 (a) Describe and evaluate the role of biological mechanisms in pattern recognition. (12 marks)

(b) Describe and evaluate the role of context in pattern recognition. (12 marks)

FACE RECOGNITION

BRUCE AND YOUNG (1986)

OUTLINE OF THEORY
- For recognising familiar or unfamiliar faces.
- Processing modules linked in **sequence** and in **parallel**.

▼

EXPANSION
- Model shows how a face is processed:
  1 Unfamiliar faces – analyse expression and speech, identify specific features.
  2 Familiar faces – attempt to recognise person, access identity and name.
  3 Structural encoding takes information from those units that recognise attributes (i.e. everything but PINs and name generation).
  4 Cognitive system – available to provide extra information.

▼

FURTHER EXPANSION
Mainly for unfamiliar faces

Expression analysis
('Guess' emotional state from facial expression)

Facial speech analysis
('Lip-reading' to help decipher speech)

Directed visual processing
(e.g. Person has moustache – doesn't involve identification)

Structural encoding
Combines information from:
- **view-centred descriptions** (above)

and

- **expression-independent descriptions** (above and below excluding expression and facial speech analysis).

Cognitive system
Holds additional details to aid recognition, e.g. where a person is likely to be seen.

Mainly for familiar faces

Face recognition units (FRUs)
(Familiar faces)

Person identity nodes (PINs)
(Personal details)

Name generation
(Name stored separately)

MODIFIED THEORY (BURTON AND BRUCE 1993)

OUTLINE OF THEORY
- More **precise** model.
- No separate store for **names**.
- **Person-identity nodes** (not FRUs) for decisions about familiarity.

▼

- Application: used in computer simulations.
- Limited – can't account for learning new faces and new identities.

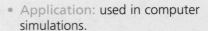
Could use modified theory as commentary.

- Faces processed differently – e.g. Yin (1969) – face recognition better than buildings, but not when turned upside down; configuration important for faces.
- Supported by: research showing independent routes for facial expressions, facial speech and familiar recognition:
  – **Young et al. (1993)**: ex-servicemen with missile wounds had difficulty with familiar *or* unfamiliar faces *or* expressions.
  – **Sergent and Signoret (1992)**: PET scans showed different regions of brain active.
- Challenged by: one patient (ME) could name famous faces but didn't know anything (**de Haan et al., 1991**).
- Weak explanation – 'Cognitive system' not well explained – a catch-all category.

META-COMMENTARY
- Experiments – well-controlled but may be unrepresentative.
- Brain-damaged patients – data unreliable because can't be certain that primary cause identified and process of damage is traumatic.

TYPICAL QUESTION...

Outline and evaluate **one or more** theories of face recognition. (24 marks)

For practice in answering A2 Psychology questions, why not use *Collins Do Brilliantly A2 Psychology*?

STRUCTURE AND FUNCTIONS OF THE VISUAL SYSTEM

THE EYE

Structure

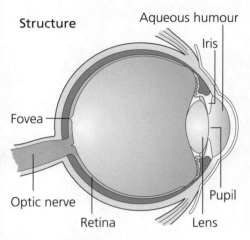

FUNCTIONS
- Eye socket and eye lid: protect from damage and dirt.
- Cornea: gather and concentrate light.
- Iris: regulates size of pupil according to external stimuli – automatic.
- Lens: focuses light on retina (= accommodation); becomes fatter to focus more distant objects; yellow tint screens out some UV light.

- Accommodation doesn't work for very close objects.
- Lens not functional in infants – fixed focus about distance of mother's breast.
- Lens loses elasticity with age.
- The eye is a mechanism for collecting light. Primitive animals (e.g. limpets) have a 'cup eye' which records unfocused multiple images.

THE RETINA
Structure
- More rods than cones (5 million: 50,000).
- Cones mainly in fovea.

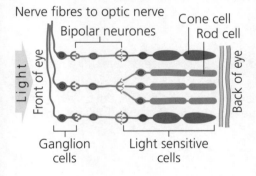

FUNCTIONS
- Changes light into a neural impulse (= transduction).
- Layer 1 (outermost): photoreceptors are light-sensitive.
- Rods: for dim lighting (scotopic system).
- Cones: for colour, detailed vision in bright light (photopic system).
- Layer 2: bipolar cells (neurones) – summarises data.
- Layer 3: ganglion cells – continues neural processing of sense data.

- Value of having two types of photoreceptors – to provide vision in different viewing conditions.
- Backward arrangement because eye is outgrowth of brain.
- Blind spot necessary because axons from retina have to leave eye. Doesn't cause disrupted vision because:
  – there are two eyes
  – the eye 'fills in' information.

VISUAL PATHWAYS
Structure

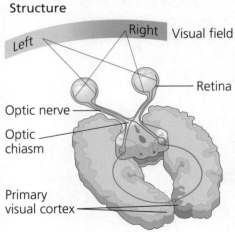

FUNCTIONS
- Optic chiasm means that data from right visual field (RTF) of both eyes goes to opposite area of visual cortex (RVF to left cortex).
- Primary visual cortex performs more processing, e.g. line detection.
- Visual association cortex: information from modules combined to produce perception of whole visual scenes.

- Supported by: Kluver and Bucy (1939) – removed monkeys' temporal lobe → they could walk around OK but not recognise objects.

TYPICAL QUESTIONS...

1 Discuss the structure and functions of the visual system. (24 marks)

2 (a) Critically consider the structure and functions of the eye. (12 marks)

(b) Critically consider the structure and functions of the retina. (12 marks)

NATURE OF VISUAL INFORMATION PROCESSING

VISUAL INFORMATION PROCESSING

What is it?
Visual information processing is the transformation of original input stimulus into a meaningful perceptual experience.

SENSORY ADAPTATION

What is it?
Sensory adaptation is the **ability to adapt to changes in the environment** (e.g. dark–light adaptation to cope with changing lighting).

- **Dark adaptation:** light to darkness (e.g. cinema) takes a few minutes. In bright light there are lots of **bleached cells** – thus system less responsive. Cells soon become unbleached and responsive again.
- **Light adaptation:** dark to light conditions – we squint to adjust to light. Light adaptation quicker. Molecules recombine quickly to be ready to respond to light.

- Evolutionary significance – permits the system to ignore stimuli once observed and be alert to changes in the environment.

CONTRAST PROCESSING

What is it?
Contrast processing is a **means of detecting brightness** by contrasting adjoining areas.

- **Lateral inhibition:** activity in one cell inhibits activity of neighbouring cells. The more one cell is illuminated and the closer the adjoining cells, the greater the inhibition.

- Supported by: **Hartline et al. (1956)** – light shone on one photoreceptor of horseshoe crab.
- Can explain simultaneous contrast effect (light-coloured square appears brightest when surrounded by darker colour) – occurs because less inhibition by darker colour.

COLOUR PROCESSING

What is it?
Colour processing is registering all the different hues.

TRICHROMATIC THEORY
- Young/von Helmholtz (1896): proposed three colour receptors: **red, green and blue.**
- **Synthesis** of these three produces all colours, e.g. red + green = yellow.

- Supported by: existence of three different cones.
- Can't explain some colour blindness, e.g. people who are red–green colour blind still see yellow.

OPPONENT PROCESS THEORY (HERING, 1870)
- Cones receptive to **red–green** (red increases activity; green decreases it) or **yellow–blue.**
- **Black–white** opponent process gives brightness perception (Hurvich and Jameson, 1957).

- Explains why people can't see reddish green.
- Supported by: ganglion cells and cells in LGN with this pattern of activity.
- Afterimages in opponent colours.

FEATURE PROCESSING

What is it?
Feature processing is **detecting objects** using contours and line orientations.

- Hubel and Wiesel (1959) – cats' visual cortex:
  – simple cells respond to unique orientation
  – complex cells respond to orientation and movement
  – hypercomplex cells respond to orientation and length = **feature detectors.**

- Supported by: DeValois and deValois (1980) – found feature detectors for corners and angles.
- Fits in with theories of pattern recognition.

TYPICAL QUESTION...

Outline and evaluate research (theories **and/or** studies) into the nature of visual information processing. (24 marks)

CONSTRUCTIVIST THEORIES OF VISUAL PERCEPTION

Constructivist theory in a nutshell

Top-down/concept-driven processing uses context and expectations to aid interpretation of sensory data.

1 Ambiguous data
• Visual stimuli are ambiguous or degraded (impoverished data). If we relied on this alone, we couldn't always make sense of the environment.

3 Importance of context
• We have hypotheses – context helps us select an appropriate one, e.g. Necker cube, changes from front to back because can't decide which hypothesis is right – no context.
• Research: Palmer (1975) – participants recognised line drawings of nose, ear, etc. when set in context of a face, but not otherwise.

2 Hypothesis-testing
• Visual stimuli act as a starting point for making informed guesses about their meaning.
• Hypotheses generated to make sense of that data based on expectations/past experience.
• Perception is the end product of an interaction between the original stimulus and internal expectations and knowledge.

GREGORY'S CONSTRUCTIVIST THEORY

• Supported by: **carpentered world hypothesis** (see Segall et al.,1963 on page 56).
• Challenged by: version with circles (see bottom right) – illusion persists.
• Alternative explanation: **conflicting cues theory (Day, 1990)** – we estimate length of vertical line from its length plus the overall length of the figure which is why left line appears longer.
• Visual illusions are artificial and can't tell us much about perception in the real world and under good visual conditions.
• Visual illusions persist (e.g. Ponzo, see page 53) even when explained.

4 Visual illusions
• Müller-Lyer illusion explained by Gregory as misapplied size constancy.
• We apply rules for interpreting 2D images.
• Outward fins (left) interpreted as a corner of a room.
• Inward fins interpreted as edge of a building and therefore seems closer to observer, so vertical line appears shorter.

Necker cube

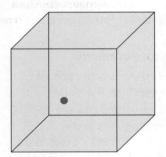

The Müller-Lyer illusion with fins

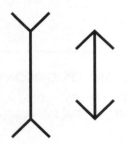

COMMENTARY ON GREGORY'S CONSTRUCTIVIST THEORY

• Supported by: studies on expectations generated by context, e.g. Bruner and Minturn (1955) showed that the number 13 will be perceived as the letter B if displayed in a set of letters.
• Artificial, ambiguous data used in experiments require top-down processes, so importance of context and experience are magnified.
• Over-emphasis on errors – perception is often very accurate.
• Doesn't reflect real life – viewing conditions not always degraded.
• Doesn't explain infants' perception – they have no prior experience.
• Alternative explanation: **direct theory (Gibson)** emphasises bottom-up processes. Perception is probably a combination of bottom-up and top-down processes.
• Acknowledges direct theory – Gregory acknowledges the role of bottom-up processes in depth perception, e.g. texture gradient and motion parallax.

The Müller-Lyer illusion with circles

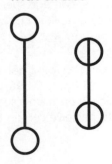

TYPICAL QUESTION...

Discuss **one or more** constructivist theories of visual perception. (24 marks)

DIRECT THEORIES OF VISUAL PERCEPTION

MUST KNOW...
• One direct theory of visual perception.

Direct theory in a nutshell
Bottom-up/data driven by physical stimulus, which is all that is needed for perception.

1 The optic array
• The optic array is the **pattern of light** reaching the eye, e.g. surfaces and textures.
• Contains all **necessary information** for perception.
• Light is **structured** by objects, e.g. surfaces and textures (optic array).

2 Movement
• The **optic array changes** when you move, e.g. move head, stand up or walk, but some elements remain the same.

GIBSONS'S DIRECT THEORY
An 'ecological approach' because perception studied in real-world environment.

3 Recognising objects
• All objects have **behavioural significance**.
• They offer (**afford**) certain responses to be made, e.g. a door handle **affords** turning.
• Affordance related to **circumstances**, e.g. bed for sleeping (when tired) or stepping on (when reaching cupboard).

4 Invariant information
• Information **remains constant** as observer moves.
• Invariant information leads **directly** to perception.

Texture gradient
• Texture = collection of objects in the visual field.
• Gradient = change in relative size and compactness of elements.
• Provides information about depth (increasing closeness of object elements) and orientation (e.g. shift from floor to wall).

Horizon ratio
• Objects of same height are cut by horizon in same ratio.
• Objects of different height have different horizon ratios.
• Provides information about size and distance.

Optic flow patterns (OFPs)
• Visual environment moves past observer.
• Provides information about position and depth.
• Information coming towards you is expanding; moving away is contracting.
• Closer objects move faster and backwards; more distant move slower and forwards.

COMMENTARY ON GIBSON'S DIRECT THEORY

• Ecological validity: rooted in real world rather than artificial settings/stimuli.
• Application:
  – constructing markings at airports which aid OFPs and help pilots landing
  – road markings approaching roundabouts encourage speed reduction because they give illusion of accelerating: they restructure perceived world.
• Supported by physiological evidence: Logothetis and Pauls (1995) – identified neurons which learn from visual experience to perceive certain forms.

• Supported by biological motion: Johannson (1975) – 'point light walkers': pattern of lights meaningless when walkers stationary but recognisable as a person when the lights are moving.
• Alternative explanation: constructivist theory (Gregory) emphasises bottom-up processes. Perception is probably a combination of bottom-up and top-down processes.
• Challenged by: studies of the effects of context (see constructivist theory).
• Affordances: inadequate to explain human perception though may explain, e.g. guided behaviour of insects (Bruce and Green, 1990).

CONSTRUCTIVIST VS DIRECT
• Each appropriate for different viewing conditions.
• Each related to different part of visual process: constructivist/top-down for ventral system (object recognition) and direct/bottom-up for dorsal system (movement) (Norman, 2001).

TYPICAL QUESTION...

1 (a) Outline and evaluate **one** constructivist theory of visual perception. (12 marks)

(b) Outline and evaluate **one** direct theory of visual perception. (12 marks)

EXPLANATIONS OF PERCEPTUAL ORGANISATION

DEPTH PERCEPTION

Needed because retinal image is 2D, and we need to perceive 3D.

BINOCULAR DEPTH CUES

- Convergence – eyes turn inwards to focus.
- Binocular disparity – difference between images presented to both eyes.

MONOCULAR DEPTH CUES

- Overlap – blocked objects are more distant.
- Linear perspective – converging lines indicate distance.
- Relative height – base of object below horizon appears more distant when higher in visual plane. Reverse if base above horizon.
- Relative size – smaller means further.
- Aerial perspective – bluer hue in distance.
- Shadowing – lighter means closer.
- Texture gradient – pebbles on beach look more distant when closely packed.
- Motion parallax – closer objects move more swiftly in opposite direction.

- Binocular and monocular cues work **in combination** – cues individually not strong but in combination give **3D**.
- Visual illusions can be explained by **depth cues**, e.g.
  – Ponzo illusion uses linear perspective
  – Kanizsa triangle uses overlap.
  (See below.)

Innate or learned?
- Direct theorists suggest we recognise cues **innately**. Constructivist theorists suggest we learn them **through experience**.
- Cross-cultural study found some depth cues learned (Hudson, 1960).
- Other research (Hochberg and Brooks, 1962) suggests innate use of pictorial cues (see page 56).
- May be a mixture. May learn to use cues more quickly/efficiently.

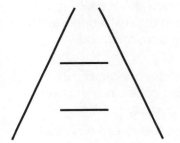

PERCEIVING MOVEMENT

The problem
Moving image is a series of separate pictures moving across retina, sometimes 'seen' as movement and sometimes seen as stationary.

GIBSON'S EXPLANATIONS FOR RECOGNISING MOVEMENT

Local movement signal
A moving object covers and uncovers background objects indicating movement. Works when tracking a moving object and retinal image is stationary, or when gaze is steady and object moves across retina.

Global optic flow
When observer moves, the retinal image moves but feedback to brain adjusts for this so that objects perceived as stationary.

- Research support: from studies of **motion agnosia** – inability to see movement, just snapshots (Zihl et al., 1983).
- Gibson's explanations can't explain:
  – **autokinetic effect** (apparent motion of light in dark room): movement perceived even though image doesn't move across retina nor is there background information;
  – **phi phenomenon** (apparent motion when adjacent lights turn on and off, used in neon light displays) shows that there are other explanations for movement.
- Constructivist explanations: high-level cognitive processes contribute to movement perception, e.g. object placed in path of apparent movement – observers 'see' movement being deflected around the barrier (Berbaum and Lenel, 1983).

VISUAL CONSTANCIES

Aspects of visual world remain stable despite changing retinal image (due to movement).

SIZE CONSTANCY

(e.g. Person walking away from you doesn't appear to shrink even though retinal image gets smaller.)

- Constructivist explanation: past experience and stored knowledge, e.g. we know that people don't change size, therefore if a person becomes larger we infer they are approaching us.
- Direct explanation: objects appear to stay the same because they maintain same size relative to nearby objects.

SHAPE CONSTANCY

(e.g. As door opens, retinal image becomes a trapezoid but we see a rectangle.)

- Constructivist explanation: past experience.
- Direct explanation: other information (e.g. texture) indicates that we are looking at the same door.

- Constructivist – can't be only explanation because size constancy occurs with unfamiliar objects.
- Direct – can't explain perceptual errors, e.g. being unable to see shapes below as same.

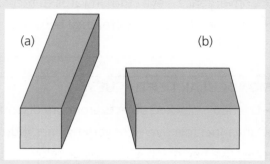

(a)   (b)

- Müller-Lyer illusion can be explained as misapplied size constancy, or may be conflicting cues (Day, 1990).

VISUAL ILLUSIONS

Visual illusions demonstrate mistaken perceptions that might explain how we organise perception.

Paradoxical figures
(e.g. Penrose triangle.)

- Shows that perceptual cues can be misleading.

Ambiguous figure
(e.g. Necker cube (see page 51).)

- Shows role of context in resolving ambiguity.

Fictitious figures
(e.g. Kanisza triangle (see page 53).)

- Shows that overlap provides depth perception.

Distortions
(e.g. Müller-Lyer illusion (see page 51).)

- Shows size constancy.

- No single explanation for illusions; occur as a combination of factors.
- Ecological validity – illusions may not tell us that much about perceptual organisation in the real world – apply only to ambiguous/degraded situations.
- Constructivist theory can be used to explain Necker cube – no data present to resolve ambiguity.
- Constructivist theory can be used to explain Müller-Lyer illusion – expectations generated about corners of buildings.
- Challenged by: evidence that illusion persists even when fins replaced with circles.
- Direct theory can be used to explain Müller-Lyer – illusion disappears if particicipants move around life-size 3D version wearing blindfolds (Wraga et al., 2000).

TYPICAL QUESTION...

Outline and evaluate explanations of perceptual organisation. (24 marks)

For practice in answering A2 Psychology questions, why not use *Collins Do Brilliantly A2 Psychology*?

INFANT STUDIES OF PERCEPTUAL DEVELOPMENT

Why?
To see what abilities are innate.

OUTLINE OF STUDIES

Acuity (ability to perceive details) (Haith,1990)

- Acuity poor at birth.
- Reaches adult level by about one year old.

→

- Can be explained by physiological factors – rapid development of neurons in visual cortex from 3–6 months (Conel, 1951).
- However, babies can recognise mother's face at close range (see Walton et al., below).

Face recognition (Fantz, 1961)

- Infants aged 4 days to 6 months preferred face-like stimuli to scrambled one.

→

- Suggests that infants have an innate preference for faces.
- Preference may be due to contours; Flavell (1985) found no preference for faces when other stimuli had similar amounts of contour.

Recognition of familiar face (Walton et al., 1992)

- Videoed pairs of women's faces – matched for hair colour, etc.
- Babies as young as one day old (sucking on dummy) had preference for mother's face.

→

- Has adaptive value for attachment.

Depth perception (Gibson and Walk, 1960)

- Infants aged 6 months wouldn't crawl over glass-covered visual cliff to mother.
- Newborn animals also wouldn't cross.

→

- Suggests that depth perception is innate.
- However, infants were 6 months old and therefore may have learned depth perception.
- However, depth perception apparent at 2 months – increased heart rate when infants dragged across visual cliff (Campos et al., 1970).

Pictorial cues (Granrud and Yonas, 1985)

- Used overlap to indicate which of three cards was closest.
- 7-month infants but not 5-month infants reached for closest card.

→

- Suggests that some aspects of depth perception are learned, i.e. pictorial cues.

Size constancy (Bower, 1965)

- Infants of 6–8 weeks conditioned to respond to 30cm cube placed at 1m.
- Placed same cube at different distances (different retinal image) or different cube at different distances (same retinal image).
- Found that retinal image didn't affect response.

→

- Suggests innate size constancy.
- However, findings not easy to replicate.
- Easy to misinterpret infant movements so findings not reliable.

GENERAL COMMENTARY

- Research with infants hampered because it is hard to:
  - attract and hold their attention
  - know what they can perceive: can't give a verbal response, and infant may perceive stimulus but not have the behavioural repertoire to demonstrate this.

CONCLUSIONS

- Research suggests that some perceptual abilities are innate, e.g. Campos et al.
- Learning necessary to develop full potential.

TYPICAL QUESTIONS...

1 Critically consider infant studies of the development of perceptual abilities. (24 marks)

2 (a) Outline **two or more** infant studies of the development of perceptual abilities. (12 marks)

(b) To what extent do such studies support the view that perceptual abilities are innate rather than learned? (12 marks)

CROSS-CULTURAL STUDIES OF PERCEPTUAL DEVELOPMENT

Why?
Innate abilities should be present in all cultures; cultural differences must be due to experience.

OUTLINE OF STUDIES

Visual illusions (Segall et al.,1963)
- European participants more affected by Müller-Lyer illusion than non-Europeans.
- True for children and adults.

- Explained by: carpentered world hypothesis – interpretation of angular objects automatic in people raised in carpentered environments:
  – Europeans more likely to interpret 2D image as 3D object and use misapplied size constancy rules
  – non-Europeans take picture at face value.
- Alternative biological explanation: retinal pigmentation may be denser in dark-skinned people – associated with poorer contour detection so individual less likely to be affected by Müller-Lyer illusion (Silvar and Pollack, 1967).

Pictorial cues: depth (Hudson, 1960)
- Showed line drawings with depth cues such as overlap and familiar size.
- Non-Western participants had difficulty interpreting pictorial depth.

- Suggests importance of experience.
- Challenged by: Hochberg and Brooks (1962) – whose son saw no pictures until 1½ years, but then fully able to interpret simple line drawings. Suggests innate use of pictorial cues.

Pictorial cues: movement (Duncan et al., 1973)
- Showed cartoons that had cues implying movement, e.g. head in three different positions.
- Rural African children thought the boy was deformed.

- Suggests importance of experience.
- Alternative explanation: differences in interpreting pictorial cues may be due to cultural aesthetic rather than perceptual experience, e.g. Africans prefer split-style drawings (Deregowski, 1972). All children prefer split-style but this is suppressed in Western culture because using depth cues helps to convey more information.

Size constancy (Turnbull, 1961)
- Kenge (pygmy) thought buffalo in distance were ants.
- Grew up in dense forest so no experience of depth cues.

- Suggests that the environment plays a strong role in the development of perceptual abilities.

Shape constancy (Allport and Pettigrew, 1957)
- Used trapezoid window illusion (rotating object flips back and forth if perceived as rectangular).
- Urban Zulus (familiar with windows) did see it, but not rural Zulus.

- Supports the view that environmental experiences predispose individuals to certain perceptions.
- Rural Zulus may have been confused by the instructions and have responded to experimenter's cues.

GENERAL COMMENTARY
- Often anecdotal and poorly controlled studies.
- Participants may not have understood instructions.

CONCLUSIONS
- Research suggests that, in general, environment plays a strong role in the development of perceptual abilities.
- Some evidence of innate abilities.

TYPICAL QUESTIONS...

1 Critically consider cross-cultural studies of the development of perceptual abilities. (24 marks)

2 (a) Discuss **two or more** infant studies of the development of perceptual abilities. (12 marks)

  (b) Discuss **two or more** cross-cultural studies of the development of perceptual abilities. (12 marks)

EXPLANATIONS OF PERCEPTUAL DEVELOPMENT

NATIVIST EXPLANATIONS
Nativist: born with perceptual abilities which change through maturation but owe nothing to learning.

EMPIRICIST EXPLANATIONS
Empiricist: born with basic sensory capacities; perceptual abilities develop through experience.

GIBSON (MR): DIRECT THEORY
- **Bottom-up** processing.
- **Sensory** (direct) information is all that is required for perception, e.g. **optic array**, cues from **movement** and **invariant information**.
- Perceptual abilities are **innate**.

- Supported by:
  - Gibson and Walk's research with visual cliff. Shows innate depth perception.
  - biological motion (see page 52).
- Challenged by: evidence for constructivist theory.

GREGORY: CONSTRUCTIVIST THEORY
- **Top-down** processing.
- Visual stimuli are starting point for **informed guesses** about their meaning.
- Perception is the end product of an **interaction** between the original stimulus and expectations.

- Supported by:
  - importance of contextual cues (see page 51)
  - evidence from visual illusions.
- Challenged by: accuracy of perception, evidence for direct theory.

GIBSON (MRS) AND GIBSON, 1955: DIFFERENTIATION THEORY
- Perceptual development = process of learning to see **differences** between objects.
- Experience leads us to **identify properties** that make two objects different.
- **Amodal infants** = children born with little differentiation between the different sensory modalities (vision, hearing, etc.).

- Supported by: Aronson and Rosenbloom (1911) – showed that one-month infants became quite distressed when they saw their mother but heard her voice coming from a different place. Suggests that the senses are integrated at birth.
- Challenged by: e.g. McGurk and Lewis (1974) – who found no distress from dislocation.

PIAGET, 1954: ENRICHMENT THEORY
- Sensory data is often impoverished and ambiguous, and **needs 'enriching'**.
- We draw on available cognitive **schemas** (expectations).
- Infants develop **sensori-motor schemas** to coordinate motor feedback with sensory data.
- Gradually build more **complex** schema to enable the development of full perceptual abilities.

- Supported by: Held and Hein (1963) – kitten carousel showed that sensory and motor experiences are necessary to develop perception (active kitten developed normal vision but not true for passive kitten who had only sensory input).

GENERAL COMMENTARY
- At least some aspects of perceptual development rely on learning schemas and cognitive input.
- Each appropriate for different viewing conditions.
- Each related to different part of visual process: constructivist/top-down for ventral system (object recognition) and direct/bottom-up for dorsal system (movement) (Norman, 2001).

TYPICAL QUESTION...
Discuss **one or more** explanations of perceptual development. (24 marks)

For practice in answering A2 Psychology questions, why not use *Collins Do Brilliantly A2 Psychology*?

THE NATURE–NURTURE DEBATE IN PERCEPTION

OUTLINE THE DEBATE
- Nature: abilities present at birth or that develop through maturation rather than experience, i.e. abilities determined by genes.
- Nurture: abilities that develop as a result of experience.

It's the same material as on page 56 just organised differently.

NATURE: EXPLANATIONS
- Direct theory: sensory (direct) information is all that is required for perception.
- Differentiation theory: perceptual abilities are innate; infants learn to discriminate between things.

EVIDENCE FOR NATURE: INFANT STUDIES
- Preference for faces in newborns (Fantz, 1961).
- Depth perception demonstrated using visual cliff (Gibson and Walk, 1960).
- Size constancy shown using cubes of different and same retinal size (Bower, 1965).

- Preference for face-like stimulus may be due to **contours** (Flavell, 1985).
- But would make **adaptive sense**.

- Infants were six months old so depth perception **may be due to experience**.
- However, infants aged two months showed anxiety (Campos et al., 1970).

- Cross-cultural case study of Kenge (Turnbull, 1961) suggests size constancy learned.
- Research with infants hampered for many reasons, e.g. can't really know what they perceive.

NURTURE: EXPLANATIONS
- Constructivist theory: top-down processes generate hypotheses based on past experience.
- Enrichment theory: schema used to enrich impoverished sensory input.

EVIDENCE FOR NURTURE: CROSS-CULTURAL STUDIES
- Europeans more affected by Müller-Lyer illusion because exposed to carpentered world.
- Some pictorial cues learned, e.g. familiar size and overlap (Hudson, 1960).

EVIDENCE FOR NURTURE: DEPRIVATION STUDIES
- Riesen (1965) – neurons in visual cortex of dark-reared chimpanzees wasted away.

- Alternative explanation: dark-skinned people poorer at contour detection (Pollack and Silvar, 1967).

- Challenged by: Hochberg and Brooks (1962) – son could interpret cues aged 1½ without previous experience.
- Alternative explanation: may be due to cultural aesthetic rather than perceptual experience, e.g. split-style drawing (Deregowski, 1972).

- **Difficult to generalise** from research with non-human animals.
- Supported by: Dennis (1960) – babies in Iranian orphanages showed major deficits in perceptual and motor skills.

CONCLUSIONS
- Some perceptual abilities are innate but learning necessary to develop full potential.
- Interaction – deprivation studies show that innate system may disappear if no appropriate experience.

TYPICAL QUESTION...

Discuss the nature–nurture debate in perception. (24 marks)

PIAGET'S THEORY

DESCRIPTION

PIAGET'S THEORY

* Qualitative change: the *type* of thinking changes rather than just acquiring more knowledge (a quantitative change).
* Biological process: cognitive development takes place due to maturation ('readiness').
* Invariant processes: assimilation and accommodation (see below).
* Variant structures: schemas and operations (see below).
* Stages: the type of thinking changes in a fixed sequence of age-related stages.

WHAT **CAUSES** THE DEVELOPMENTAL CHANGES?

* The driving force behind changes is **equilibration**.
* Innate schema: everything an infant knows about an object, e.g. innate recognition of human face (Fantz, 1961).
* Assimilation: fitting new experiences into existing schema.
* Accommodation: changing existing schema to fit new experiences.

WHAT CHANGES?

1 SENSORIMOTOR (0–2 YEARS)
* Knowledge of what can be sensed (sensory) coordinated with what can be done (motor experiences).
* Object permanence develops.

EXPANSION
* Early movements are uncoordinated, e.g. movement of hand.
* Sensory information matched to motor input to construct new schemas.
* Up to eight months infants don't realise that objects continue to exist when they're out of sight.
* Object permanence develops by one year.

2 PRE-OPERATIONAL (2–7 YEARS)
* Use of symbols, e.g. language.
* Unable to use operations; rules lack logic.
* Thought guided by external appearance and not internal consistency.
* Egocentric thought.

EXPANSION
* Operations are logical mental rules, e.g. arithmetic.
* Preconceptual sub-stage: e.g. concepts not fully formed (all men are 'Daddy').
* Intuitive sub-stage: based on intuition; underlying principles can't be explained.
* Egocentricism – inability to take another's perspective, e.g. three mountains task with doll.

3 CONCRETE OPERATIONAL (7–11 YEARS)
* Use of logical rules but only concrete examples.
* Seriation (ordering) can only be done with concrete examples.
* Can conserve quantity.

EXPANSION
* Can't cope with abstract or hypothetical problems.
* Seriation, e.g. putting dolls in order of size.
* Conservation tasks, e.g. beads (number) or beakers (volume).

Remember the stages: SPoCoFo.

4 FORMAL OPERATIONAL (11+ YEARS)
* Abstract thought.
* Can solve problems with systematic overall plan = abstract deductive reasoning.

EXPANSION
* Beaker problem – four beakers of colourless liquid can be combined to produce yellow.
* Stage 3 thinkers try random combinations.
* Stage 4 thinkers – principle → hypothesis → test to confirm.

EVALUATION OF PIAGET'S THEORY

COMMENTARY ON STAGES

1 SENSORIMOTOR

- Underestimating infant abilities – Bower (1981) found five-month olds had object permanence when object placed behind a screen.
- However, still supports the age-related appearance of this ability.

MUST TAKE CARE...
To use research studies effectively.

2 PRE-OPERATIONAL

- Three mountains task – doesn't relate to everyday experiences. Hughes (1975) used two policemen; 90% of 3–5 year olds could cope when their errors were explained to them.
- Shows that:
  – practice can improve performance (i.e. not just maturation)
  – everyday tasks are easier.

3 CONCRETE OPERATIONAL

- Demand characteristics – Rose and Blank (1974) – two questions in conservation task may confuse younger children; did better with one question.
- More real-life task – McGarrigle and Donaldson (1974) – deliberate change of display in number conservation may suggest a different response required. Accidental change by 'naughty teddy' led to improved performance.

However...
Moore and Frye (1986) – children didn't notice if naughty teddy actually did add a counter, therefore teddy is a distraction so children simply don't notice the transformation.

4 FORMAL OPERATIONAL

- Universal? – Dasen (1994) – only third of adults ever reach this stage.
- Four-card selection task (Wason and Shapiro, 1971) – only 10% of college students cope with abstract version; 62% did concrete version.

PRACTICAL APPLICATION

Implications of theory for education

- Children learn by constructing their own knowledge, for assimilation and accommodation to take place.
- Teacher should use appropriate materials related to stage of development, e.g. concrete materials in concrete operational stage.
- Readiness – premature learning results in incomplete understanding.

GENERAL COMMENTARY

- Age underestimated – didn't distinguish between competence and performance. Other research has focused on competence and found children could do more than Piaget suggested.
- Cross-cultural research (e.g. Smith et al., 1998) supports qualitative biologically regulated cognitive changes.
- Practice does improve performance, e.g. Bryant and Trabasso (1971) trained children to do transivity tasks; if changes due to maturation, practice shouldn't matter.
- Underplayed role of language and social factors.

TYPICAL QUESTIONS...

1 Discuss Piaget's theory of cognitive development. (24 marks)

2 Describe and evaluate **one** theory of cognitive development. (24 marks)

VYGOTSKY'S THEORY

DESCRIPTION

VYGOTSKY'S THEORY

- Social construction of knowledge.
- Culture transforms elementary into higher mental functions.
- Language and other cultural symbols (**semiotics**) are the medium through which knowledge is transmitted.
- Experts move child through ZPD (see below).
- Learn what and how – learn content of knowledge and the processes (how to think).

THE INFLUENCE OF CULTURE

CULTURE TRANSFORMS ELEMENTARY INTO HIGHER MENTAL FUNCTIONS
- **Elementary** mental functions, e.g. attention and sensation – present at birth.
- **Higher** mental functions, e.g. decision-making and comprehension of language.
- **Culture**, e.g. books and experts (people with more knowledge).
- Culture transmitted through language.

THE PROCESS OF CULTURAL INFLUENCE

ZONE OF PROXIMAL DEVELOPMENT (ZPD)
- Distance between child's **current** and **potential** abilities.
- Potential achieved through guidance of **experts** and **scaffolding**.

EXPANSION
- Expert is sensitive to learner's capabilities.
- Greatest teaching input occurs at edge of ZPD, point at which the child can still cope.
- Scaffolding enables learner to cope with difficult tasks.

SEMIOTIC MEDIATION
- Semiotics = **language** and other **cultural symbols**.
- Means by which **knowledge transmitted**.

EXPANSION
- Semiotics transform elementary to higher mental functions.
- A social process.

SOCIAL AND INDIVIDUAL PLANES
- Learning starts as a **social, shared** activity.
- Shifts to an **individual, self-regulated** activity.

EXPANSION
- Dialogues between instructor and learner enable learner to take responsibility for own learning.

ROLE OF LANGUAGE
- **Pre-intellectual language** – language for social and emotional functions.
- **Pre-linguistic thought** – mental activities conducted without language.
- **Language and thought** – after age of two, language used to assist problem-solving.

EXPANSION
- Egocentric speech – young children talk out loud when problem-solving.
- Inner speech – after age of seven.

STAGES IN THE DEVELOPMENT OF THINKING

PROCESS OF CONCEPT FORMATION
1 Vague syncretic stage: largely trial and error without understanding.
2 Complexes stage: some strategies but main attributes not identified.
3 Potential concept stage: one attribute only dealt with at a time (e.g. tall).
4 Mature concept stage: several attributes simultaneously (e.g. tall, square).

EVALUATION OF VYGOTSKY'S THEORY

THE INFLUENCE OF CULTURE

- Papua New Guinea counting systems – Gredler (1992) – difficult to add/subtract just using fingers, arms, etc. (cultural system) – culture limits mathematical abilities.
- Increase in IQ over recent decades attributed to increased knowledge that surrounds children and enhances cognitive development.

THE PROCESS OF CULTURAL INFLUENCE

ZONE OF PROXIMAL DEVELOPMENT

- **Supported by: McNaughton and Leyland (1990)** – can define ZPD by comparing how well children could cope with jigsaw puzzles of increasing difficulty on own or with mother's help.
- **Scaffolding:** when puzzles easy – mothers sat back; 2nd level (within ZPD) – mothers helped children solve puzzle; 3rd level (beyond child's ZPD) – mothers took over.

SOCIAL AND INDIVIDUAL PLANES

- Self-regulation increases with age – Wertsch (1985) observed children doing jigsaw puzzles with mothers; children's gazes decreased with age.

MUST REMEMBER...
To balance AO1 and AO2.

ROLE OF LANGUAGE

Supported by:

- **Vygotsky (1934)** – inner speech increased when obstacles introduced.
- **Berk (1994)** – children talk to themselves more when doing difficult tasks.
- **Berk and Garvin (1984)** – inner speech less developed in Appalachian children than middle-class children because parents talk less to children (i.e. lack of social communication related to less developed inner speech).

PRACTICAL APPLICATION

Implications of theory for education

- Knowledge is socially constructed:
  - **scaffolding:** teachers should help students through ZPD using scaffolding
  - **collaborative learning:** working in groups
  - **peer tutoring:** peers can act as experts.

GENERAL COMMENTARY

- Lack of research support because theory less conducive to research as it focuses on process rather than outcome, but research base is growing.
- Overemphasis on social factors – learning should be faster if social factors are sufficient.
- Underemphasis on biological and individual factors.

COMPARING PIAGET AND VYGOTSKY

- **Individual versus social construction:** Piaget – child creates knowledge from him/herself (individualist); Vygotsky – knowledge is a collaborative, social process (collectivist).
- **Role of egocentric speech:** Piaget – individual to social world, able to share other's perspective; Vygotsky – social to individual.
- **Scope for assisted learning in Vygotsky's theory:** Piaget said learner must wait.
- **Individual differences in learning:** some learners cope better with individual learning (Piagetian); others prefer expert guidance (Vygoyskian).
- **Theories similar at central core (Glassman, 1999):** can integrate both views.

TYPICAL QUESTIONS...

1 Discuss Vygotsky's theory of cognitive development. (24 marks)

2 (a) Outline and evaluate Piaget's theory of cognitive development. (12 marks)
   (b) Outline and evaluate Vygotsky's theory of cognitive development. (12 marks)

APPLICATIONS OF PIAGET'S AND VYGOTSKY'S THEORIES

APPLICATIONS OF PIAGET'S THEORY

THE APPROACH
- Child-centred approach.
- Active, discovery learning.
- Motivation – children do not need to be taught; they learn because they are drawn into experiences.
- If a child is taught something prematurely, this prevents them from ever completely understanding it.

OUTLINE

1 Children learn by constructing own knowledge
- Teacher should provide **suitable materials**.
- Teacher should ask questions which **challenge existing schema**.
- Peers can provide **conflict**.

2 Logic is not an innate mental process →
- Logic must be **taught**.
- **Maths and science** should be taught in primary school to facilitate this.
- But have to wait until child is '**ready**'.

3 Use appropriate materials →
- **Concrete materials** in concrete operational stage, e.g. do maths tasks with objects.
- **Logical relationships** after pre-operational stage.

4 Readiness →
- Children can't **acquire new abilities** until they are old enough.
- Premature learning results in **incomplete understanding**.

COMMENTARY
- Very influential – e.g. on primary education in UK – Plowden report (1960s) recommended change from teacher- to child-centred education.
- Supported by: e.g. Danner and Day (1977) – students doing formal operational tasks. Coaching helped 17-year olds but not 13-year olds.
- Challenged by: e.g. Bryant and Trabasso (1971) – found practice helped.
- Criticisms of Piaget's theory are relevant, e.g. underestimation of age-related abilities.
- May reduce real learning – Modgil et al. (1983) – time spent on activities reduces time spent on content learning.
- Not practical – many teachers don't have time and/or skill to assess child's stage of maturation.

 However...
Piaget's theory may not have been the cause of such changes but provided theoretical background to *justify* them.

 However...
The content learning may be superficial because student's not actively involved.

APPLICATIONS OF VYGOTSKY'S THEORY

THE APPROACH

- Teacher-centred approach.
- Active, discovery learning.
- Motivation – desire to learn is an outcome of learning rather than being a prerequisite for learning.
- Expert guidance moves the child through the ZPD; without active intervention the child learns less.

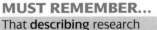

MUST REMEMBER...
That **describing** research evidence is AO1, **using it effectively** makes it AO2.

OUTLINE

1 Scaffolding

Stages involved in scaffolding:

1 Recruitment – gaining child's interest.
2 Reduction of degrees of freedom – breaking the task down.
3 Direction maintenance – encouraging and motivating.
4 Marking critical features – which will help further progress.
5 Demonstration – tutor finishes the task off so that the learner can imitate.

EXPANSION

- Teacher or more knowledgeable other (MKO) provides suitable assistance.
- Gives more or less assistance depending on whether task within or beyond ZPD (see McNaughton and Leyland, 1990 on page 62).
- Wood et al. (1976) found that most efficient strategy was combining general and specific instructions.

2 Collaborative learning

- **Cooperative group work** – groups of children working together with common goal.
- Increases interest and promotes **critical thinking**.
- Each individual brings different skills and **perspectives**.

3 Peer tutoring

- Peers act as **experts**.
- Promotes learning in **tutee and tutor** (because best way to learn something is to teach it).

COMMENTARY

- Research support for **collaborative learning**:
  – Bennett and Dunne (1991) – children less competitive and more likely to show evidence of logical thinking;
  – Blaye et al. (1991) – children who had worked in pairs were later more successful on problem-solving task when working on own than those who had worked individually at the start.
- Research support for **peer tutoring** – Cloward (1967) – may have greatest benefit for peer tutor.
- Individual differences – works for some but not all learners, e.g. Blaye et al. – some children didn't do better in pairs.
- Role of experts – must be sensitive to needs of learner; requires skill and time.

COMPARING PIAGET AND VYGOTSKY

- Both are **discovery learning** – knowledge constructed individually (Piaget) or socially (Vygotsky), in contrast with Behaviourist notion that learning is passive (occurs as a consequence of external reinforcements).
- **Combined approach** – e.g. CASE (cognitive acceleration through science education): create situations with conflict (Piaget) and use collaborative learning (Vygotsky). Adey and Shayer (1993) found pupils improved in Maths, Science and English.

TYPICAL QUESTIONS...

1 Discuss applications of **one or more** theories of cognitive development (e.g. to education). (24 marks)

2 (a) Outline Piaget's theory of cognitive development. (12 marks)

(b) To what extent has this theory been successfully applied (e.g. to education)? (12 marks)

DEVELOPMENT OF INTELLIGENCE TEST PERFORMANCE

ROLE OF GENETICS

MUST KNOW...
- Research into the role of genetics in the development of intelligence test performance.
- Research into the role of environmental factors (e.g. cultural differences) in the development of intelligence test performance.

- Twin studies and other kinship studies: natural experiments where either genetics or environment vary.
- Adoption studies: compare adopted children with adoptive family or biological family; thus controlling genetics and environment.
- Gene-mapping studies: provide direct genetic evidence.

Twin studies
Examples
- Shields (1962):
  - MZ twins reared apart – 0.77 correlation in IQ
  - MZ twins together – 0.76
  - DZ twins together – 0.51.
- SATSA adoption/twin study (Pederson et al., 1992) – twins tested late in life:
  - MZ twins apart – 0.78
  - MZ twins together – 0.80
  - DZ twins together – 0.22.

- Suggests that environment has very little influence and may decrease with age.
- Reared apart twins **may spend time together** and be reared in similar environments (Kamin, 1977).
- MZ twins may not be MZ because of erroneous identification (Scarr and Carter-Saltzman, 1979).
- **Microenvironment** – children in same home not sharing same environment because **different temperaments at birth** shape their environment – affects developing IQ.

THE EVIDENCE FOR THE ROLE OF GENETICS

Adoption studies
Example
- Texas Adoption Project (Horn, 1983) – adoptive children's IQ:
  - closer to biological (0.28) than adoptive mother (0.15)
  - biological correlation increased and adoptive one decreased when tested years later (Plomin et al., 1988).
  - same pattern for correlation with adoptive siblings: 0.26 at age 8 dropped to zero by age 18 (Loehlin et al., 1989).

Gene-mapping studies
- Chorney et al. (1998) identified gene (IGF2R) present in 33% of 'super-brights' but in only 17% of average participants.

Other kinship studies
- We would expect IQ to be more similar, the more closely related two individuals are, e.g. Bouchard and McGue (1981) – meta-analysis of relatives living together:
  - MZ twins – 0.86 correlation
  - DZ twins – 0.60
  - siblings – 0.47
  - parents and offspring – 0.38.

- **Niche picking** (Scarr and McCartney, 1983) can explain decrease in similarity – because genetically-related people progressively select **more similar environments** which affects development.
- Challenged by: trans-racial adoption studies (Scarr and Weinberg, 1976) – **environment more important** black children raised in white middle-class families had IQs of 106 aged 7; those in low-income black families had IQs of 97. However, by age 17, IQs were all 97 (Weinberg et al., 1992) supporting niche-picking hypothesis.

- IQ not determined by one gene – will need a variety of high quality (plus) genes; IGF2R is just one such 'plus gene'. On its own doesn't guarantee high IQ; may add 4 IQ points.

- Suggests that genetic factors are at least partly responsible.
- Also shows there are environmental effects.
- Drawback of meta-analysis – combines data from different studies with different methods so may not be reliable data.

THE ALTERNATIVE VIEW
Research support for environmental factors, e.g.
- Correlation between family factors and IQ scores, e.g. Sameroff et al. (1993).
- 'Flynn effect' (steady increases in IQ over 60 years) can only be explained by environmental changes.
- Nature–nurture interaction – genetic factors emphasised when looking at wealthy individuals; environmental factors appear strongest in children from low income families.

MUST REMEMBER...
That nothing is inherently 'AO2' – it's how **you** use it that makes it AO2.

ENVIRONMENTAL FACTORS

DEFINITION
Environment = **physical** and **social** (family, cultural) factors.

Home background
Examples
- Rochester Longitudinal Study (Sameroff et al., 1993):
  - identified 10 factors, e.g. mother has serious anxiety, mother didn't go to high school, father doesn't live with family
  - each factor decreased IQ by about 4 points
  - factors accounted for 50% of variability in IQ scores.
- Caldwell and Bradley (1978) – HOME checklist – high IQ in pre-school children from families who are:
  - emotionally responsive
  - provide opportunities for play and exploring
  - have high expectations.

- Correlational data – therefore risk factors do not *cause* low IQ; may be that there is a genetic link: parents with low IQ more likely to have risk factors.
- HOME scores and IQ have lower correlation in middle childhood, possibly because genetic factors gain in importance (niche picking).

THE EVIDENCE FOR THE ROLE OF THE ENVIRONMENT

Cultural factors: racial differences
- Suggest genetic factors strongest, e.g.
  - Jensen (1969) found black Americans' IQs 15 points lower than whites.
  - Scarr and Weinberg (1976) – black children raised in white families had IQs 17 points lower than white children adopted to white families.

- Race doesn't equal culture – black individuals come from various cultures.
- IQ tests are culture-biased – Williams (1972) designed BITCH test which favoured black Americans.

The Flynn effect
- IQ scores have been increasing all over the word for last 60 years (Flynn, 1996), between 5 and 25 points:
  - people may be getting better at doing IQ tests
  - improved environment (diet, information from books/internet) maximises an individual's reaction range (Gottesman, 1963).

Compensatory programmes
- Additional enrichment to boost IQ, e.g. Head Start (1960s) pre-school academic/social/medical support:
  - more advanced social and cognitive behaviour (Lee et al., 1990)
  - initial positive effects disappeared
  - 'sleeper effect': later showed higher attainment levels and more likely to go to college (Lazar and Darlington, 1982).

- Design flaws, e.g. choice of control groups not random.
- Gains not just IQ, also life-style changes.

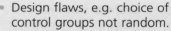

- Supported by: studies of diet, e.g. Benton and Cook (1991) – mineral and vitamin supplements led to IQ increases.

GENERAL COMMENTARY
- Nature–nurture interaction – variations in similar environments due to genetic factors; variations when comparing children reared in different environments are environmental.
- Turkheimer et al. (2003) found low IQ heritability (0.10) in poor children but high (0.72) in wealthy children ('heritability' is measure of extent to which a trait is inherited).

TYPICAL QUESTIONS...

1 Discuss research into the role of genetic factors in the development of intelligence test performance. (24 marks)

2 Discuss research into the role of environmental factors in the development of intelligence test performance. (24 marks)

3 (a) Outline research into the role of environmental factors in the development of intelligence test performance. (12 marks)

(b) To what extent does such research suggest that IQ test performance can be explained solely in terms of environmental factors? (12 marks)

THEORIES OF MORAL UNDERSTANDING/ PRO-SOCIAL REASONING

MUST KNOW...
- Two theories of moral understanding/ pro-social reasoning.

DESCRIPTION

KOHLBERG'S THEORY

- **Moral understanding** underlies moral behaviour.
- **Type of thinking** changes in fixed sequence of age-related stages.
- Development through **maturation** (invariant stages) and experience.

EISENBERG'S THEORY

- **Pro-social behaviour** – helping others at a possible personal cost.
- **Empathy and role-taking skills** enable pro-social behaviour.
- **Levels** of development related to maturation of general cognitive abilities.

BASIC ASSUMPTIONS

- **Moral thinking** is linked to moral behaviour.
- Moral development proceeds through **innately determined** stages with an **invariant** sequence.
- Each stage is a more **equilibrated** (balanced) stage of moral understanding, resulting in more **logically consistent** understanding.
- Development also related to experience – **disequilibrium** challenges current thinking, but only if person is 'cognitively ready'.

BASIC ASSUMPTIONS

- **Empathy** enabled by taking on the role of another person and seeing their perspective.
- **Personal distress** experienced when someone else is suffering, but action taken only if empathy felt.
  - A young child feels **'primitive' distress** at seeing someone else suffering but has no empathy and therefore doesn't take action.
  - **'Sympathetic distress'** develops with perspective-taking and leads to pro-social behaviour.

STAGES

- Focus on *how* people think rather than *what*.
- Developed from research with moral dilemmas (Kohlberg, 1976).

LEVELS

- Developed using different moral dilemmas (Eisenberg et al., 1983).

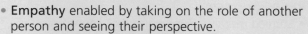

Level 1: Preconventional morality

- Stage 1 – Punishment and obedience orientation: child obeys because adults have superior power.
- Stage 2 – Individualism, instrumental purpose and exchange: children follow rules when it's in their immediate interest.

Level 1: Hedonistic (self-centred)

- Pre-school/early primary pupils: pro-social behaviour related to personal benefit.

Level 2: Needs oriented

- Mainly primary: will consider needs of others, but not much evidence of sympathy or guilt.

Level 2: Conventional morality

- Stage 3 – Mutual interpersonal expectations, relationships and interpersonal conformity: 'being good' becomes important for its own sake and for mutual relationships.
- Stage 4 – Social system and conscience (law and order): a shift in focus from family and close groups to the larger society.

Level 3: Approval oriented

- Primary and some secondary: pro-social behaviour in return for approval and praise from others.

Level 4: Empathetic or transitional

- Older primary and secondary: evidence of sympathy and guilt; some reference to abstract principles, duties and values.

Level 3: Principled or post-conventional morality

- Stage 5 – Social contract or utility and individual rights: 'greatest good for the greatest number'. Laws can be changed but there are some basic non-relative values, such as life and liberty.
- Stage 6 – Universal ethical principles: when there is a difference between law and conscience, conscience dominates.

Level 5: Strongly internalised

- Perhaps some primary, some secondary, mainly adults: strong sense of internalised principles.

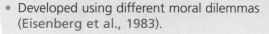

Can use research studies as AO1 or AO2.

EVALUATION OF KOHLBERG'S THEORY

RESEARCH STUDIES

Kohlberg (1963)
- 10 moral dilemmas (e.g. Heinz story) – 72 boys aged 10–16 years interviewed about why they would make certain decisions.
- Reasoning not consistent but overall tendency to one type of reasoning → stage theory.

Colby et al. (1983)
- Followed initial sample for 26 years, interviewing them every three years.
- Confirmed the sequence of development.
- At age 10 mainly Stage 2, but some 1 and 3.
- By age 36, about 65% were at Stage 4 and only 5% at Stage 5.

Kohlberg (1969)
- Studied moral reasoning in other countries.
- Found same pattern of development.
- But slower in non-industrialised countries.

SUPPORT FOR THE THEORY

- Cross-cultural support – Eckensberger (1983) and Snarey et al. (1985) examined a total of 94 cross-cultural studies and found support for invariant sequence and increased incidence in urban areas.
- Value of experience and social interactions supported by Berkowitz and Gibbs' (1983) concept of transitive interactions (discussions around 'what would happen if …') as the key to moral progression.

LIMITATIONS

- Stage 6 is a moral ideal and same for Stage 5.
- Artificial dilemmas – people respond differently when tested on real life dilemmas, e.g. Gilligan (1982), interviewing women about abortions.
- Gender bias:
  – androcentric: dilemmas reflect a male morality (justice); females use an 'ethic of care' (Gilligan, 1982)
  – stage theory based on responses from male participants.
- Cultural bias – dilemmas are typical of middle-class Western Europeans; needs of individual greater than of community.

EVALUATION OF EISENBERG'S THEORY

RESEARCH STUDIES

Eisenberg-Berg and Hand (1979)
- Each dilemma involved having to decide whether to help someone or not (at a cost to the helper).
- Tested pre-school children; reasoning not consistent – functioning at several different levels.
- When tested a few years later, reasoning had developed.

Eisenberg et al. (1983, 1987, 1991)
- Longitudinal study from 4 years to adolescence.
- Continuing support for levels.

Eisenberg et al. (1999)
- Children, who showed spontaneous pro-social behaviour at aged 5, were the same in early adulthood.

SUPPORT FOR THE THEORY

- Primitive versus sympathetic distress – Caplan and Hay (1989) found that children aged 3–5 were upset but didn't help someone in distress.
- Pro-social behaviour motivated by distress suggested by Batson (1991) – empathy–altruism theory.
- However, negative state relief hypothesis (Cialdini et al., 1982) suggests the opposite.
- Evidence to support both views, e.g. Batson et al. (1981) found pro-social behaviour due to empathy; Cialdini et al. (1987) found this was lessened if participants experienced 'mood-lifting' event.

COMPARING KOHLBERG AND EISENBERG

Kohlberg and Eisenberg differ:
- Eisenberg emphasises the importance of emotional factors.
- Eisenberg focuses on pro-social reasoning rather than issues of wrongdoing.

Kohlberg and Eisenberg are similar:
- Both see progression from self-centred, reward-based morality to ethical principles.
- Both include role for cognitive maturation.
- Both explain moral behaviour in terms of underlying reasoning.

MUST REMEMBER...
That for AO2, credit studies must be used effectively.

TYPICAL QUESTIONS...

1 Outline and evaluate **two or more** theories of the development of moral understanding/pro-social behaviour. (24 marks)

2 Describe and evaluate **one** theory of the development of moral understanding/pro-social behaviour. (24 marks)

INFLUENCES ON MORAL UNDERSTANDING

THE INFLUENCE OF GENDER

KOHLBERG'S VIEW

Women are morally inferior to men.

Explanations

- Women do not attain higher levels because they cannot move beyond personal concerns.
- Women have a life lived mainly in the home; lack of outside experience means moral thinking is not challenged.

- Outdated view – women no longer 'home-bound'.
- Female inferiority more likely to be due to assessment using a male standard (justice-based dilemmas).

RESEARCH EVIDENCE

- Kohlberg and Kramer (1969) interviewed females and found most at Stage 3.

- But remember, this was using justice-based dilemmas.

GILLIGAN'S VIEW

Two different moralities:

- Women use an 'ethic of care'.
- Men are concerned with justice and rights.

Gilligan's stage theory

- Stage 1 – Self-interest: (pre-conventional, similar to Kohlberg's level 1).
- Stage 2 – Self-sacrifice: (conventional stage, caring for others at personal cost).
- Stage 3 – Integration: (post-conventional, balancing own and others' needs).

Explanation

- Gilligan et al. (1990): women have a stronger sense of interconnectedness:
  - interconnectedness is outcome of close maternal attachment
  - boys develop 'separateness' – at early age they become independent from mothers; need to coordinate with others leads to greater concern for fairness/justice
  - girls have continued attachment and therefore have less need to interact with others.

- Unrepresentative samples – Sommers (2000) – urban US women in Gilligan's initial interviews; not sound basis for universal theory.

ALPHA BIAS OR BETA BIAS?

Alpha bias: assumes there are real differences (true for both Kohlberg and Gilligan). The result may be that male or female behaviour may be portrayed as inferior – which was the case for Kohlberg.

Beta bias: ignores sex differences. True of Kohlberg because he 'unthinkingly' created a form of measurement (moral dilemmas) which assumed they were universal.

- Supported by: Garmon et al. (1996) – tested 500 participants.
- Challenged by: Walker (1984) – meta-analysis of 108 studies; only eight found sex differences.

RESEARCH EVIDENCE

- Gilligan and Attanucci (1988) used moral dilemmas; found that overall men showed a justice focus and women showed a care focus, though most people showed a mixture.
- Eisenberg et al. (1987) – girls aged 10–12 gave more caring, empathetic responses than boys.

- Empathetic responses may be due to demand characteristics – Eisenberg and Lennon (1983) found girls portray themselves as empathetic when they know that's what researchers are looking for; when aim of study less clear, sex differences disappeared.

CULTURAL VARIATIONS IN MORAL UNDERSTANDING

DEFINITION
- Culture refers to the rules that bind a group of people together: their practices, attitudes, child-rearing methods and morals.

MORAL UNIVERSALISM
- Kohlberg (1969) and Snarey et al. (1985) found the same pattern of moral development in many different countries.

Studies can be AO2 if used effectively, or use as elaboration.

INDIVIDUALIST VERSUS COLLECTIVIST CULTURES
- Individualist cultures emphasise individual concerns and value independence.
- Collectivist cultures emphasise group concerns and value interdependence.
- Would expect collectivist societies to be:
  – more altruistic
  – more concerned with interpersonal moral focus.

- Whiting and Whiting (1975) found 100% of Kenyan (collectivist) children behaved altruistically; only 8% of US (individualist) did.

- Miller and Bershoff (1992) – hypothetical case of friend's wedding and missing ring; 84% of Asian Indians (collectivist) would steal (contravene moral of justice) rather than miss the wedding (moral of care) compared to 39% of Americans.

COMMENTARY
- Makes sense – collectivist societies have rules to protect communal aspects.
- May be an **oversimplification** – societies aren't simply individualist or collectivist, e.g. Miller (1994) found that Indian Muslims were collectivist and Indian Hindus were individualist.

URBAN VERSUS RURAL
- Might explain individualist-collectivist dichotomy better in terms of urban-rural.
- Pro-social behaviour higher in rural communities.
- Moral understanding advanced in urban countries, possibly because such societies pose more conflicts which leads to greater moral development.

- Hedge and Yousif (1992) found no difference in helpfulness in British (individualist) and Sudanese (collectivist), but found urban/rural differences in both countries.

- Korte and Kerr (1975) – more stamped letters returned in rural community.

- Snarey and Keljo (1991) – post-conventional understanding occurs in industrialised, urban societies.

COMMENTARY
- **Alpha bias** – implies that urban dwellers are 'better' because they are more sophisticated, but may just be a question of adapting to demands of society.

MORAL RELATIVISM VERSUS UNIVERSALISM?
- Some evidence for universalism, e.g. Kohlberg's research in different countries and similarities over serious moral issues.
- Most evidence for relativism; makes sense because morals are part of what makes a culture.

DIFFERENT KINDS OF MORALITIES
- Social conventional rules vary between cultures.
- Serious moral issues, e.g. murder – fewer differences (Berry et al., 1992).

- Shweder et al. (1987) – certain rules (e.g. having hair cut on day your father dies) rated as morally offensive by Asian Indians but an arbitrary social rule in US.

TYPICAL QUESTIONS...

1 Discuss the influence of gender on moral understanding/pro-social reasoning. (24 marks)

2 Discuss cultural variations in moral understanding/pro-social reasoning. (24 marks)

3 Discuss the influence of gender **and/or** cultural variations in moral understanding/pro-social reasoning. (24 marks)

4 (a) Outline and evaluate the influence of gender on moral understanding/pro-social reasoning. (12 marks)

(b) Outline and evaluate cultural variations in moral understanding/pro-social reasoning. (12 marks)

PSYCHODYNAMIC EXPLANATIONS OF PERSONALITY DEVELOPMENT

MUST KNOW...
- Two psychodynamic explanations of personality development.
- One theory in 24 marks worth of detail; 2nd theory in less detail.

DESCRIPTION

FREUD

Freud's explanation in a nutshell

- **Psychosexual conflicts**.
- **Biological drives** motivate interaction with the environment.
- **Early experience** plays a critical role in adult personality.
- Driving force + personality structure + organ-focus = behaviour.

DEFINITION

Psychodynamic explanations explain what motivates behaviour.

1   PERSONALITY STRUCTURES

Id	Primitive, instinctive, wants immediate satisfaction.	From birth.	Pleasure principle: seeks gratification, avoids pain.
Ego	Rational mind; modifies demands of id.	During first two years.	Reality principle: accommodates to demands of the environment.
Superego	Conscience and sense of right and wrong.	Around age of five.	Sexual conflicts (e.g. Oedipus) reconciled through identification with same-sex parent.

2   DYNAMICS OF THE PERSONALITY

- **Pleasure** and **reality** principles.
- **Ego defence mechanisms**, e.g. repression.
- **Libido** – life force, attaches to body parts during developmental stages.

EXPANSION
- Due to conflicts between id, ego and superego.
- Causes anxiety.
- Anxiety reduced unconsciously by ego defences which motivate behaviour.
- May cause abnormal personality development.

3   STAGES OF PSYCHOSEXUAL DEVELOPMENT

- **Key stages** for personality development: oral, anal and phallic.
- Severe **frustration** or excessive **overindulgence** lead to fixations as well as adult personality types.
- Problems later in life result in **regression** to stage of fixation.

EXPANSION

STAGE	Pleasure from...	Frustration leads to...	Overindulgence leads to....
Oral	Mouth.	Oral aggressive: dominating.	Oral receptive: gullible, dependent.
Anal	Expelling/ withholding faeces.	Anal-retentive: rigid, possessive.	Anal-expulsive: reckless, disorganised.
Phallic	Own and parents' genitals.	Phallic personality: vain, impulsive.	Conflict may lead to homosexuality, authority problems.
Genital	Genitals.	Unresolved issues restrict development of independence.	

ERIKSON

Erikson's explanation in a nutshell

- **Psychosocial** conflicts.
- Development is a **lifelong process**.

EIGHT STAGES OF MAN
- At each stage an individual faces a **conflict**.
- Resolved through **social interactions**.
- Successful **resolution** leads to healthy personality development.

EXPANSION

STAGE	
Age	Psychosocial conflict
1st year	Trust versus mistrust.
2nd year	Autonomy versus shame and doubt.
3–6 years	Initiative versus guilt.
To puberty	Industry versus inferiority.
Adolescence	Identity versus identity confusion.
Early adulthood	Intimacy versus isolation.
Middle age	Generativity versus stagnation.
Old age	Integrity versus despair.

EVALUATION OF PSYCHODYNAMIC EXPLANATIONS

RESEARCH EVIDENCE RELATED TO FREUD'S THEORY

- Freud observed patients during psychoanalysis.

Case study: Little Hans (Freud, 1909)

- Hans resented father and sister because in competition with him for his mother's affections.
- Created anxiety, projected elsewhere (an ego defence).
- Led to phobia for horses.
- Recovery occurred when Hans admitted to his feelings and came to identify with his father.

Repression

- Myers and Brewin (1994) – 'repressors' (low on anxiety, high on defensiveness) took longer to recall negative childhood memories.

Perceptual defence

- McGinnies (1949) – participants took longer to identify emotionally-threatening words than other words.

→

- **Not objective** – didn't make notes in case it interfered with therapy but later recall may have been biased.
- But **meticulous observations** of human nature.

→

- Supported his predictions of events during the phallic stage of development (Oedipus conflict).
- Data reported indirectly to Freud from Hans' father – may not be accurate.
- **Alternative explanation** for boy's phobia (classical conditioning).

→

- Shows link between personality type and ego defences.
- Recollection of childhood memories may be unreliable.

MUST REMEMBER...
That **describing** research evidence is AO1; **using it effectively** makes it AO2.

COMMENTARY ON FREUD'S THEORY

Strengths	Limitations
• One of the **best known and enduring theories** in Psychology, and beyond. • View of human nature 'broad and deep' (Hall and Lindzey, 1970). • Accounts for **rationality** and **irrationality** using idea of the **unconscious mind**; fits with our own experiences of different motivations (Jarvis, 2000).	• Study of **abnormal individuals** not suitable basis for theory about normal personality development. • Patients were a **biased sample** (white, middle-class female, Europeans) and their recollections from childhood may be unreliable. • **Over-emphasis on sex** may have been true in 19th C. but not applicable now. Neo-Freudians have incorporated social influences. • **Gender bias** – women portrayed as inferior; reflected women's role in Victorian times but not in all times. • **Lacks falsifiabilty** – cannot disprove Freud's interpretations; if patient disagreed with interpretation seen as a sign of repression.

COMMENTARY ON ERIKSON'S THEORY

Strengths	Limitations
• Influential in establishing **lifespan approach**. • **Social influences** recognised. • Some **research support**, e.g. Marcia (1966) – confirmation of identity crisis in adolescence.	• **Difficult to test** the theory except through interviews. • **Gender bias** – androcentric; ignores female values such as interdependence. • **Culture bias** – based on individualist society, e.g. emphasis on identity which is less relevant in collectivist societies. • **Historical bias** – details are outdated, e.g. finding a 'job for life'.

TYPICAL QUESTIONS...

1 Critically consider **one or more** psychodynamic explanationS of personality development. (24 marks)

2 Discuss **one** psychodynamic explanation of personality development. (24 marks)

SOCIAL LEARNING EXPLANATIONS OF PERSONALITY DEVELOPMENT

DESCRIPTION

BANDURA

Social learning theory in a nutshell
- Incorporates **indirect** and **direct** reinforcement.
- Important difference between **learning** and **production**.
- Observation → vicarious reinforcement → imitation → maintenance through direct reinforcement.

KEY PRINCIPLES: OBSERVATION AND MODELLING
- Novel behaviours are learned directly or indirectly.
- Far more can be learned through observation (indirectly).
- Observation leads to learning a behaviour.
- Vicarious reinforcement increases likelihood that a behaviour will be repeated (modelling).
- Individual needs suitable opportunity and necessary skills.
- Once repeated, direct reinforcement/punishment will increase/decrease likelihood that behaviour will be further repeated.

DEMONSTRATING MODELLING
Bandura et al. (1961)
- Children who saw model behave aggressively towards Bobo were more aggressive when playing with Bobo, and imitated specific acts.

Bandura (1965)
- Children who saw model rewarded were more likely to behave aggressively.

KEY CONCEPTS
Reciprocal determinism
- Learning is not passive.
- As individual acts, this changes their environment, affecting subsequent behaviour.
- Also people can self-reinforce and make choices.

Self-efficacy
- A person's sense of their own competence.
- Learned directly from own performance.
- Or learned indirectly, e.g. Schunk (1983) – test score improved if children told classmates did well.

MISCHEL

Situationalism in a nutshell
- Personality is **not stable** – people are not consistent in their behaviour but are only consistent in the same situations.
- **Situational** rather than dispositional explanation of personality.
- Explains personality paradox – we think we are consistent but acknowledge inconsistency.

KEY PRINCIPLES: BEHAVIOURAL SPECIFICITY
- Behaviour related to specific situation.
- Behaviour determined by past rewards/punishments received in that situation.
- Leads to different probabilities for each situation.
- We learn through selective reinforcement (similar to context-dependent learning).

DEMONSTRATING SITUATIONISM
Mischel and Peake (1982)
- Family, friends and strangers rated 63 students in various situations.
- Correlation in same situation across time = 0.29.
- Correlation across situations = 0.08.

KEY CONCEPT: PERSON VARIABLES
- Individuals differ in terms of 'person variables'.
- Examples: competencies, encoding strategies, expectancies based on experience, subjective values.
- Person variables determine how one will respond in any situation.

Social learning explanations emphasise the role of experience and reinforcement.

EVALUATION

STRENGTHS

- **Testable** propositions.
- Well-supported by laboratory experiments.
- **Confirmed** in real-life studies, e.g. Bandura used live clown instead of Bobo.
- **Useful applications**, e.g. concept of self-efficacy is applied to improving people's health behaviour.

LIMITATIONS
Research studies

- Laboratory experiments do not represent complexities of life.
- **Demand characteristics** in the Bobo studies.
- Focuses on **short-term effects** which may not show how long-term behaviours are learned.

LIMITATIONS
Theory

- Not intended specifically as a theory of personality.
- **Lacks detail**, e.g. how do we influence the environment?
- Lacks cohesiveness – how do the different concepts relate to each other?
- **Denies free will** – suggests we are controlled by the environment.
- Focuses too much on situation with little attention on personality traits.
- **Lacks biological perspective**, e.g. Eysenck's type theory and research by Thomas and Chess (1980) suggest we inherit our temperament.

STRENGTHS

- Correctly **challenges trait-only view** of personality.
- Can explain personality inconsistency.
- Promoted idea that biology and learning interact with situations to produce personality.

LIMITATIONS
Research studies

- **Erroneous analysis** (Epstein, 1979) – moment-to-moment correlations inevitably low (when you correlate only two scores); if you aggregate correlations (i.e. average scores over a number of days), they are higher.
- Re-analysis of Mischel and Peak data using aggregation found 0.65 for consistency across time and 0.13 across situations.
- Fleeson (2001) found high correlation on the 'Big 5 personality factors' (OCEAN) when aggregation used (about 0.90).

LIMITATIONS
Theory

- **Determinist** – suggests we are controlled by rewards/punishments.
- **Ignores consistency** – evidence that people are consistent but can resolve this:
  - combine situationalism and consistency (Mischel and Shoda, 1998) – people are consistent in each situation
  - situational factors may be strong in novel, formal, brief situations where there is little choice; dispositional factors stronger in informal situations where one is freer (Buss, 1989).

> For practice in answering A2 Psychology questions, why not use *Collins Do Brilliantly A2 Psychology*?

TYPICAL QUESTIONS...

1 Discuss **one or more** social learning explanations of personality development. (24 marks)

2 (a) Outline and evaluate **one** psychodynamic explanation of personality development. (12 marks)

  (b) Outline and evaluate **one** social learning explanation of personality development. (12 marks)

EXPLANATIONS OF GENDER DEVELOPMENT

EXPLANATION I: SOCIAL COGNITIVE THEORY (BUSSEY AND BANDURA, 1992)

1 MODELLING (INDIRECT REINFORCEMENT)

- Children acquire knowledge of gender stereotypes from observing others, e.g. in the media.
- Children most likely to imitate rewarded behaviours.
- In absence of rewards, stereotypes can still act as a model.

Evidence of influence of the media

- Williams (1985) – noted children's gender attitudes; became more stereotyped after two years of TV.

3 DIRECT TUITION

- Parents tell children what is and isn't appropriate.

2 ENACTIVE EXPERIENCE

- Children perform (enact) gender behaviours which are selectively reinforced, creating 'outcome expectancies'.

Influence of parents

- Parents reward gender-appropriate behaviour, punish gender-inappropriate behaviour, e.g. girl wearing feminine clothes, boy wearing feminine clothes.
- Smith and Lloyd (1978) – women selected feminine toy (e.g. doll) if thought baby was a girl or masculine toy (e.g. squeaky hammer) for a boy.

Influence of peers

- Lamb and Roopnarine (1979) – nursery children: reinforced gender-appropriate play (e.g. gave more attention) and criticised gender-inappropriate play.

COMMENTARY ON STUDIES

- **Demand characteristics** – Smith and Lloyd study: gender of infant was a cue in a contrived situation.
- Contrived studies are not always natural situations so may not apply in real world.
- **Conflicting evidence**, e.g.
  - Jacklin and Maccoby (1978) – boys and girls don't receive different reinforcements;
  - Smith and Daglish (1977) – children whose parents were more gender stereotyped were not more stereotyped themselves – the theory would predict such a link.

STRENGTHS OF THEORY

- **Testable** propositions.
- **Useful applications** – can reduce gender stereotypes using counter-conditioning, i.e. present children with non-traditional stereotypes.
- **Explains cultural differences** – Whiting and Edwards (1988) found gender stereotype differences in a study of 11 different cultures.

However, may lack effectiveness because:

- contradicted by direct experience which may have stronger effect (e.g. female rather than male nurses)
- people prefer evidence that confirms rather than challenges stereotypes (confirmatory bias).

However...

There is also evidence of cultural universalism, e.g. in most cultures women care for children. The evolutionary approach suggests that different male and female behaviours exist as a consequence of adaptive pressure.

LIMITATIONS OF THEORY

- Children **not consistently reinforced** so it is difficult to see how learning occurs.
- Children may pay **little attention** to adult instructions and models.
- **Adevelopmental** – does not explain how children's behaviour changes qualitatively as they get older in contrast with cognitive-developmental theory.
- Alternative perspectives – not sufficient on own; **omits biological explanations**, e.g. hormones lead to gender-related behaviours as in the case of girls receiving male hormones prenatally and becoming more tomboyish (Money and Ehrhardt, 1972).

EXPLANATION 2: COGNITIVE-DEVELOPMENTAL THEORY

Cognitive-developmental theory in a nutshell
- Focuses on **how** thinking changes (qualitatively as children get older).
- Changes are a consequence of **maturation**.
- Stage theory – sequence is **invariant**.

GENGER CONSISTENCY THEORY (KOHLBERG, 1966)

2–3 years	Gender identity.	Recognises own gender.
3–7 years	Gender stability.	Aware that gender is fixed.
7–12 years	Gender consistency.	Superficial changes don't alter gender (like ability to conserve).

Research

- **Slaby and Frey (1975):**
  - children over 2 years can identify whether they are a boy or a girl
  - children of 3–4 years can give appropriate answer to 'When you were little, were you a boy/girl?'
  - children who were rated as gender-consistent looked more at same-gender actors in a film – focused on obtaining gender-appropriate information. Suggests that gender consistency is cause not effect of gender identification.

- **Universal sequence** – confirmed by Munroe et al. (1984), supports biological basis.
- **Ages for stages may vary** – may be due to methods used in testing, e.g. Emmerlich et al. (1977) – if drawings used, children not able to show gender stability. However, they could if photographs of real children used (Bem, 1989).
- **Stages questioned** – Martin and Halverson (1983) found that pre-schoolers showed gender consistency if asked if they would change gender if they wore gender-inappropriate clothing.
- **Further challenge** from Martin and Little (1990) – found pre-schoolers had rudimentary gender understanding but **strong gender stereotypes**, therefore stereotypes before not after understanding.

GENDER SCHEMA THEORY (MARTIN AND HALVERSON, 1983)

- Children **motivated** to learn about gender as soon as identity clear (around 3 years).
  - **Readiness** to categorise gender drives gender development.
    - Search for gender 'rules' or schema.
      - Gender schemas are '**theories**' about how men/women behave.
- Pre-schoolers should have more interest in 'in-group schemas' and less in 'out-group schemas'.

Research

- **Martin et al. (1995)** – boys (4–5 years) more likely to play with toys identified as 'boys toys'; same for girls. Shows that gender identity triggers search for in-group schemas and leads to acting on that information.
- **Liben and Signorella** (1993) – young children ignored information inconsistent with stereotypes. Shows how schema affects processing of information.

- Can explain why children not affected by all stereotypes – because only attending to in-group schema.
- Can explain why children not affected by opposite-gender reinforcement, e.g. Fagot (1985) found that teachers reinforce feminine behaviours in boys and girls, but boys and girls behave differently.

COMPARE AND CONTRAST

Bussey and Bandura	Gender behaviour is **cause** of gender identity.	Stereotypes learned first.
Kohlberg	Gender consistency is **cause** of gender identity.	Stereotypes learned later.
Martin and Halverson	Gender consistency is **effect** of gender identity.	Schema learned first.

TYPICAL QUESTION...

Describe and evaluate **two or more** explanations of the development of gender identity/gender roles. (24 marks)

> For practice in answering A2 Psychology questions, why not use *Collins Do Brilliantly A2 Psychology*?

SOCIAL DEVELOPMENT AND FORMATION OF IDENTITY IN ADOLESCENCE

MUST KNOW...
- Research into social development in adolescence.
- Research related to the formation of identity in adolescence.

SOCIAL DEVELOPMENT IN ADOLESCENCE

AUTONOMY

- Freud – genital stage leads to independence.
- Blos (1967) – adolescence is second period of 'individuation' (first in infancy) = re-individuation.
- Adolescent task is to become independent from parents and assert individuality.
- This independence (separation) results in:
  - emotional emptiness, satisfied by group experiences
  - regression to child-like behaviour to receive substitute parenting, or to hero worship to gain substitute parent.
- Rebellion is an ego defence to prevent becoming dependent again.

- Independence alone may not be sufficient for healthy development – continuing secure attachment enables exploration = **connectedness**.
- Empirical support from Cooper et al. (1998) found adolescents who are securely attached have fewer emotional, behavioural and physical problems.

STORM AND STRESS

- Common view that adolescence is stressful (Hall, 1904).
- Research evidence:
  - Smith and Crawford (1986) – high rate of suicidal thoughts in adolescents.
  - Csikszentmihalyi and Larson (1984) – used pages to record adolescent frequent and drastic mood swings.
- Cross-cultural evidence:
  - Mead (1928) – in Samoa relatively easy passage from child to adulthood, maybe because no pressures from job choices as they are in a non-industrialised society; also sexual maturity dealt with more openly;
  - Bronfenbrenner (1974) – in USSR adolescents less segregated and encouraged more to enter adulthood, behaved more pro-socially than US adolescents.

- Suggests that Western society **creates stress** rather than transition itself.
- Cross-cultural research may not be reliable:
  - Mead's research has been challenged by Freeman (1983) suggesting she 'saw' what she wanted to see
  - Mead only studied women
  - many other factors may explain cross-cultural differences.

FOCAL THEORY

- Explains why some adolescents are stressed while others aren't.
- Coleman (1974) proposed that adolescents have to deal with various issues, e.g. changing appearance, sexual maturity, peer relationships, etc.
- Stress occurs when have to cope with too many issues at one time.
- No stress if can focus on one issue at a time.
- Research evidence – Rutter et al. (1976, Isle of Wight study) found little turmoil in study of 2,000 adolescents; did find 1:5 clinically depressed.

- Further research support: Coleman and Hendry (1990) studied 800 adolescents; found that each issue peaked at different ages and there were individual differences. Most adolescents navigating carefully through this period by putting some issues on hold.
- Practical applications for counselling adolescents.
- Storm and stress view – may stem from research by psychiatrists (e.g. Blos, Erikson) who looked at troubled adolescents.
- Alternative explanation: Eccles et al. (1993) – stress may occur because of mismatch between adolescent's developing needs and role offered to them in Western society.

FORMATION OF IDENTITY IN ADOLESCENCE

ERIKSON'S PSYCHOSOCIAL THEORY

General theory
- Eight stages of man.
- A psychodynamic theory – proposed conflicts during development.
- Erikson's conflicts were psychosocial.
- Conflicts resolved through social interactions.
- Successful resolution leads to healthy personality development.

Adolescent stage
- 12–18 years – 'identity versus role confusion'.
- Role confusion *is* healthy.
- Psychosocial **moratorium** – temporary suspension of activity to try out different attitudes/roles.
- **Role sampling** leads to formation of adult identity.
- **Identity confusion** is *not* healthy; 4 kinds of behaviour:

Intimacy is avoided to protect fragile identity – leads to isolation or stereotyped relationships.

Negative identity – adopting an extreme identity.

Time perspective – plans for future avoided.

Industry – compulsive overwork or underwork.

STRENGTHS
- Evidence from Erikson's (1968) own experiences as psychoanalyst and interviewing Dakota Indians.
- Empirical support from Marcia, Smith and Crawford and Csikszentmihalyi and Larson.

LIMITATIONS
- Adolescence not necessarily a time of turmoil, e.g. Rutter et al. and Coleman and Hendry.
- Gender bias – androcentric; ignores female values such as interdependence.
- Culture bias – based on individualist society, e.g. emphasis on identity which is less relevant in collectivist societies.
- Historical bias – details outdated, e.g. finding a 'job for life'.

MARCIA'S APPROACH

General theory
- Marcia (1966) developed method to test Erikson's theory.
- Interviewed adolescents about their identity status in areas such as politics, religion and sex.
- Analysis of answers showed four categories/identity statuses which differ in terms of degree of crisis and commitment.
- No fixed order, statuses may be skipped.
- Moratorium is a pre-requisite for identity achievement.

Identity diffusion status (low low)

Moratorium status (high low)

Foreclosure status (low high)

Identity achievement status (high high)

STRENGTHS
- An empirical theory – designed so that more could be found out about adolescent development, e.g. Waterman (1985) studied 11–21 year olds; identity diffusion decreased and achievement increased as predicted; moratorium uncommon at all ages, 34% in foreclosure.

LIMITATIONS
- Oversimplifcation – Archer (1982) found that 90% of those interviewed were in different statuses for different areas (politics, religion, sex, etc.) rather than just one status at any time.

TYPICAL QUESTIONS...

1 Describe and evaluate research (explanations **and/or** studies) into social development in adolescence. (24 marks)

2 Discuss research (explanations **and/or** studies) into the formation of identity in adolescence. (24 marks)

3 Discuss research (explanations **and/or** studies) into social development in adolescence, including the formation of identity. (24 marks)

ADOLESCENT RELATIONSHIPS AND CULTURAL DIFFERENCES IN BEHAVIOUR

RELATIONSHIPS WITH PARENTS AND PEERS DURING ADOLESCENCE

RELATIONSHIPS WITH PARENTS

Autonomy
- Blos – separation leads to autonomy.
- Independence alone may not be sufficient for healthy development; attachment/connectedness enables exploration.

Identity formation
- Identity foreclosure associated with domineering parenting; moratorium/identity achievement with democratic parenting (Waterman, 1982).
- Connectedness provides secure base for exploration and identity formation.

Conflict with parents
- Mainly mild conflict (e.g. having to tidy room) rather than major (e.g. politics).
- Permissive/authoritarian parents may have more conflicts (Steinberg and Morris, 2001).

RESEARCH SUPPORT
- Cooper et al. (1998) – adolescents who are securely attached have fewer problems.
- Archer and Waterman (1994) found weak connectedness associated with adolescents in identity confusion.
- Laursen (1995) – most conflicts were between mothers and daughters, possibly because boys more independent.

COMMENTARY
- Oversimplification of family relationships – parents don't use just one parenting style.
- Two-way process – parents develop as a consequence of their adolescent children, e.g. Montemayor et al. (1993) – fathers less stressed if closer to adolescent children.
- Gender differences – parental relationships more important for girls (Frey and Rothlisberger, 1996).
- Cultural differences, e.g. in India adolescents have close and subordinate relationships with parents (Larsen, 1999).

RELATIONSHIPS WITH PEERS

- Peer relationships take over – adolescents have **twice** as many peer as family relationships (Frey and Rothlisberger, 1996).

Autonomy
- Peers become attachment figures; may act as a secure base.
- Peers help adolescents avoid loneliness (Blos, 1967) – 'way-station' on road to independence.

Identity formation
- Peers help adolescents explore new ideologies (Erikson, 1968).
- Cliques provide adolescent with social identity (Coleman, 1961).

Peer conformity
- Highest in early to mid-adolescence.
- Peer groups associated with anti-social behaviour but...

RESEARCH SUPPORT
- Steinberg and Silverberg (1986) – 10–16 year-olds: autonomy increased as peer involvements increased.
- Brown and Lohr (1987) – adolescents who didn't belong to cliques had lowest self-esteem.
- Berndt (1979) – evidence that peer conformity more related to pro-social behaviour.

COMMENTARY
- Research correlational, e.g. could be that low self-esteem was reason for non-membership of cliques.
- Parent–peer relationships interdependent – Fuligni and Eccles (1993) interviewed 2,000 11-year olds; those with authoritarian parents rated peers more highly than those with democratic parents.

CULTURAL DIFFERENCES IN ADOLESCENT BEHAVIOUR

CULTURAL DIFFERENCES

AUTONOMY

- Only individualist cultures value individual needs and independence (Jensen, 1999).
- In Japan (collectivist society), dependence is central aim for adulthood (Doi, 1973).

Supported by: Gilani (1995) – compared UK Asian (collectivist) and white (individualist) families; for Asian teenage girls family came first and were expected to conform rather than become independent.

CONFLICT

- 'Storm and stress' not universal:
  - Mead (1928) – in Samoa, relatively easy passage from child to adulthood, maybe because no pressures from job choices as they are in a non-industrialised society; also sexual maturity dealt with more openly.
- 'Rites of passage' may help transition, e.g. religious rites that mark distinct change rather than Western transitional period where individual is neither child nor adult.
- Historical change – adolescent crisis may be 'invention' of 20th C.

- Mead's research has been challenged by Freeman (1983) suggesting she 'saw' what she wanted to see; and she only studied women.

IDENTITY FORMATION

Individualist versus collectivist

- In collectivist cultures, group identities contribute to individual identity, e.g. in China – successful development related to interdependence between individual and group identity (Dien, 1983).

Urban versus rural

- Urban, industrialised cultures have more choices – leads to more delay in transition from child to adulthood because too many choices (Chosholm and Hurrelmann, 1995).
- Rural culture, e.g. Samoa, youths had no choices and no period of adolescence; adult roles decided by community (Tupuola, 1993).

However...
In some inner cities, youths often have little choice because job shortage makes identity achievement difficult (Wilson, 1987).

Ethnic minorities

- Ethnicity is part of identity.
- Not easy to resolve ethnicity because lack of suitable role models may delay identity achievement.
- Berry (1997) outlined four options: assimilation (identify with dominant culture), integration (identify with both), separation (reject dominant culture, focus on ethnic group), marginality (remain on fringes of both).

However...
Integration is best route to take (White and Burke, 1987).

GENERAL COMMENTARY

- Suggests that Western society creates stress rather than transition itself.
- Problems with cross-cultural research:
  - Western psychologists' observations may be biased
  - individuals may present stereotyped behaviour to psychologist, even indigenous ones
  - may use assessment tools developed by Western psychologists (imposed etic).

TYPICAL QUESTIONS...

1 Discuss research (explanations **and/or** studies) into relationships with parents and peers during adolescence. (24 marks)

2 Discuss research (explanations **and/or** studies) into relationships with parents **and/or** peers during adolescence. (24 marks)

3 Describe and evaluate research (explanations **and/or** studies) related to cultural differences in adolescent behaviour. (24 marks)

EVOLUTIONARY EXPLANATIONS OF THE BEHAVIOUR OF NON-HUMAN ANIMALS

MUST KNOW...
- Evolutionary explanations of the behaviour of non-human animals.
- Biological explanations of apparent altruism.

EVOLUTIONARY EXPLANATIONS

MUST REMEMBER...
This is about the evolution of **behaviour** in non-human animals, and **not** the evolution of physical characteristics.

SURVIVAL OF THE FITTEST
- In evolution, *fitness* is measured in terms of **reproductive success**.
- Individuals who leave the **most surviving offspring** have the greatest chance of evolutionary success.
- **Differential reproductive success** among individual members of a species is at the centre of the process of evolution.

APPARENT ALTRUISM
- **Altruism** – any act of helping which increases the fitness of another individual, at some cost to the fitness of the helper.
- **Kin selection theory** (Hamilton, 1963) proposes that individuals pass on their genes *directly* through their own offspring, and *indirectly* by helping the reproductive success of their genetic relatives (**inclusive fitness**).
- **Trivers (1971)** proposed a theory of **reciprocal altruism**, where one animal will show altruistic behaviour toward another if the recipient returns the favour in the future.
- Each of these types of 'apparent' altruism are advantageous to the 'altruist', either at an individual level or at a genetic level, and therefore offer an *adaptive* advantage.

EEA = Environment of Evolutionary Adaptiveness (the environment to which a species is adapted).

WHY DO YOUNG ANIMALS CRY?
- **Trivers (1974)** – each offspring must try to **maximise the presence of its own genes** in succeeding generations (i.e. fitness).
- **Exaggerated indications of need** would secure a greater share of parental resources, thus increasing the likelihood of their survival.
- As a result, this would be favoured by natural selection, leading to more and more ostentatious demands by offspring in the future.
- **Furlow (2000)** suggests that when resources are limited, parents may not invest in all offspring equally, particularly if some have little chance of surviving to reproductive age.
- Such potentially costly displays (in terms of energy and attracting predators) may have evolved because they reveal an offspring's health and vigour, indicating that they are worth investing in.

Nature or nurture?
- The fact that all members of a species demonstrate the same behaviour does not exclude the possibility that they all share common learning experiences.
- The Baldwin Effect proposes that initially, some aspect of the environment promotes a certain behaviour or trait (learning). This useful trait then becomes widespread within the population.
- Animals who have a genetic predisposition to that trait (nature) thus gain a selective advantage over others, and so the trait becomes more widespread in future generations.

Ultimate or proximate causes?
- **Gould (1984)** claims that evolutionary explanations, which explain behaviours in terms of their possible ultimate cause (i.e. their function in the **EEA**) are unnecessary.
- This is because we are able to successfully explain most behaviour in terms of its proximate (e.g. developmental or physiological) causes.

← EVALUATION →

Levels of selection
- A problem faced by Darwin in his theory of natural selection was that he focused on the adaptive advantage to *individual* animals rather than focusing on the gene as the unit of selection.
- This would explain the apparently selfless behaviour of social insects.

Natural and sexual selection
- Some characteristics of animals appear to have nothing to do with an animal's chances of survival.
- Some (such as the bright plumage of peacocks) appear to *impede* survival.
- This is because some characteristics have evolved because they give an advantage in sexual reproduction.
- If one sex (usually female) has a preference for a particular characteristic (e.g. bright plumage might indicate vigour and health in a potential mate), then it gradually becomes more prominent in the gene pool over time (sexual selection).

BIOLOGICAL EXPLANATIONS OF APPARENT ALTRUISM

KIN SELECTION THEORY (Hamilton, 1963)
- Individuals pass on their genes *directly* through their own offspring, and *indirectly* by facilitating the reproductive success of their genetic relatives (inclusive fitness).
- Helping a close relative can therefore be considered a form of genetic selfishness.

Example: nepotism
- In Belding's ground squirrel, females recognise genetic relatives (kin) and treat them with special deference (nepotism).
- Females who are close relatives help each other in defending offspring from predators (Sherman, 1981).
- There is a correlation between cooperation of two individuals and their degree of relatedness.

Kin recognition
- Kin selection requires that animals recognise kin.
- Stuart (1991) suggests two mechanisms by which kin recognise each other:
  - spatial proximity (family groups tend to stay together)
  - phenotype matching (related individuals have common characteristics such as appearance, smell and behaviour).

Altruism = any act of helping which increases the reproductive fitness of the individual who is helped, at some cost to the fitness of the helper.

MUST TAKE CARE...
Not to use too many examples in lieu of explanation.

RECIPROCAL ALTRUISM (TRIVERS, 1971)
- One animal might show altruistic behaviour toward another if the recipient of this 'favour' reciprocates (returns the favour) in the future.
- This will increase the fitness of each individual involved, provided benefits of reciprocating outweigh costs over time, and cheaters can be excluded.

Example: vampire bats
- Food-sharing reduces mortality (Wilkinson, 1984).
- The benefit of receiving food outweighs the cost of sharing a meal.
- A recipient of food-sharing gains 18 hours of time until starvation, while a donor only loses six hours.
- Over a lifetime of reciprocating, each bat gains far more hours than it loses.

Detecting cheats
- Trivers suggested that reciprocal altruism would only evolve in species where individuals could recognise cheats.
- Axelrod and Hamilton (1981) proposed 'tit-for-tat' strategy – cooperation is met with mutual cooperation and defection (taking but not returning) with defection.

RESEARCH SUPPORT
- Using DNA matching tests, researchers were able to show that females show more altruistic behaviour towards full sisters than towards half sisters (Holmes and Sherman, 1982).
- This supports the claim that animals increase their fitness by helping those with whom they share the most genes.

EVIDENCE FOR PHENOTYPE MATCHING
- Mateo and Johnston (2000) provided support for the use of phenotype matching in kin recognition.
- Hamsters that were reared only with non-kin since birth later responded differently to odours of unfamiliar relatives and non-relatives.

IMPORTANCE OF KIN SELECTION
- Kin selection is important because:
  - parents who fail to recognise their own offspring would waste resources on non-relatives (at some cost to their fitness)
  - related individuals who collaborate are more likely to fend off aggression from non-relatives.

RESEARCH SUPPORT
- Manning and Dawkins (1998) claim that the example of vampire bats fits assumptions of reciprocal altruism because:
  - they can provide help at little personal cost
  - bats associate with the same individuals over a long time therefore are able to detect cheats who do not reciprocate.

LACK OF EVIDENCE
- Stevens and Hauser (2004) argue that although there is plenty of evidence for cooperation among kin, the evidence for reciprocity among non-kin is still slim for primates.
- However, some studies (e.g. deWaal, 1996) do appear to show clear evidence of reciprocity operating among non-kin.

TIT-FOR-TAT
- Stevens and Stephens (2004) found some supporting evidence for a tit-for-tat strategy operating in captive blue jays. Jays attend only to short-term consequences; they do not cooperate in the absence of an immediate benefit.

TYPICAL QUESTIONS...

1 Discuss evolutionary explanations of the behaviour of non-human animals. (24 marks)

2 Discuss evolutionary explanations for two or more forms of non-human animal behaviour. (24 marks)

3 Critically consider two biological explanations for apparent altruism. (24 marks)

CLASSICAL CONDITIONING AND ITS ROLE IN THE BEHAVIOUR OF NON-HUMAN ANIMALS

DESCRIPTION OF CLASSICAL CONDITIONING

Acquisition
- Initially a neutral stimulus does not bring about a reflex response by itself.
- After many pairings of the NS with a UCS this changes, and the NS acquires the ability to produce the response in question.

Timing
- For classical conditioning to work effectively, the NS must precede the UCS but overlap with it – this means the NS can be used to predict the UCS.
- Other arrangements (e.g. NS and UCS presented at the same time, or UCS precedes NS) tend to fail.

Extinction and spontaneous recovery
- The CR does not become permanently established as a response.
- It does not last long after the removal of the UCS (i.e. it undergoes extinction).
- Under the right conditions the CR can reappear (spontaneous recovery).
- After extinction, if the organism is retrained using the same CS–UCS pairings, the CR is quickly re-installed.

THE PROCESS OF CLASSICAL CONDITIONING

Before conditioning

Food (UCS) → Salivation (UCR)

Buzzer (NS) → No response

During conditioning

Buzzer (NS) + Food (UCS) → Salivation (UCR)

After conditioning

Buzzer (CS) → Salivation (CR)

Stimulus generalisation
- Although conditioning may involve only one stimulus, the response itself may be generalised to other stimuli.
- If a stimulus is presented that is similar, but not identical to the original CS, the same CR can occur.
- The more similar the new stimulus is to the CR, the stronger the response to it.

Stimulus discrimination
- During conditioning, when the CS–UCS pairing is made, other similar stimuli are introduced, but these are not paired with the UCS.
- The outcome of this is that eventually only the CS produces a CR, and the other similar stimuli do not.

Higher order conditioning
- A second neutral stimulus can be paired with an established CS, and eventually will produce a weaker version of the CR.

NS → CS → CR

Eventually...

NS → CR

REMEMBERING THE FEATURES OF CLASSICAL CONDITIONING

Timing
Higher order conditioning
Extinction

Discrimination
Acquisition
Generalisation
Spontaneous recovery

THE DAGS

EVALUTION OF CLASSICAL CONDITIONING

BIOLOGICAL PREPAREDNESS

Classical conditioning does not work in the same way for all species – some relationships between CS and UCS are more difficult for some species to learn than for others:

- Animals are **prepared** to learn associations that are significant in terms of their survival needs (i.e. they make the CS–UCS association easily).

- Animals are **unprepared** to learn associations that are *not* significant to their survival needs (i.e. they make the CS–UCS association with difficulty).

- Animals are **contraprepared** to learn associations that are opposite to some naturally occurring predisposition (i.e. they cannot make the CS–UCS association).

With care, each of these (evaluation and role of CC) can be used to elaborate the other.

TASTE-AVERSION CONDITIONING

In taste-aversion conditioning (TAC), an animal may become sick (UCS) after eating food with a particular taste (CS), and later avoids foods that taste the same. This challenges CC because:

- Classical conditioning requires **many associations** between the CS and UCS, but in TAC, learning takes place after just one association.

- In CC, the **longer the delay** between the NS and the UCS, the less likely it is that an association will be made. In TAC, conditioning can still take place despite a delay of hours between NS and UCS.

- In CC, **extinction** takes place shortly after the removal of the UCS, whereas in TAC, the association is remarkably resistant to extinction.

ROLE OF CLASSICAL CONDITIONING IN ANIMAL BEHAVIOUR

CONDITIONED TASTE AVERSION

- Conditioned taste aversion (CTA) has been applied successfully to wildlife management problems, including the preservation of wolves and other endangered species.

- In CTA, the taste–illness association suppresses the killing of prey (e.g. sheep), by predators (e.g. wolves).

- Wolves and coyotes, which have consumed a mutton bait containing an undetectable dose of an illness-causing substance, will later avoid live sheep as long as they taste and smell like the baits (**Garcia et al., 1977**).

- **Nicolaus et al. (1983)** demonstrated that free-ranging crows in a particular breeding territory very quickly acquired CTA by eating green-coloured eggs treated with a small amount of illness-inducing agent.

- As a result, attacks upon eggs of that colour decreased significantly for these crows. Crows occupying other breeding territories that had not undergone CTA consumed untreated eggs freely.

MUST REMEMBER...
That this material tends to form part of an AO2 response, so must make it sound like AO2 in an answer!

BEHAVIOUR TOWARDS CONSPECIFICS

- Animals that are able to change their behaviour in response to a CS have a selective advantage.

- Through CC, an animal can respond more rapidly or appropriately to important environmental stimuli, such as those associated with food or other members of its species (conspecifics).

- In some species, territorial males attack females during the breeding season, delaying the breeding process.

- **Hollis et al. (1990)** trained male gouramis using CC to *court* rather attack females. As courtship is more likely to lead to reproduction, natural selection would favour those who could learn in this way.

- Later research by **Hollis et al. (1997)** showed that males conditioned in this way fathered 10 times as many young as males who were not conditioned.

MUST TAKE CARE ...
To be seen to be **assessing** the role of CC in animal behaviour here, e.g. by saying 'The importance of CC in reproductive success is demonstrated in research on...'

TYPICAL QUESTIONS...

1 Discuss the nature of classical conditioning. (24 marks)

2 (a) Outline the main features of classical conditioning. (12 marks)

(b) Assess the role of classical conditioning in the behaviour of non-human animals. (12 marks)

OPERANT CONDITIONING AND ITS ROLE IN THE BEHAVIOUR OF NON-HUMAN ANIMALS

MUST KNOW...

- Description and evaluation of operant conditioning, including an assessment of the role of operant conditioning in the behaviour of non-human animals.

DESCRIPTION OF OPERANT CONDITIONING

THE NATURE OF OPERANT CONDITIONING

This is an explanation of learning that sees the consequences of a behaviour as being of vital importance to the future appearance of that behaviour.

Punishment

- Punishment occurs when a behaviour is followed by the addition of an unpleasant stimulus (positive punishment) or the removal of a pleasant stimulus (negative punishment).
- Both serve to reduce the future likelihood of that behaviour occurring.

REINFORCEMENT

The principles of reinforcement are:

- Consequences which are rewarding *increase* a behaviour.
- Consequences which are punishing *decrease* a behaviour.
- Consequences which are neither rewarding nor punishing have little effect on that behaviour.

Schedules of reinforcement

- In continuous reinforcement, an animal is reinforced for every correct response.
- This brings about rapid learning but also rapid extinction if reinforcement is stopped.
- In partial reinforcement, an animal is reinforced according to a schedule (e.g. fixed interval, variable ratio, etc.).
- This brings about slower initial learning but also slower extinction.

Timing

- The time interval between the response and the reinforcer is crucial.
- If reinforcer (or punishment) follows immediately after the response, conditioning is more effective than if it is delayed.

Positive reinforcement

- These are something like rewards (e.g. food, money, etc.).
- Positive reinforcement has occurred when three conditions have been met:
  1. Consequence occurs which is dependent on a specific behaviour (e.g. a child receives praise for good behaviour).
  2. That behaviour then becomes more likely to occur.
  3. It becomes more likely to occur only because the reward is dependent on that behaviour occurring.

Negative reinforcement

- Basic principle of negative reinforcement is that if a behaviour stops something unpleasant, then that behaviour is likely to occur again in similar situations.
- That behaviour is therefore strengthened (reinforced) by the desirable consequence of escaping from an unpleasant situation.

REMEMBERING THE FEATURES OF CLASSICAL CONDITIONING

Reinforcement
Timing
Punishment
Positive reinforcement
Negative reinforcement
Schedules of reinforcement

Really **T**ough **P**arents **P**unish **N**aughty **S**ons

MUST TAKE CARE ...

Not to confuse negative reinforcement (**NR**) and punishment (**Pt**):

- **NR** *strengthens* a behaviour because an unpleasant (i.e. negative) condition is removed as a consequence of the behaviour.
- **Pt** *weakens* a behaviour because an unpleasant condition is introduced as a consequence of the behaviour.

EVALUATION OF OPERANT CONDITIONING

Instinctive drift
- According to operant conditioning theory, it should be possible for any behaviour to be conditioned through modification of reinforcement.
- Breland and Breland (1951) discovered that **instinctive behaviour patterns** can interfere with the operant conditioning of arbitrary responses.
- These tendencies then override the temporary changes that are brought about by operant conditioning.

Instinctive drift and preparedness
- Instinctive drift relates to **preparedness** which states that certain animals are **evolutionarily prepared** to make some associations readily and unprepared to make others.
- Some types of conditioning would be unlikely to occur in the natural environment of animals and would therefore be difficult to learn or maintain.

EVALUATION OF OC

The problem of novel behaviour
- Operant conditioning cannot account for the production of **novel behaviour**. Only behaviours that already exist in the repertoire of an animal can be reinforced.
- However, social learning *can* explain how animals can acquire new behaviours as a consequence of watching other animals perform effective responses.

Classical or operant conditioning?
- One of the main assumptions of OC is that the **consequences** of a behaviour determine the probability of it recurring.
- Mackintosh (1981) claims that many studies of OC where an animal responds to a stimulus (e.g. pigeon pecking a key) are really examples of CC instead.
- What is actually learned is an association between stimulus (key) and reinforcer (food), with the pigeon's response being irrelevant to this process.

With care, each of these (evaluation and role of OC) can be used to elaborate the other.

ROLE OF OC IN ANIMAL BEHAVIOUR

SELECTIVE ADVANTAGE OF FLEXIBILITY THROUGH LEARNING

- Unpredictable environmental changes during an animal's lifetime cannot be anticipated. As a result, pre-programmed forms of behaviour would not be able to adapt to these changes.
- The ability to modify behaviour in the light of these changes gives animals a selective advantage.
- Operant conditioning thus allows animals to 'correct the faults of evolution'. Behaviours are selected as a result of their consequences with the animal's present environment and in its lifetime, rather than over generations as a result of natural selection.

The ability of various species to modify their behaviour as a result of reinforcement is demonstrated in studies by:
- Dews (1959) – taught octopi to pull a lever for food (**positive reinforcement**).
- Davidson (1966) – taught alligators to respond correctly in a discrimination task to escape heat (**negative reinforcement**).
- Brower et al. (1960) – found that toads learned to avoid bumblebees after being stung by one (**punishment**).

MATING PREFERENCES

- Patterns of courtship behaviour in birds can be socially transmitted across generations as a result of learning by operant conditioning.
- The learning experiences of young birds affect male birdsong, female preferences for males as mates, and the courtship interactions between males and females.
- Research has demonstrated that young birds learn to sing from older birds and because birds can also learn other species' songs, this shows that social influence is very strong in this process.

- West and King (1988) discovered that male cowbirds raised in isolation can later match their courtship songs to 'match' the preferences of local female cowbirds.
  When the male birds sang, the female responded to some elements of the song but not others.
  As a result, the frequency of the rewarded elements increased and the un-reinforced elements were eliminated.

TYPICAL QUESTIONS...

1 Discuss the nature of operant conditioning. (24 marks)

2 (a) Outline the main features of operant conditioning. (12 marks)

(b) Assess the role of operant conditioning in the behaviour of non-human animals. (12 marks)

EXPLANATIONS AND RESEARCH STUDIES OF SOCIAL LEARNING

- Bugnyar and Huber (1997) studied marmosets who learned either to push or pull a door to get food. After they had learned this, other marmosets observed them performing the response to get food. The 'observer' marmosets were then tested, but showed little evidence of imitation.

- Russon and Galdikas (1995) studied orang-utans in a natural setting. They found that orang-utans showed a preference for imitating animals with whom they had a established relationship. Status was important, with subordinate animals appearing to imitate dominant animals.

- A study which provides supporting evidence for imitation in chimps showed that animals raised in close contact with humans were superior in their ability to imitate after a 48-hour delay to both mother-reared chimps and human children (Nagell et al., 1993).

IMITATION

Hayes (1993) – difference between imitation and other form of social learning: non-imitative social learning involves learning *about* a particular stimulus whereas imitation involves learning a specific behaviour from observing others.

- Nagell et al. (1993) claimed that Japanese macaques seen to wash sweet potatoes in a stream were *not* imitating, but demonstrating **stimulus enhancement** (non-imitative learning where an animal's attention is simply drawn to whatever another animal is doing).

Social learning enables animals to learn from observing the behaviour of other animals.

Foraging
- Young Norwegian rats prefer to feed where others are feeding or have recently been feeding. This ensures that they will only eat what will not harm them (Shettleworth, 1998).

Do animals teach others?
- Some animals appear to modify their behaviour in the presence of young animals as if to facilitate their learning.
- This reduces the time they must spend finding food for offspring as they become more efficient foragers.
- In the long term this increases their inclusive fitness.

- Galef and Wigmore (1983) tested the feeding preferences of rats exposed to the food preferences of other rats. They found that rats who had interacted with 'demonstrator' rats (who had already fed) later showed the same food preference.
- A commonly cited example of social learning in birds is the behaviour of blue tits removing the foil tops of milk bottles to get at the cream underneath.

- Boesch (1991) observed many cases where chimpanzee mothers left stone 'hammers' and coula nuts near stone 'anvils' to stimulate and facilitate learning.
- Examples of 'direct learning' were relatively rare, although some mothers actively intervened when their infants were unable to break nuts. In these cases, the mothers correctly positioned either the nut or hammer for the infant.

Other explanations...

Make the social learning explanation unnecessary:
- Pecking and tearing (of bark) are an important part of the blue tit's *natural* foraging behaviour (Shettleworth, 1998).
- Birds that come across an opened bottle (and so can feed from it) come to associate bottles with food. When they come across an unopened bottle they engage in natural pecking and tearing behaviour which would then be reinforced (Hinde and Fisher, 1951).

However...
- Other research (e.g. Inoue-Nakamura and Matsuzawa, 1997) has failed to find evidence of *intentional* teaching among chimpanzees.
- There are two problems with assuming that animals *teach* others:
  - it is impossible for researchers to assess the mothers' **intention**
  - there is little evidence that mothers understand what knowledge another animal possesses (they lack a **theory of mind**).

TYPICAL QUESTION...

Discuss research (explanations and/or studies) into social learning in non-human animals. (24 marks)

INTELLIGENCE IN NON-HUMAN ANIMALS

MUST KNOW...
• Research evidence for intelligence in non-human animals.

SELF-AWARENESS

SELF-RECOGNITION

• The ability to recognise oneself in a mirror is seen as indicating self-awareness in animals.
• Gallup (1970) found that chimpanzees initially ignored a red mark on their forehead (put there under anaesthetic) but touched it when viewed in a mirror.
• Gallup (1983) argues that the use of mirrors for self-recognition requires self-awareness, an indication of intelligence.

LACK OF RESEARCH SUPPORT

• Heyes (1998) – argues there is little reliable evidence that any non-human primates are able to use a mirror to gain information about their own bodies.

ANAESTHETIC ARTEFACT HYPOTHESIS

• Heyes (1998) suggests an alternative explanation which does not require the skill of self-recognition. Chimps had no lingering effects of the anaesthetic in the second (mirror) condition, and so were more active and interested in the red spot.

THEORY OF MIND

THEORY OF MIND

• Early research by Premack and Woodruff (1978) suggested that chimps may possess theory of mind – i.e. to make inferences about the intentions, knowledge and state of mind of other animals.

DECEPTION

• Woodruff and Premack (1979) found that chimps could misdirect trainers in order to keep a food reward for themselves. This reflects the need in the wild to prevent food resources being stolen by others.

EVALUATION OF DECEPTION EVIDENCE

• Chimps needed many attempts before they could distinguish which behaviour was most appropriate for which trainer. This challenges the claim that they were showing theory of mind, and the behaviour can better be explained as a form of conditioning.

ATTRIBUTIONS TO OTHERS

• Povinelli et al. (1990) found that chimps were able to make use of information from experimenters who had knowledge of the location of a food reward, yet tended to ignore 'guesses' from experimenters who they knew lacked this information.

EVALUATION OF ATTRIBUTIONS TO OTHERS EVIDENCE

• An alternative explanation is that picking the person who stayed in the room (and coincidentally had information about the location of the food), rather than picking the person who did not, led to a reward. This would therefore be more likely as a response.

SOCIAL INTELLIGENCE

SOCIAL INTELLIGENCE

• Some species must also be able to solve social problems as well as physical problems, therefore must develop *social* intelligence, e.g. learning each other's identity over time and returning favours or holding grudges.
• Social intelligence is thought to have developed out of the need to detect cheats in social relationships.

THE ADVANTAGES OF COALITIONS

• Primate coalitions enable an animal to achieve something that they would otherwise be unable to achieve on their own. It is therefore 'intelligent' behaviour to cooperate with others in order to meet selfish goals.

MACHIAVELLIAN INTELLIGENCE

• The intelligence of primates is an adaptation to the special complexities of primate social life. Relationships in primate societies are frequently manipulative, e.g. dominant males rarely share food with rivals but do share food with those who are allies (Nishida et al., 1992).

BRAIN SIZE AND MACHIAVELLIAN INTELLIGENCE

• Dunbar (1995) found that the best predictor of increased brain size is not environmental complexity but the size of the social group. This supports the claim that social intelligence arises out of social complexity.

TYPICAL QUESTION...

Critically consider evidence for intelligence in non-human animals. (24 marks)

SEXUAL SELECTION AND HUMAN REPRODUCTIVE BEHAVIOUR

SEXUAL SELECTION
Competition for mates between individuals of the species leads to the evolution of certain traits.

- e.g. Pagel and Bodmer (2003) suggest that relative hairlessness in humans allowed early humans to advertise their reduced susceptibility to parasitic infection (desirable in a mate), and so males became less hairy over evolutionary time.

MUST KNOW...
- Explanations and research studies relating to the way that human reproductive behaviour is shaped by sexual selection.

MUST TAKE CARE...
Not to spend an inappropriate amount of time writing about non-human reproductive behaviour.

THE NATURE OF SEXUAL SELECTION
Sexual selection and reproductive success
- Individuals possess features that make them attractive to the opposite sex or help them compete with their own.
- If a characteristic becomes established as a universal preference among females, then males who possess the best examples will have greater reproductive success.

Intrasexual and intersexual selection
- If conditions favour polygyny – males must compete with other males, leading to intrasexual selection.
- Females are choosy in their choice of mate as implications of a wrong choice are more serious for them. This leads to intersexual selection.

THE ORIGINS OF MATE CHOICE
- Mate choice is a product of mate preferences formed in EEA.
- Our ancestors evolved neural adaptations that favoured mating with individuals possessing particular traits.
- Mate choice operates among modern-day humans by individuals accepting some potential mates and rejecting others on the basis of these traits.

Selection for indicators
- An important criterion is the preference for viability and fertility.
- These indicators reveal traits that are passed on to offspring (good genes) or might result in protection and support for offspring (good parents).
- Indicators are subject to the 'handicap principle' (must be costly to produce or could be faked easily).

Selection for provisioning
- Females can gain benefits from mate choice if they favour males that offer gifts.
- Male provisioning is useful to females because it eases their reproductive burden.
- In hunter-gatherer societies, the best hunters have the most wives and the most extra-marital affairs (Hill and Kaplan, 1988).

CONSEQUENCES
- The pressures of inter- and intra-sexual selection have led to a number of consequences for human morphology that are criteria used when choosing a mate.

Facial features
- Individuals who possess attractive facial features are preferred as mates because benefits associated with these features can be passed on to offspring.
- Little and Hancock (2002) found that 'average' faces are preferred because less likely to carry harmful genetic mutations.

COMMENTARY ON SEXUAL SELECTION

Evidence for evolutionary influences on facial preferences
- Differential interest in attractive adult female faces emerges early in first year of infancy – suggesting that this is an evolved rather than learned response (Langlois et al.,1987).
- Also a significant degree of cross-cultural agreement in ratings of facial attractiveness (Perrett et al.,1994; Cardwell, 2004).
- These studies support the view that facial preferences are shaped by sexual selection, and disprove the argument that criteria are shaped by cultural factors alone.

Limitations of evolutionary psychology
- Nicholson (1999) argues that the relevance of sexual selection is overemphasised in human reproductive behaviour.
- She claims that this is not how people really choose partners – decisions are more likely to be made on a range of different issues.
- Evolutionary influences on human reproductive behaviour are probably lost in the context of modern human relationships.

Facial preferences and women's menstrual cycles
- Despite predictions of sexual selection theory, research suggests that women's preferences for male faces are not static, but vary according to their position in the menstrual cycle.
- Penton-Voak et al. (1999) found evidence that women are attracted to more masculine faces during the most fertile time of their menstrual cycle and slightly feminised faces at other times.
- This suggests that a less masculine-looking male may make the best *long-term* partner (more caring, etc.), but that masculine-looking males might produce the strongest, healthiest children.

TYPICAL QUESTION...

Discuss the relationship between sexual selection and human reproductive behaviour. (24 marks)

EVOLUTIONARY EXPLANATIONS OF PARENTAL INVESTMENT

MUST KNOW...
- Description and evaluation of evolutionary explanations of parental investment (sex differences and parent–offspring conflict).

PARENTAL INVESTMENT THEORY (TRIVERS, 1972)

- PI is any investment by the parent in an individual offspring that increases that offspring's chance of surviving at the cost of the parent's ability to invest in other offspring.
- Choosiness in females is a direct result of the fact that they invest more in offspring than do males.
- Female investment tends to be more because female gametes are less numerous and more costly to produce than male gametes.
- Males tend to compete for females who have more to lose from a poor choice of partner.

Parental investment and mating behaviour

- Because of the differential investment of males and females, the optimum number of offspring for males and females would be different.
- Females would be more disposed towards **monogamy** because of the level of resources she would receive for her offspring.
- Because it is more profitable for males to divert energy into mating than parenting, males are more disposed to **polygyny**.

Paternal investment

- Males of most species expend more effort on courtship and mating than on parental care (Daly and Wilson, 1978).
- Males do not have the same degree of parental certainty and may use up valuable resources raising children who are not their own (cuckoldry).
- Buss (1995) suggested that sexual jealousy in males evolved as a solution to this problem.

Maternal investment

- Females usually put more time and effort into rearing offspring.
- Although the young of most species become independent relatively quickly, human young remain dependent for many years.
- A possible explanation for greater maternal investment in humans is because of **greater certainty they *were* the mother** (because of internal fertilisation).

MUST REMEMBER...
Material on PI can also be used to answer questions on sexual selection and reproductive behaviour.

EVALUATION

Maternal investment and parental certainty

- Laham et al. (2005) studied the investment of maternal and paternal *grandparents*.
- Maternal grandmothers know with certainty that their genes have passed to their grandchildren but a paternal grandfather has double uncertainty (no certainty that either his son or his grandchildren carry his genes).
- They found that maternal grandmothers were closer to their grandchildren than other grandparents. Next closest relationship was between maternal grandfathers and grandchildren.

Evidence for sex differences in jealousy

- Buss et al. (1992) found that males showed more emotional arousal when asked to imagine sexual infidelity of their partner whereas females showed more concern about emotional infidelity.

However...

- Harris (2003) questions whether this sex difference reflects an adaptive response, as males respond with greater arousal to any form of sexual imagery.

Willing fathers

- According to PI theory, males are more likely to share resources with children they *know* are their own.
- However, a study by Anderson et al. (1999) found that when investing financially, men did not discriminate between a stepchild and their own child from a previous relationship.
- Why? A man may invest less in children from a failed relationship because he cannot be certain he is the father, but invest in a stepchild to convince the mother he is a good provider and so bring about future mating possibilities.

TYPICAL QUESTION...

Discuss evolutionary explanations of parental investment. (24 marks)

For practice in answering A2 Psychology questions, why not use *Collins Do Brilliantly A2 Psychology*?

EVOLUTIONARY EXPLANATIONS OF MENTAL DISORDERS

EXPLANATIONS OF DEPRESSION

DEPRESSION

Evolutionary explanations of depression argue that genes for depression would not have evolved unless the beneficial effect was greater (from an adaptive point of view) than the costs incurred.

MUST REMEMBER...
That some questions ask for evolutionary explanations of **two** mental disorders, in which case should use just one of these explanations for depression.

MUST KNOW...
- Explanation of depression and anxiety disorders from an evolutionary perspective.

SOCIAL COMPETITION HYPOTHESIS (PRICE ET AL., 1994)
- Depression is an adaptive response for an individual who loses a conflict over status within a group.
- It is adaptive because it helps them adjust to fact that they have lost and now must occupy a subordinate position in the dominance hierarchy.
- When defeated, an involuntary process operates preventing the individual from continuing to compete. This results in loss of energy, depressed mood and loss of confidence.
- Over the course of time the depressive response may be triggered by other situations that involve loss (e.g. of a relationship), i.e. the response may now be activated in situations where it is psychologically maladaptive.

Depression as a yielding signal
- The real value of depression may be that it acts as a signal that the loser has yielded to the winner, thus restoring social harmony.
- This is supported by clinical evidence of episodes of depression that have been triggered by competition and resolved by reconciliation (Brown et al., 1995).

Is depression an adaptation?
- Cyranowski et al. (2000) claim that depression may be maladaptive for the *individual* but adaptive for the *group*.
- Among ancestral hunter-gatherers, when an individual lost their mate, the survival of the tribe was enhanced by the decreased food intake, and eventual death of the survivor.
- This would leave more food for those still successfully reproducing.
- The genes of the depressed individual would be carried by a close relative, whose survival chances would be enhanced.

Social rumination function
- Social situations that trigger a depressive episode are difficult to deal with, so the individual must shut down involvement with other activities to focus on them.
- Key aspect of depression is anhedonia (loss of interest in previously enjoyed activities).
- As a result of this enhanced cognitive effort, depression is associated with an enhanced analysis of social information.

MUST TAKE CARE...
Not to give lots of **clinical** detail about depression.

SOCIAL NAVIGATION HYPOTHESIS (WATSON AND ANDREWS, 2002)
- Depression evolved to perform two related problem-solving functions:
  – it focuses limited cognitive resources on solving complex social problems (social rumination function)
  – it provides an honest signal of need such that others will be willing to help, particularly if the fitness of the individual is intertwined with their own (social motivation function).

Evidence for social rumination
- Hartlage et al. (1993) – people with depression show diminished performance on cognitively demanding tasks of a non-social nature.
- This is to be expected if their cognitive resources are directed elsewhere.

Evidence for social motivation
- Hawton and Fagg (1992) – suicide attempts generally stop when relationships improve.
- Person with depression trades risk of death against benefits of motivating close social partners to help them.

Social motivation function
- The many personal costs suffered by the depressed individual also impose costs on close social partners.
- When mental mechanisms that underlie depression are activated, they cause the individual to engage in 'unintentional fitness extortion'.
- This elicits help from partners who perceive it is better to help than suffer the rising costs of the other person's depression.

Anti-depressant medication
- Implication of the SNH is that anti-depressant medications may handicap a depressed individual's ability to control their social environment and improve their quality of life by masking the functions of a potentially adaptive depressive episode.

EXPLANATIONS OF ANXIETY DISORDERS

ANXIETY DISORDERS

Fears are natural human emotions that bear some relationship to the source of danger. Phobias are fears that are wildly out of proportion to the actual hazards faced. Fears are adaptive; phobias are not. The most common phobias reflect ancestral hazards encountered in the EEA.

THE UNIVERSAL NATURE OF HUMAN FEARS

- Daly and Wilson (1988) found that the risk of infanticide is 100 times greater for stepchild than child with natural parents.
- Consistent with fact that the fear reaction of young children to strange males is found in most cultures (Smith, 1979).

Evidence from animal studies

- Cook and Mineka (1989) – monkeys that had never seen a snake before rapidly acquired intense fear when shown a toy snake if they saw a wild-reared monkey behaving fearfully.
- Same monkeys did not display fear towards less snake-like stimuli.
- Because they learned so rapidly, suggests this is due to evolutionary factors in fear acquisition.

PREPAREDNESS AND PHOBIAS

- Humans do not inherit rigid behavioural responses to situations that may change over time.
- Instead they have an innate readiness to *learn* about dangerous situations.
- We are predisposed to form some associations rather than others.
- Most phobias are focused on stimuli that would have presented a survival threat to our ancestors.
- Selection pressures generated by these hazardous stimuli resulted in the evolution of predispositions to associate them with danger.

Cultural differences

- Biological preparedness assumes that all members of a species have the same predisposition. Davey (1994) claims this is not the case.
- Fear of spiders is not a universal phenomenon, with many cultures believing spiders to be symbols of good fortune rather than fear (Bristowe, 1958).

OBSESSIVE–COMPULSIVE DISORDER

- Abed and de Pauw (1999) argue that OCD is an accentuated version of an adaptive strategy which had enhanced the reproductive fitness of ancestral humans.
- Intrusive thoughts and compulsive rituals are universal phenomena across cultures (Osborn, 1998).
- Specific tasks would have been selected because of their contribution to inclusive fitness.
- The 'Involuntary Risk Scenario Generating System' (IRSCS) allows individuals to develop behavioural strategies to avoid harmful situations.
- The adaptive function of this system is that it saves the individual from having to experience dangers in real life.
- Over time this has led to obsessional traits becoming widespread.
- However, extreme expressions of this trait would be maladaptive and so *reduce* reproductive fitness.

OCD is universal

- Evolutionary explanation of OCD assumes that most humans would have the same adaptation. Research supports this, as OCDs appear to occur universally across cultures (Rapoport and Fiske, 1998).

Gender differences

- Research has consistently shown that females engage in risk-taking behaviour less than males.
- Females are more likely to develop OCD *after* puberty and males *before* puberty.
- Both findings are consistent with the claim that females were exposed to increased risks after puberty in the EEA, and this would have led to increased activity of IRSCS and greater incidence of OCD.

TYPICAL QUESTIONS...

1 Discuss two mental disorders from an evolutionary perspective. (24 marks)

2 Describe and evaluate **one or more** evolutionary explanations of depression. (24 marks)

3 Describe and evaluate **one or more** evolutionary explanations of anxiety disorders. (24 marks)

4 (a) Outline and evaluate the explanation of depression from an evolutionary perspective. (12 marks)

(b) Outline and evaluate the explanation of anxiety disorders from an evolutionary perspective. (12 marks)

EVOLUTION OF INTELLIGENCE

EVOLUTIONARY FACTORS IN THE DEVELOPMENT OF HUMAN INTELLIGENCE

ECOLOGICAL THEORIES OF INTELLIGENCE

Foraging
- Need for superior memory and navigational abilities created adaptive problems for ancestral humans.
- Also a need for social/communicative skills as *groups* of hunter-gatherers more successful than individuals.
- Comparative brain size related to diet with foliovores having proportionally less neocortex than frugivores.
- Dunbar (1992) claimed that evolution of intelligence among frugivores indicated increased cognitive demand to monitor widely dispersed food supply.
- Foliovores have smaller home ranges, and monitor food supply easily – so less demand for complex cognitive skills.

Extracting food and tool use
- Boesche et al. (2002) studied chimps in West Africa – they used stones as hammers to crack open nuts.
- Similar to evidence from early human archaeological sites in East Africa.
- !Kung San use highly elaborate tools whereas others (e.g. Tasmanian Aborigines) use only simple tools.
- From such evidence, it appears that groups that evolve sophisticated tool use are more successful. Development of such tools for foraging requires intelligence.

Foraging advantages versus problems of a large brain
- Animals with large brains are relatively rare because of the costs involved.
- A large brain is extremely demanding in terms of energy and must compete with other body organs for resources.
- A large brain takes a long time to mature, meaning infants are heavily dependent on their parents for longer.

Tool use – a cause or consequence of intelligence?
- Parker and Gibson (1979) claim that tool use is not necessarily a *cause* of intelligence, but a *consequence*.
- Intelligent species can adapt to the ecological pressures of seasonally available food by developing appropriate tools.
- Less intelligent species have no need to do this. Their food is available all year round.

Intelligence comes at a cost
- Change from eating vegetation and fruit to eating meat and fish led to improvements in brain function but had an undesirable side effect – an increasing incidence of schizophrenic behaviours.
- Horrobin (1998) claims that these were initially kept in check by sufficient levels of essential fatty acids, but these are replaced in the modern diet by saturated fatty acids.

SOCIAL THEORIES OF INTELLIGENCE

Machiavellian intelligence (Whiten and Byrne, 1988)
- The demands of the social world led to the growth in primate intelligence.
- Individuals who are able to use and exploit others in their social world without causing aggression are able to increase their reproductive fitness.
- Example is the formation of alliances. Harcourt (1992) suggests that only apes and humans form alliances on the basis of an individual's ability to provide help.
- As groups become larger, this trait becomes essential and so spreads through the population.

Neocortex size and group size
- Dunbar (1993) found no relationship between neocortex volume and environmental complexity but strong correlation between neocortex volume and group size.
- Supports Machiavellian hypothesis because it shows the complexity of the human cortex is due more to the demands of the social environment than the physical environment.

The meat-sharing hypothesis
- Hill and Kaplan (1988) – supporting evidence among the Ache of Paraguay.
- Plant food is not shared outside the family but meat is.
- Skilled hunters are rewarded with majority of hunting spoils and with sexual favours from women, who regularly exchange sex for meat.

Meat-sharing (Stanford, 1999)
- For ancestral humans in the EEA, meat was an important source of saturated fat, yet was not readily available.
- Stanford believed the strategic sharing of meat paved the way for human intelligence.
- Meat could be used to forge and maintain alliances and to persuade females to mate.
- Strategic meat-sharing required considerable cognitive abilities to recognise other individuals and keep 'running scorecard' of debts, credits and relationships over the years.

The 'sharing under pressure hypothesis' (Wrangham, 1975)
- This offers a simpler explanation for meat-sharing by arguing that a male with meat can conserve energy by not trying to defend his kill from others.

BRAIN SIZE AND INTELLIGENCE

THE PRIMATE LIFE STYLE

- Early humans had to develop skilled movements that allowed them to hunt and forage successfully.
- They also had to learn cognitive maps of their environment and seasonal changes in food sources.
- Each of these complex skills required evolution of new brain regions or development of existing regions.

The problems with large brains

- The brain represents 2% of body mass, but uses 20% of basal metabolic rate.
- Unless large brains contributed significantly to reproductive fitness, they would not have evolved (Rushton, 1995).
- This might indicate that a **sexual selection process** was at work (Miller, 1996).

BRAIN SIZE IN HUMANS AND OTHER MAMMALS

- Actual body size relative to expected brain size for a particular body mass = encephalisation quotient (EQ).
- Humans have highest EQ (7), primates score 2.34 and dolphins 4.5 (Jerison, 1973).

Limits of encephalisation as a measure of intelligence

- It has proved difficult to establish a strong correlation between EQ and intelligence.
- Animals vary considerably in body and brain weight at different times of the year, making it hard to establish an accurate brain to body ratio.
- Some animals appear to have a low EQ, but are not unintelligent.

GENDER DIFFERENCES

- Brains of men are heavier than the brains of women (Ankney, 1992).
- Ankney (1995) – selection for hunting abilities would have led to relatively larger brains in men in order to process spatial information.
- The 'man as hunter' hypothesis (Washburn and Lancaster, 1968) places the selective pressure for the evolution of the brain solidly in the male, who hunted, rather than the female, who did not.

Evaluation of 'man as hunter' hypothesis

- This hypothesis largely neglects the role of the female in this process.
- However, anthropological evidence from traditional societies has shown that food gathering by females was more nutritionally important for these groups (Zihlmann and Tanner, 1978).

RACIAL DIFFERENCES

- Beals et al. (1984) found differences in cranial capacity between East Asians (largest), Europeans and Africans (smallest).
- Differences in cranial capacity suggest differences in brain size.
- Evolutionary selection pressures were different for each population.
- Rushton (1995) – the 'out of Africa hypotheis': the further north populations migrated, the more cognitively demanding the environment they faced.

Evaluation of racial differences

- Estimating intelligence through cranial size has been shown to be an unreliable measure (Reed and Jensen, 1993).
- Other explanations exist for racial differences, e.g. among East Asians, intelligence is culturally valued more than in other populations.

INNOVATION, SOCIAL LEARNING AND TOOL USE

- Reader and Laland (2002) searched major primate journals for evidence of:
  - **innovation**: displaying novel solutions to environmental or social problems
  - **social learning**: the acquisition of information from others
  - **tool use**.
- Each provided a measure of the behavioural flexibility of a species.
- Among 116 primate species, frequency of these behaviours was correlated with brain size.

This finding challenges the view that...

- Large brains arose because of the unique problems faced during human evolution.
- Reader and Laland claim that intellectual accomplishments that are specific to humans (e.g. language use) may have played a less significant role in the evolution of our large brains than previously thought.

MUST REMEMBER...
That material about brain size in other species is also relevant here.

TYPICAL QUESTIONS...

1 Discuss evolutionary factors in the development of human intelligence. (24 marks)

2 Discuss the relationship between brain size and intelligence. (24 marks)

PSYCHOPATHOLOGY – CLINICAL CHARACTERISTICS OF SCHIZOPHRENIA, DEPRESSION AND ANXIETY DISORDERS

MUST KNOW...
- An outline of the main clinical characteristics (e.g. types, symptoms, etc.) of schizophrenia, depression and one anxiety disorder.

SCHIZOPHRENIA

What is schizophrenia?
Schizophrenia is a serious mental disorder characterised by **severe disruptions in psychological functioning** and a loss of contact with reality.

SYMPTOMS (ICD-10)

For schizophrenia to be diagnosed, there is a minimum requirement of at least *one* of the symptoms listed under 1 or *two* of those listed under 2 to be present for at least one month:

1 (a) **Thought control:** e.g. thought withdrawal – thoughts are extracted from the person's mind.
  (b) **Delusions:** distorted beliefs – the individual does not feel in control of their thoughts, feelings and will.
  (c) **Hallucinatory voices:** voices that don't exist, but feel real to the person hearing them, e.g. a running commentary on the person's behaviour.
  (d) **Other persistent delusions:** distorted beliefs that are culturally inappropriate or involve impossible powers or capabilities.

2 (a) **Persistent hallucinations:** distorted perceptions arising from any of the senses and may be accompanied by delusions.
  (b) **Incoherent or irrelevant speech:** the individual's train of thought is disrupted and their speech is so jumbled that it becomes meaningless.
  (c) **Catatonic behaviour:** unusual body movements, including the adoption of odd postures and sometimes frozen immobility.
  (d) **Negative symptoms:** these include apathy, flattened affect and a general lack of drive and motivation.

TYPE I AND TYPE II SCHIZOPHRENIA

Type I
An acute (sudden onset) disorder characterised by positive symptoms (hallucinations, delusions and thought disorder).

Type II
A chronic (gradual) disorder characterised by negative symptoms such as flattening of affect (emotional response), apathy and poverty of speech.

MUST REMEMBER...
That 'clinical characteristics' can include any of this material. Don't need to include **all** these symptoms, but should try to retain some detail in those used.

DEPRESSION

What is depression?
Depression (unipolar disorder) is a type of **mood disorder** where the person experiences feelings of great sadness, worthlessness and guilt, and finds the challenges of life overwhelming.

SYMPTOMS (DSM-IV) OF UNIPOLAR DEPRESSION

Diagnosis requires presence of *five* of the following symptoms (*including* depressed mood). The symptoms must also cause clinically significant distress or impairment in general functioning. They should be present all or most of the time, and should persist for longer than two weeks.

- **Sad, depressed mood:** indicated by either subjective report or observation made by others.
- **Loss of interest and pleasure in usual activities.**
- **Difficulties in sleeping (insomnia):** in some patients a desire to sleep all the time (hypersomnia).
- **Shift in activity level, becoming either lethargic or agitated:** observable by others; not merely restlessness.
- **Poor appetite and weight loss, or increased appetite and weight gain:** significant weight loss when not dieting or a significant change in appetite.
- **Loss of energy and great fatigue.**
- **Negative self-concept, feelings of worthlessness and guilt:** feelings of worthlessness or excessive or inappropriate guilt.
- **Difficulty in concentrating:** e.g. slowed thinking and indecisiveness.
- **Recurrent thoughts of death or suicide.**

CATEGORIES OF DEPRESSION

Reactive depression
A reaction to **stressful events outside ourselves,** such as the death of someone close, redundancy or failing exams.

Endogenous depression
Depression that has **no obvious cause** – i.e. was not brought on by a specific life event or circumstance, but rather appears to come from nowhere.

Specification allows for unipolar or bipolar depression. Questions can't specify which should be written about.

ANXIETY DISORDERS: PHOBIAS

What are phobias?
These are a type of anxiety disorder where there is a **persistent and unreasonable fear** of an object or situation.

SYMPTOMS

Type I
- Fear that is excessive or unreasonable, cued by the presence or anticipation of a specific object or situation (e.g. flying, animals).
- Exposure to the phobic stimulus provokes an immediate anxiety response.
- The person recognises that the fear is excessive or unreasonable.
- The phobic situation is avoided or endured with intense anxiety.

Social phobia
- Marked fear of social or performance situations in which the person is exposed to unfamiliar people or to possible scrutiny by others.
- The person fears they will act in a way that will be humiliating for them.
- Exposure to the feared social situation provokes anxiety, e.g. a panic attack.
- The person recognises that their fear is excessive or unreasonable.
- The feared situations are avoided or endured with intense anxiety.

Agoraphobia
- Anxiety about being in places from which escape might be difficult or in which help may not be available in the event of having a panic attack.
- The feared situations are avoided or endured with intense anxiety.

TYPES OF SPECIFIC PHOBIA
- Animal type: e.g. fear of spiders (arachnophobia) or dogs (cynophobia).
- Situational types: e.g. fear of flying (aerophobia) or enclosed spaces (claustrophobia).
- Natural environment types: e.g. fear of heights (acrophobia) or water (hydrophobia).
- Blood-injection types: e.g. fear of blood (hematophobia) or injections (trypanophobia).

MUST REMEMBER...
That the specification only requires **one** type of anxiety disorder, so can choose **either** phobias **or** OCD.

ANXIETY DISORDERS: OBSESSIVE–COMPULSIVE DISORDER

What is OCD?
OCD is an anxiety disorder in which the individual is plagued with **uncontrollable thoughts** (obsessions) and performs seemingly **senseless rituals** (compulsive behaviours).

SYMPTOMS (DSM-IV)

Obsessions
- Recurrent and persistent thoughts, impulses, or images that are experienced as intrusive and inappropriate and that cause marked anxiety or distress.
- These are not simply excessive worries about real-life problems.
- The person attempts to ignore or suppress these thoughts or impulses, or to neutralise them with some other thought or action.
- The person recognises that these obsessional thoughts are a product of their own mind.

Compulsions
- Repetitive behaviours (e.g. hand-washing or checking) or mental acts (e.g. counting or repeating words silently) that the person feels driven to perform in response to an obsession.
- These are aimed at preventing or reducing distress or preventing some dreaded event or situation. However, they are not connected in a realistic way with what they are designed to prevent or are clearly excessive.

The obsessions or compulsions cause marked distress, are time-consuming, or significantly interfere with the person's normal routine or ability to function.

OBSESSIONS AND COMPULSIVE BEHAVIOURS

Obsessions
Obsessions are persistent and recurrent thoughts, images, beliefs and impulses, which enter the mind apparently uninvited and cannot be removed.

Compulsions
The compulsive element of OCD is the irresistible urge to carry out repetitive acts ritualistically in order to ward off some imagined dire consequence.

TYPICAL QUESTIONS...

*NB Each of these are **parts** of questions.*

1 Outline the clinical characteristics of schizophrenia. (5 marks)

2 Describe the clinical characteristics of depression. (15 marks)

3 Outline two or more clinical characteristics of **one** type of anxiety disorder. (5 marks)

SCHIZOPHRENIA

BIOLOGICAL EXPLANATIONS OF SCHIZOPHRENIA

MUST KNOW...
• At least two biological and two psychological explanations of schizophrenia, and research related to these explanations.

GENETIC EXPLANATIONS
• Those who have genetic relatives with schizophrenia have a higher likelihood of developing it than the general population.
• The current belief is that there are a number of genes that contribute to schizophrenia, but none are solely responsible for the disorder.

Limitations
The genetic explanation cannot account for people who develop schizophrenia yet have no close relatives with the disorder – about two thirds of patients (Stirling and Hellewell, 1999).

FAMILY STUDIES
• Kety et al. (1962) – identified 207 offspring of mothers with schizophrenia; 16% later developed schizophrenia, compared to 2% in a matched group with non-schizophrenic mothers.
• Kendler et al. (1985) – first-degree relatives of people with schizophrenia were 18 times more at risk than general population.

TWIN STUDIES
• Gottesman and Shields (1982) – found that 58% of MZ (identical) twins were concordant for schizophrenia.
• Cardno et al. (1999) – found a concordance rate of 40% for MZ twins compared to 5.3% for DZ twins.

Degree of risk
MZ twins (who share 100% of their genes) have only a 50% chance of developing schizophrenia if the other twin has the disorder, leaving a substantial role for environmental factors.

ADOPTION STUDIES
• Finnish adoption study (Tienari et al., 1987) found that 7% of adoptees whose biological mothers had schizophrenia later developed the disorder compared to 1.5% of matched control group whose natural mothers didn't.
• Danish adoption study (Kety et al., 1994) found high rates for adoptees whose biological parents had schizophrenia even when adopted by 'healthy' parents.

THE DOPAMINE HYPOTHESIS
• Messages from neurons that transmit dopamine fire too easily or too often, leading to the symptoms of schizophrenia.
• Schizophrenics are thought to have abnormally high numbers of D-2 receptors on receiving neurons, resulting in more dopamine binding and so more neurons firing.

Cause or effect?
Neither post-mortems nor scans can reveal whether increased dopamine activity causes schizophrenia, or whether schizophrenia interferes with dopamine metabolism.

EVIDENCE
• Post-mortems of schizophrenics have shown an increase of dopamine in the left amygdala (Falkai et al., 1988) and increased dopamine density in the caudate nucleus (Owen et al., 1978). Low levels of dopamine activity are found in people with Parkinson's disease.
• Some people who take the drug L-dopa to raise their levels of dopamine also develop schizophrenic-type symptoms (Grilly, 2002).

Role of dopamine in other disorders
Dopamine is unlikely to be the only biological factor in schizophrenia because people with many other disorders respond to antipsychotic medication. This suggests that dopamine abnormalities are not only related to symptoms of schizophrenia but may be generic symptoms of all mental disorders.

NEUROANATOMICAL EXPLANATIONS
• Many schizophrenics have brain ventricles that are about 15% bigger than normal (Torrey, 2002). Enlarged ventricles are the result of either poor brain development or tissue damage, and therefore it may be these problems that lead to the development of schizophrenia.

Cause or effect?
As most studies are carried out on people already diagnosed with schizophrenia, it is not clear whether these abnormalities cause the symptoms of schizophrenia or whether the onset of symptoms causes the observed structural changes.

EVIDENCE
• Brown et al. (1986) found decreased brain weight and enlarged ventricles in schizophrenics. Structural brain abnormalities are found more often in those with negative/chronic symptoms rather than those with positive/acute symptoms (Bornstein et al., 1992).

Supporting evidence
Patients with Type II schizophrenia also have smaller amounts of grey matter and smaller temporal and frontal lobes (Sigmundssen et al., 2001). This suggests that enlarged ventricles are only significant because they are a consequence of reduced brain matter, which may indicate brain damage in other areas.

PSYCHOLOGICAL EXPLANATIONS OF SCHIZOPHRENIA

Expressed emotion: e.g. hostility, criticism, over-involvement and over-concern.

1 FAMILIES AND EXPRESSED EMOTION

- Fromm-Reichmann (1948) claimed that families with high levels of emotional tension (schizophrenogenic families) were a factor in the development of schizophrenia.
- Bateson et al. (1956) proposed the 'double-bind hypothesis' where children receive conflicting parental messages of care and criticism which leads to withdrawal.
- Vaughn and Leff (1976) suggested that the extent of expressed emotion in a family was a strong predictor of relapse rates among discharged schizophrenics.

EVIDENCE FOR THE ROLE OF EXPRESSED EMOTION (EE)

- Brown (1972) – patients who returned to homes with high EE showed a greater tendency to relapse compared to those returning to low EE homes.
- Vaughn and Leff (1976) found a 51% relapse in high EE homes, and a 13% rate in low EE homes. They also found that relapse rates increased as face-to-face contact with high EE relatives increased.
- Kalafi and Torabi (1996) found that the high prevalence of EE in Iranian culture (overprotective mothers and rejecting fathers) was one of the main causes of schizophrenic relapses. Kalafi and Torabi claim that the negative emotional climate in these families arouses the patient and leads to stress beyond their already impaired coping mechanisms.

Relapse rates and family estrangement

- Many patients are estranged from their family and yet there is no evidence that they are less prone to relapse.
- This may not negate the model, as any form of social involvement could count as EE.

High EE as response to living with schizophrenia

- High EE is less common in families of first-episode schizophrenics than those with frequent re-admissions, therefore high EE may develop as a response to the burden of living with schizophrenia.

2 COGNITIVE EXPLANATIONS

- Cognitive psychologists suggest that disturbed thinking processes are the cause rather than the consequence of schizophrenia, in particular the role of attention.
- Research has shown that some people with schizophrenia are poor at tasks that require them to pay attention to some stimuli but to ignore others.

Genetic links for cognitive malfunctions

- Faraone et al. (1999) claim that memory and attentional impairments are an expression of the genetic predisposition for schizophrenia and are the main cause of the symptoms found in the disorder.

Physiological abnormality and cognitive malfunction

- Hemsley (1993) – because of a breakdown in the relationship between existing schema and new sensory information, people with schizophrenia are subjected to sensory overload and do not know which aspects of a situation to attend to and which to ignore.

Underlying neurological structures

Hemsley (1993) has tried to link his cognitive model to dysfunction in the hippocampus and related brain structures. As yet there is little evidence to support this.

Brain injury and mental disorder

If cognitive impairments were a function of brain dysfunction, then brain injury as a result of stroke or accident would lead to mental disorder, but this rarely happens.

Scope of cognitive explanations

Cognitive explanations do not explain the *causes* of schizophrenia but merely describe its symptoms. To do this, they need to be combined with biological explanations.

Explaining symptoms

Although cognitive models may not offer a full explanation of schizophrenia, they may help to explain some of its symptoms (e.g. hallucinations and delusions).

TYPICAL QUESTIONS...

1 Discuss two or more biological explanations of schizophrenia, including the evidence on which they are based. (30 marks)

2 Describe and evaluate one biological and one psychological explanation of schizophrenia. (30 marks)

3 Compare and contrast biological and psychological explanations of schizophrenia. (30 marks)

DEPRESSION

BIOLOGICAL EXPLANATIONS OF DEPRESSION

Evidence from family studies
- Gershon (1990) – rates of unipolar depression in first-degree relatives ranged between 7% and 30% in 10 family studies.
- Harrington et al. (1993) – around 20% of the relatives of depressives also have depression, compared to a figure of around 10% for the general population.

Depression seems to run in families, which suggests there is a genetic basis for this disorder.

Genes or environment?
- Although these studies appear to show evidence for genetic basis for depression, in most cases people have shared the same environment, so may be a learned behaviour.

Evidence from twin studies
- McGuffin et al. (1996) – found 46% concordance among MZ twins with no shared environment, compared to 20% for DZ twins.
- Bierut et al. (1999) – heritability ranged from 36% to 44% for women and 1% to 24% for men, showing that environmental factors played a larger role in the development of male depression.

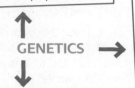
GENETICS →

Risk factor only
- Genetic factors may only act as a risk factor, requiring environmental factors to trigger depression.
- Kendler et al. (1995) found the highest levels of depression were in a group who were exposed to significant negative life events *and* were most genetically at risk for depression.

Evidence from adoption studies
- Adoption studies disentangle the effects of genetic and environmental factors by looking at people adopted at an early age away from the influence of their biological families.
- Wender et al. (1986) – biological relatives eight times more likely to have depression than adoptive relatives.

Norepinephrine and noradrenaline are the same!

BIOCHEMICAL EXPLANATIONS

NEUROTRANSMITTER THEORIES
Depression stems from a deficiency of noradrenaline or serotonin in brain circuits, which independently or together produce its symptoms.

- Noradrenaline:
  – Drugs that are able to block noradrenaline reuptake (and increase available norepinephrine in synapses) are effective antidepressants.
  – The drug reserpine which reduces levels of noradrenaline can produce depressive symptoms as a side effect.

- Serotonin:
  – Drugs that block reuptake transporters from drawing serotonin out of the synapse (SSRIs) are effective antidepressants.
  – Mann et al. (1996) found evidence of impaired serotonergic transmission in people with depression.

Role of neurotransmitters
Theories based on deficit of neurotransmitters are too simple, e.g. anti-depressant drugs have an immediate effect on increasing the availability of neurotransmitters but typically take several weeks to have a significant effect on mood.

Isolating cause and effect
Difficult to establish cause and effect in these studies, as depression may cause biochemical changes rather than the other way round.

Depression and the stress-response system
Irregularities in the cortisol levels, and the stress-response system in general are not found in all people with depression and are sometimes found in people with other types of mental disorder.

THE ROLE OF HORMONES
- Levels of cortisol are found to be high in people suffering from depression, and suppressing cortisol secretion is effective in the treatment of depressive patients (Carroll, 1982).
- Nemeroff et al. (1992) found evidence of a marked adrenal gland enlargement in people suffering from depression, but not in controls.

Role of female hormones in depression
Evidence for the role of hormones in depression is weak, e.g. only a small minority of women suffer from severe post-natal depression, so this is not an automatic response to hormonal changes.

PSYCHOLOGICAL EXPLANATIONS OF DEPRESSION

THE PSYCHODYNAMIC EXPLANATION
- Freud (1917) believed that when a loved one is lost (e.g. through bereavement or loss of the mother figure) the person first goes through a mourning period before life eventually returns to normal.
- In some people this mourning period never seems to end and they continue to exist in a state of depression.
- Freud also believed that we have unconscious negative feelings towards those we love. When we lose a loved one, these feelings are turned upon ourselves.
- In some cases the individual continues this pattern of self-abuse and self-blame for a prolonged period.

RESEARCH SUPPORT
- There is some research support for the claim that early loss may lead to depression. Some studies have found that many people who are suffering from depression describe their parents as 'affectionless' (Shah and Waller, 2000).

However...
The loss of a parent also affects the child's environment as well as their psychological functioning. The social hardship that such loss brings may create a vulnerability to depression.

BEHAVIOURAL EXPLANATIONS
Learning theory
- Lewinsohn (1974) suggests depression is caused by a reduction in positive reinforcement.
- However, the depressive behaviour may be positively reinforced by others in the form of sympathy or concern.

Learned helplessness (Seligman, 1974)
- When a person tries but fails to control unpleasant experiences, they may acquire a sense of being unable to exercise control over their life, and so become depressed.
- This 'learned helplessness' then prevents them from trying to exercise any control over their lives.

INCONSISTENT FINDINGS
- A number of studies have supported these predictions, e.g. Miller and Seligman (1974), but others have not found evidence of the adverse effects of learned helplessness. Some have found that helplessness actually facilitates later performance (Wortman and Brehm, 1975).

Links with biological explanations of depression
Wu et al. (1999) found that uncontrollable negative events led to lower levels of noradrenaline and serotonin, thus providing a link with biological explanations of depression.

COGNITIVE–BEHAVIOURAL EXPLANATIONS
- The hopelessness theory (Abramson et al., 1989) explains depression in terms of a person's pessimistic expectations of the future.
- Depressed people develop a maladaptive attributional style whereby they consistently attribute failure to internal (i.e. personal), stable (i.e. will always be like this) and global (i.e. all encompassing) causes.
- The hopeless person therefore expects bad things to happen in important areas of their life and does not believe they have the resources to change that situation.

RESEARCH SUPPORT
- Kwon and Laurenceau (2002) provided evidence to support the hopelessness model. They found that participants with a more negative attributional style also showed more of the symptoms associated with depression when stressed.

Perception of control
A key element is that depressed people believe they have little control over their lives. However, Ford and Neale (1985) found that depressed students did not underestimate their level of control.

COGNITIVE EXPLANATIONS
- Beck (1967) believed that depression is the result of negative thinking, i.e. the person is biased towards negative interpretations of the world.
- This negative view of the world is subject to cognitive biases (e.g. overgeneralisation).
- Negative thinking and cognitive biases maintain the cognitive triad, a negative view of the self as worthless, the world as full of obstacles, and the future as continuing in much the same way.

NEGATIVE THINKING AS A CAUSE OR CONSEQUENCE OF DEPRESSION?
- Segal and Ingram (1994) reviewed a number of studies that have compared non-depressed and depressed patients.
- These studies found no difference on a variety of cognitive vulnerability measures (such as negative thinking).
- This suggests that negative thinking is a *consequence* of having depression rather than a cause.

TYPICAL QUESTIONS...

1 Discuss two or more psychological explanations of depression, including the evidence on which they are based. (30 marks)

2 Describe and evaluate one biological and one psychological explanation of depression. (30 marks)

3 (a) Outline the main clinical characteristics of depression. (5 marks)

   (b) Discuss two explanations of depression. (25 marks)

4 Compare and contrast biological and psychological explanations of depression. (30 marks)

ANXIETY DISORDERS (I)

BIOLOGICAL EXPLANATIONS OF PHOBIAS

MUST REMEMBER...
That only need to cover **one** type of anxiety disorder: either phobias **or** OCD.

MUST KNOW...
- At least two biological and two psychological explanations of one anxiety disorder, and research related to these explanations.

GENETIC EXPLANATIONS
- Research suggests there is a genetic predisposition to phobias, although many psychologists believe the cause of phobias lies is a combination of genetic predisposition together with environmental and social causes.

FAMILY STUDIES
- Solyom et al. (1974) found a family history of psychiatric disorder in 45% of phobic patients compared to 19% in non-phobic group.
- Noyes et al. (1986) found a higher than normal rate (11.6%) of agoraphobia in first-degree relatives of people with this disorder.

TWIN STUDIES
- Slater and Shields (1969) found 41% concordance for MZ twins compared to just 4% for DZ twins.
- Torgersen (1983) found 31% concordance in MZ twins for agoraphobia compared to 0% for DZ twins.
- Kendler et al. (1992) found a much lower concordance rate for agoraphobia for MZ twins compared to DZ twins.
- Hettema et al. (2003) found that MZ twins were more likely to have similar responses in a fear-conditioning experiment than DZ twins. As MZ twins share the same genes, this supports the idea that genes play a significant role in the development of phobias.

EVALUATION OF GENETIC EXPLANATIONS
Family studies
There are significant methodological problems with family studies. In most cases, the family members in these studies would have shared similar backgrounds meaning that their phobic behaviour could have been acquired through social learning.

Twin studies
Few twin studies have been conducted in this area, and the numbers of twins used have been quite small. Adoption studies would provide a more convincing test of genetic contributions but they are rare in this area.

Role of genetic factors
Although genetic factors may predispose a person to develop a phobia, in most cases it requires a trigger from the environment for the full blown development of the disorder. This is an example of the diathesis-stress model.

Kendler et al.'s study
These findings appear to contradict the genetic hypothesis but might be explained in terms of the protective effect of the close emotional bond between MZ twins which prevented the development of anxiety in these children.

BIOCHEMICAL EXPLANATIONS
- Phobias are thought to arise because of a dysfunction in neurons that inhibit anxiety.
- GABA is automatically released in response to high levels of anxiety, inhibiting the activity of excited neurons.
- This leads to a reduction of arousal levels and a decrease in anxiety.
- Ameli et al. (2005) suggest that reduced GABA may predispose some people to an exaggerated anxiety response.
- Studies of people treated with BZs, which imitate the action of GABA, have demonstrated a reduction in levels of anxiety associated with phobias (Davidson et al., 1993).

EVALUATION OF BIOCHEMICAL EXPLANATIONS
Low levels of GABA activity
Research has supported the proposed relationship between GABA levels and panic disorder. In one study, people with panic disorder were found to have a 22% reduction in GABA compared to people without panic disorder (Goddard et al., 2001).

Effects of BZs
There is some evidence for the anxiety-reducing effects of BZs in adults, but these effects seem to be short term. Physical dependency can actually lead to an *increase* in anxiety as a result of tolerance and withdrawal. This suggests that a biochemical explanation is insufficient on its own to explain the causes of phobic anxiety disorder.

MUST TAKE CARE...
Not to include **psychological** explanations unless being used as part of a critical commentary.

MUST REMEMBER...
That questions require at least **two** types of biological explanation.

PSYCHOLOGICAL EXPLANATIONS OF PHOBIAS

THE PSYCHODYNAMIC EXPLANATION

The psychodynamic view is that anxiety expressed towards an object or situation is a displacement of internal underlying anxiety.

- Freud's theory of phobias was based on a case study of Little Hans (Freud, 1909) who developed a fear of horses. Freud believed this fear was directly related to his unconscious fear of his father (Oedipus conflict).
- Freud claimed that phobias are associated with unconscious sexual fears (id impulses) and operate through defence mechanisms of repression and displacement.
- The original source of the fear is repressed into the unconscious and the fear is displaced onto some other object or situation.

Link between phobias and 'strict' cultures

- Whiting (1966) found that anxieties and phobias are more common in cultures characterised by strict upbringing and punishment, supporting the view that parental rejection may be displaced onto another object or situation.

No evidence of symptom substitution

The theory predicts that treatment of a phobia will simply result in the development of another displaced fear, but when phobias *are* removed, no evidence of symptom substitution.

PREPAREDNESS THEORY

There is a species-specific, biological predisposition to fear certain stimuli, dating back to our ancestors.

- Seligman (1971) proposed that all species are innately prepared to avoid certain stimuli because they are potentially dangerous and a threat to survival.
- Garcia and Koelling (1966) showed that rats could easily be conditioned to avoid life-threatening stimuli (such as toxic liquids), but not those that carried no adverse consequences (such as flashing lights).
- Human phobias, such as fear of the dark or fear of heights, are consistent with this theory because they would have posed survival threats to our ancestors.
- Ohman et al. (1976) conditioned students using a variety of prepared (e.g. snakes or spiders) and unprepared (e.g. faces or flowers). They found that fear conditioning occurred rapidly (after one trial) in the prepared condition, but it took much longer to condition a fear response in the unprepared condition.

Doesn't explain all types of phobia

This theory can account for the fact that some objects and situations are more likely to induce phobic reactions than others, but cannot explain why some people develop phobias to less dangerous objects such as feathers and buttons.

Explains the persistence of phobias

In Ohman's study, conditioned fear to non-prepared stimuli extinguished when no more shocks were given, yet the conditioned fear response to the prepared stimuli was much harder to extinguish. This shows that the learned association had survival value so was resistant to extinction.

Criticism of preparedness theory

McNally and Steketee (1985) found that in 91% of cases of snake and spider phobia, the *real* fear was not one of harm but of having a panic attack. This undermines the claim that people develop phobias because of the potential danger.

BEHAVIOURAL EXPLANATIONS

People acquire fear reactions to objects or situations that are not dangerous through conditioning and social learning.

- Classical conditioning involves a learned association between two stimuli that occur close together in time. The person begins to react similarly to both of them. If one stimulus triggers a fear response, the other may also.
- We may also acquire a fear reaction through modelling: the observation and imitation of others' behaviour. A person observes that others are afraid of objects or situations and develops fears of the same things.
- Behaviourists believe that after learning a fear response, people then attempt to *avoid* the feared object or situation. These avoidance behaviours are then reinforced through operant conditioning because the individual is rewarded by a reduction in anxiety whenever they avoid what they fear.

Research support for classical conditioning

Miller (1948) showed that animals and humans can be taught to fear objects through classical conditioning, and that animals learn to *avoid* a feared situation through a learned response.

Research support for modelling

Bandura and Rosenthal (1966) found that participants later developed a fear reaction to a buzzer after *observing* others receiving electric shocks whenever the buzzer sounded.

Criticisms

Several laboratory studies have failed to condition fear reactions in participants (e.g. Bancroft, 1971) and a number of studies have failed to trace a phobia back to an instance of conditioning or modelling (e.g. King et al., 1998). Therefore it is not clear that *all* phobias are acquired in this way.

ANXIETY DISORDERS (2)

MUST REMEMBER...
That only need to know phobias **or** OCD, but must know biological **and** psychological explanations of the one chosen.

BIOLOGICAL EXPLANATIONS OF OCD

GENETIC EXPLANATIONS

- Although no specific genes for OCD have been identified, research suggests that genes can play a role in the development of OCD.
- OCD tends to run in families. When a parent has OCD, there is a slightly increased risk that their child will also develop this disorder.

RESEARCH EVIDENCE

- Family history studies (e.g. Hoaken and Schnurr, 1980) have found an incidence of up to 10% for OCD among first-degree relatives.
- Billett et al. (1998) carried out a meta-analysis of 14 twin studies of OCD and found that, on average, MZ twins were more than twice as likely to develop OCD if the other twin had the disorder compared to DZ twins.

BIOCHEMICAL EXPLANATIONS

- OCD may involve problems in communication between the orbital cortex and the basal ganglia.
- These brain structures use serotonin to communicate, and OCD has been linked with low levels of serotonin in this brain circuit.
- Drugs that increase the brain concentration of serotonin often help improve OCD symptoms.
- People with OCD may therefore have too little serotonin for their nerve cells to communicate effectively.

RESEARCH EVIDENCE

- Drugs which inhibit the reuptake of serotonin (SSRIs) have been found to be beneficial for up to 60% of patients with OCD (Zohar et al., 1996).
- Studies using PET scans have found lower levels of serotonin in OCD patients compared to non-OCD participants

NEUROANATOMICAL EXPLANATIONS

- Rapaport and Wise (1988) suggest OCD is caused by a structural dysfunction in pathway that links the frontal cortex with the basal ganglia.
- The symptoms of OCD can be caused by degeneration of tissue in the part of the basal ganglia responsible for filtering messages coming from the frontal cortex.
- In people with OCD, the selection of messages to be passed on to other parts of the brain is performed poorly, resulting in obsessional thoughts.

RESEARCH EVIDENCE

- OCD can also occur in people with disorders such as Parkinson's disease and Tourette's syndrome, both of which involve basal ganglia damage.
- Rapoport et al. (1994) report that surgery which disconnects the basal ganglia from the frontal cortex brings relief in severe cases of OCD.

Effectiveness of psychological therapy

- Research evidence suggests that psychological therapy alone can be very effective in treating OCD.
- About 50% of patients with OCD benefit from behaviour therapy without any form of medication.
- It is difficult to account for this finding if OCD has only biological causes.

These research studies can also be used as AO2 commentary on the biological explanations of OCD.

MUST TAKE CARE...
To incorporate at least **two** biological explanations in any answer to a question in this area.

Genetics or environment?

- Although there is some evidence that OCD does have a genetic component, studies have generally found it difficult to disentangle the effects of genetics from those of a shared environment.
- Because OCD fluctuates with stress levels, a complete explanation would incorporate both genetic *and* environmental factors (i.e. the diathesis-stress model).

EVALUATION OF BIOLOGICAL EXPLANATIONS

Inconsistent findings regarding serotonin

- Studies of the role of serotonin have produced inconsistent findings.
- Many of these studies have failed to include controls to rule out the possibility that SSRIs bring relief from OCD symptoms, since they also alleviate the symptoms of depression that tend to accompany OCD.

Evidence from psychosurgery

- Dougherty et al. (2002) provided support for the influence of brain dysfunction in OCD.
- Up to 45% of patients who had been unresponsive to medication and other treatments improved after removal of the cingulate gyrus.
- However, this procedure may have affected behaviour more globally, e.g. by reducing motivation and energy levels which may explain the reduction of OCD symptoms.

PSYCHOLOGICAL EXPLANATIONS OF OCD

PSYCHODYNAMIC EXPLANATIONS

- Freud believed that OCD is caused by a fixation at an earlier stage of development.
- In the anal stage, the child must accept the will of the parents, and ignore the impulses coming from the id.
- If natural impulses are strong and parental restrictions too strict, development may be arrested at this stage.
- The issues related to this stage become issues in adulthood.
- OCD sufferers use defence mechanisms (e.g. regression and reaction formation) to reduce the anxiety associated with these impulses as they arise in adulthood.
- Impulses may intrude as obsessional thoughts. To deal with them a person may act out a compulsion to symbolically undo their unacceptable impulses (e.g. washing hands).

Psychodynamic therapy

- There is evidence that psychodynamic therapy is not effective in the treatment of OCD, and may even have a *negative* effect.
- The fact that therapy does not help resolve childhood conflicts, challenges the psychodynamic explanation of OCD.

Supporting evidence

- Adams et al. (1996) found that men who were aroused by videos of male homosexual sex were more likely to claim to be homophobic. This suggests that they dealt with their anxiety by unconsciously forming a reaction against it.

COGNITIVE–BEHAVIOURAL EXPLANATIONS

- OCD is a consequence of faulty and irrational thinking taken to an extreme.
- For some, these thoughts are a cue for self-blame and the expectation that terrible things will happen as a result.
- In order to avoid the consequences of these thoughts, the individual must find a way of 'neutralising' them.
- Compulsive rituals, e.g. hand washing due to fear of contamination, give temporary relief, before anxiety builds up again.
- People become convinced that their intrusive thoughts are dangerous, and so fear of them increases.
- The thoughts turn into obsessions, and the need to reduce the anxiety associated with them becomes even more acute.

Supporting evidence

- People with OCD do have more intrusive thoughts than 'normal' people (Clark, 1992).
- Cognitive–behavioural therapies have been shown to be reasonably effective in treating OCD (e.g. Emmelkamp et al., 1988), supporting the view that OCD is a product of faulty thinking processes.

MUST TAKE CARE...
Not to spend too long describing underlying theories (e.g. Freudian theory or conditioning theory).

BEHAVIOURAL EXPLANATIONS

- An initial event is associated with anxiety or fear.
- This is alleviated by avoidance behaviour, which eventually becomes a conditioned response.
- In OCD, some thoughts or behaviours (e.g. sexual behaviour) become aversive through their association with some traumatic event (e.g. parental punishment).
- People learn to regard such thoughts as unclean or dangerous.
- When the thought recurs in adulthood, it becomes a source of conditioned anxiety.
- The ritualistic behaviour seen in OCD is a way of avoiding these fear-associated obsessions.
- The person may link a compulsive behaviour with changing the feared situation (i.e. it is reinforced).

Supporting evidence

- Rachman and Hodgson (1980) demonstrated the ability of compulsive acts to reduce anxiety in OCD.
- OCD patients asked to carry out a 'prohibited' activity that would cause a rise in anxiety and an accompanying urge to perform the compulsive action to reduce this anxiety.
- Patients asked to delay carrying out the compulsive activity – anxiety levels persisted for a while then declined.
- This shows that compulsive behaviours provide quicker relief from anxiety than spontaneous decay alone.

TYPICAL QUESTIONS...

1 Discuss two or more biological explanations of one anxiety disorder, including the evidence on which they are based. (30 marks)

2 Describe and evaluate one or more biological explanation and one or more psychological explanation of one anxiety disorder. (30 marks)

3 (a) Outline the main clinical characteristics of one anxiety disorder. (5 marks)

(b) Discuss two explanations of the anxiety disorder you outlined in (a). (25 marks)

4 Compare and contrast biological and psychological explanations of one anxiety disorder. (30 marks)

BIOLOGICAL THERAPIES

CHEMOTHERAPY

MUST REMEMBER...

That **biological** therapies are different from **psychological** therapies in that they aim to alter abnormal behaviours by intervening directly in bodily processes.

Anti-depressant drugs

These enhance the mood of people with depression and reduce panic in people with anxiety disorders.

- MAOIs block the action of the enzyme that breaks down noradrenaline and serotonin, increasing the availability of these neurotransmitters.
- Tricyclics block the mechanism that re-absorbs serotonin and adrenaline into the pre-synaptic cell, thus prolonging their activity.
- SSRIs selectively block the re-uptake mechanism for serotonin only and so make more serotonin available in the synapse to excite adjoining cells.

Anti-anxiety drugs

These are used to combat anxiety by bringing its symptoms under control.

- Benzodiazepines (BZs) are used for the short-term relief of severe anxiety. They inhibit the excitatory action of the nervous system and produce an overall calming effect by supporting the action of GABA in the brain.
- Beta-blockers are used in the treatment of hypertension. They work by blocking the action or adrenaline and noradrenaline, and so reduce sympathetic arousal.

← **CHEMOTHERAPY** →

Anti-manic drugs

These are used to control mania in people suffering from bipolar disorder.

- Anti-manic drugs reduce excessive mood swings in people with bipolar disorder.
- Anti-manic drugs act by normalising chemical activity in the emotional centres of the brain.
- Lithium carbonate is the most common drug used to treat bipolar disorder. Lithium evens out mood swings in both directions.

MUST KNOW...

- Description of chemotherapy, ECT and psychosurgery, and commentary on the issues surrounding their use.

Anti-psychotic drugs

These are used in the treatment of schizophrenia and other psychotic disorders. They help patients function as well as possible in their life, and also increase subjective feelings of well-being.

- Conventional anti-psychotics are used primarily to combat *positive* symptoms of schizophrenia (e.g. hallucinations and thought disturbances).
- Atypical anti-psychotic drugs also combat positive symptoms, but may also have some beneficial effects on *negative* symptoms.

ECT

- ECT is used in severely depressed patients if other treatments have proved ineffective.
- Also used when there is a risk of suicide because it has much quicker results than drugs.

▶

- Patient injected with a barbiturate, so they are unconscious before shock is administered.
- Also given a nerve-blocking agent, paralysing muscles to stop them contracting during treatment.

▶

- Electrode placed above the temple on the non-dominant side of the brain, and a second in the middle of forehead. An electric current is passed between the two electrodes to create a seizure.

▶

- Small amount of electric current lasting about half a second is passed through the brain. This produces a seizure lasting up to one minute, which affects the entire brain.

▶

- ECT is thought to increase amount of serotonin available to stimulate nerve cells and causes hypothalamus to release chemicals that cause changes in areas of the body that regulate mood.

PSYCHOSURGERY

PREFRONTAL LOBOTOMY AND LEUCOTOMY

- Involved the destruction of fibres connecting higher thought centres of frontal cortex with other areas of brain.
- Intention was that patients could be relieved of their distressing thoughts and behaviours.
- Operations were performed on patients with **affective disorders** although also used on **OCD and schizophrenia**.
- *Severity* of illness was a more important factor than *type* of illness.

STEREOTACTIC PSYCHOSURGERY

- Neurosurgeons use stereotactic imaging to locate precise points within the brain and sever connections.
- In the surgical treatment of OCD, a **cingulotomy** is performed to interrupt a circuit linking the orbital frontal cortex to deeper structures in the brain which appears to be more active than normal.

MUST TAKE CARE...

To cover more than one type of biological treatment, e.g. could use drugs and ECT, or all three on this page.

ISSUES SURROUNDING THE USE OF CHEMOTHERAPY

ANTI-ANXIETY DRUGS

BZs are effective in reducing symptoms of anxiety and panic.

- Gelernter et al. (1991) – more effective than placebo in treatment of social phobia.
- Lecrubier et al. (1997) – 60% of patients with panic disorder stayed free from panic.

However...

- BZs create dependence and tolerance, so that dosage needs to be increased over time to produce the same effects.
- Anti-anxiety drugs do not treat the cause of anxiety, shown by 90% relapse rate when medication ceases (Fyer et al., 1987).

ANTI-DEPRESSANTS

- Found to be effective in reducing symptoms of severe depression in up to 75% of cases compared to placebos (e.g. Prien, 1988).
- Jarrett et al. (1999) found that MAOIs were much more effective than tricyclics for *severe* depression, although these can interact dangerously with other drugs.

However...

- Anti-depressants may not be appropriate for children. Studies on effects of anti-depressant drugs on children suggest some are both ineffective and potentially harmful (Kendall, 2004).

ANTI-PSYCHOTICS

- Newer 'atypical' drugs found to be more effective in treating psychotic symptoms than conventional drugs (Davis et al., 2003).

This suggests that...

- Atypical antipsychotics may ultimately be more appropriate in the treatment of schizophrenia because there are fewer side effects.

ISSUES SURROUNDING THE USE OF ECT

- ECT has been effective in the treatment of severe depression. Comer (2002) claims 60–70% of patients improve after treatment.
- Because it is a quick form of treatment, Klerman (1988) claims it is the most appropriate treatment for severe depression, particularly where there is a risk of suicide.

However...

- Some studies show improvement rates as high as 80% can be found with placebo alone (Lowinger and Dobie, 1969).
- Sackheim et al. (2001) found 84% of patients they studied relapsed within six months of having ECT.

- In the early days of ECT, there were serious side effects, including memory loss and confusion, making it less effective.
- More recently, studies have found little evidence of long-term memory loss or other long-term cognitive changes (Devanand et al., 1994).

However...

- Rose et al. (2003) found that at least one third of patients complained of persistent memory loss after ECT.
- DOH report (1999) found that 30% of those receiving ECT claimed that it had resulted in permanent fear and anxiety.

- MIND report (2001) found that ECT was not appropriate for all groups. Respondents from black and minority ethnic communities reported a more negative view of ECT with 50% finding it unhelpful or damaging in the short-term and 72% in the long-term.

However...

- DOH report (1999) found that more than half of detained patients did not consent to ECT treatments.
- MIND report (2001) found a third of those given ECT were not *aware* that they could refuse to give consent to treatment.

ISSUES SURROUNDING THE USE OF PSYCHOSURGERY

- Modern procedures are less invasive than the lobotomy, but there are still dangers and so this form of treatment is used as a last resort.
- Beck and Cowley (1990) claim psychosurgery can be beneficial (i.e. effective) in some cases of severe anxiety, depression and OCD.

- Cosgrove and Raugh (2001) found cingulotomy was effective in over half of OCD patients, and 65% of patients with major affective disorder.
- This procedure may be more appropriate than other forms of psychosurgery because it has fewer side effects (Cohen et al., 1999).

Safer alternative

- In **deep brain stimulation**, wires are connected to a battery pack which produces an adjustable current. This interrupts circuitry involved in OCD.
- Gabriels et al. (2003) found three quarters of OCD patients experienced relief of symptoms with this method.

TYPICAL QUESTIONS...

1 Describe and evaluate two or more biological therapies. (30 marks)

2 (a) Describe chemotherapy and ECT as methods of treating mental disorders. (15 marks)

(b) Evaluate chemotherapy and ECT in terms of the issues surrounding their use. (15 marks)

3 Discuss the issues surrounding the use of any two biological therapies (e.g. effectiveness and appropriateness). (30 marks)

BEHAVIOURAL THERAPIES

THERAPIES BASED ON CLASSICAL CONDITIONING

Systematic desensitisation

Enables individuals to **overcome their anxieties** by learning to relax in the presence of stimuli that had once made them fearful or anxious.

Patients are taught how to relax their muscles completely.	The therapist and patient construct a desensitisation hierarchy.	The patient works their way through their hierarchy, visualising each anxiety-evoking event while engaging in the competing relaxation response.	Once the patient has mastered one step in the hierarchy, they are ready to move onto the next, continuing until they have mastered the feared situation.

Flooding

- This involves **exposing clients to a phobic object** in a non-graded manner with no prior attempt to reduce anxiety.
- Client is placed alone in the phobic situation and required to remain there until there is a reduction in anxiety levels.
- In **implosion therapy**, the client would be asked to *imagine* themselves in such a situation.
- In initial stages of the treatment, anxiety is high but reduces fairly quickly as habituation sets in and the client realises nothing dreadful has happened.
- The fear is then extinguished.

THERAPIES BASED ON CLASSICAL CONDITIONING

Behaviour therapists target the symptoms of a problem rather than its underlying cause. They believe that the original cause of a maladaptive behaviour may have little to do with factors currently maintaining it.

Aversion therapy

- Developed to **deal with habits and addictions** such as smoking and alcoholism.
- Therapist attempts to remove unwanted behaviours by associating them with aversive stimuli.
- Individuals are repeatedly presented with an aversive stimulus (e.g. an electric shock) at the same time they are engaging in the undesirable behaviour.
- Aversive stimulus acts as an UCS which already produces a UCR (e.g. avoidance).
- Repeated association of the aversive stimulus and behaviour means that patients eventually lose desire to engage in the undesirable behaviour.

THERAPIES BASED ON OPERANT CONDITIONING

Classical conditioning

- A **form of learning** where a neutral stimulus is paired with a stimulus that already produces a response, such that over time, the neutral stimulus also produces that response.

THERAPIES BASED ON OPERANT CONDITIONING

Behavioural therapies based on operant conditioning principles are known as behaviour modification. If maladaptive behaviours have been acquired through the process of operant conditioning, then it should be possible to change these behaviours using the same principles.

Operant conditioning

- Sees the **consequences of a behaviour** as being of vital importance to its future appearance. If it is followed by a desirable consequence, it becomes more frequent. If it is followed by an undesirable consequence, it becomes more

Token economy

- The token economy is a behaviour modification procedure, based on the principle of behaviour shaping through positive reinforcement.
- It is used in institutions, mainly with psychotic patients, and people with severe learning difficulties.
- Patients are given tokens for socially constructive behaviour, whereas these are withheld when unwanted behaviours are exhibited.
- The aim of a token economy is to increase the frequency of a patient's desirable behaviours (e.g. personal hygiene habits) and decrease the frequency of undesirable behaviours.
- Tokens are used to signify reinforcement, and are used as part of a reinforcement schedule.
- Tokens can be exchanged for rewards (such as sweets) or other privileges.

Social skills training

- Modelling has been applied for developing assertiveness and other interpersonal skills.
- Technique involves behaviour rehearsal and feedback, and is particularly helpful for people with low self-esteem.
- People are encouraged to practise appropriate responses to replace maladaptive responses in the safety of a role-play situation.
- **Elliot et al. (2001)** – four aims of social skills training:
  - promoting social skills acquisition
  - enhancing social skills performance
  - reducing interfering problem behaviours
  - facilitating the generalisation of social skills.
- When used in a school setting, peer support and pressure is important for the success of these strategies.

ISSUES SURROUNDING THE USE OF THERAPIES BASED ON CLASSICAL CONDITIONING

SYSTEMATIC DESENSITISATION

- McGrath et al. (1990) found systematic desensitisation to be effective for 75% of people with specific phobias.
- Ost et al. (1991) found that 90% of patients who had a single session were cured of spider phobia when tested four years later.

However...

- Psychoanalytic theorists claim behaviour therapies inappropriate in treatment of phobias as treatment will simply result in a new symptom emerging if the underlying conflict is not resolved.
- Despite this claim, no evidence that such 'symptom substitution' does occur after SD or any other behavioural therapy.

AVERSION THERAPY

- Smith et al. (1997) found that aversion therapy is effective in treatment of alcoholics. Those treated with aversion therapy had higher rates of abstinence after one year than those treated with counselling alone.
- Smith (1988) reported success with smokers. Over half of those treated using shocks maintained abstinence after one year.

However...

- Miller (1978) – aversion therapy is no more effective in the treatment of alcoholism than counselling alone.
- Critics claim AT inappropriate form of treatment as it can result in serious long-term psychological effects, such as feelings of despair and depression (Harris, 1987).

FLOODING

- Flooding and implosion therapies are typically faster than SD and often reduce physiological signs of fear arousal more (Rimm and Masters, 1974).
- Barrett (1969) found implosion therapy was effective in removing symptoms in only 45% of time required with SD.

However...

- In Barrett's study, there was far more variability in results than among SD patients, i.e. while many were improved, some were made much worse.
- Bandura (1997) claims that the effectiveness of a treatment does not depend on exposure to the feared situation alone, but also the patient's perception of their ability to deal with that exposure (i.e. self-efficacy).

ISSUES SURROUNDING THE USE OF THERAPIES BASED ON OPERANT CONDITIONING

TOKEN ECONOMY

- Emmelkamp (1994) – found token economy to be very effective in reducing inappropriate behaviour in psychotic patients in psychiatric institutions.
- Paul and Lentz (1977) found after four years, 96% of patients treated under a token economy system had been released from their institution compared to 68% treated in milieu therapy.
- Token economies are appropriate for many psychotic patients because the transition to community living requires more than the reduction of symptoms; living skills must also be improved.
- Token economy programmes can also be effective with children. Reitman (2001) found that token economy therapy significantly increased attentive behaviour in children with ADHD.

However...

- Critics claim the 'success' of token economy is more to do with the need for closer interaction between patient and nurse. This suggests that it is the greater attention that is therapeutic rather than the therapy itself.
- Comer (2002) claims that token economies may have limited effectiveness in the treatment of psychotic disorders. Although an individual's behaviour may change (helping them live a more normal life), the mental illness remains.

SOCIAL SKILLS TRAINING

- Quinn et al. (1999) – meta-analysis of 35 studies to examine effectiveness of social skills training in the treatment of children with emotional and behavioural disorders. Results showed only a very modest gain for children receiving social skills training.
- Mathur et al. (1998) found social skills training more effective at promoting social interaction than fostering communication skills in students with emotional and behavioural problems.

However...

- Competing behaviours (inappropriate social skills) may be stronger and difficult to change because of their reinforcement history.
- Hung, (2000) failed to find any improvement in social behaviour in *children* after training, suggesting that social skills training is most appropriate for adolescents.

TYPICAL QUESTIONS...

1 Describe and evaluate two or more behavioural therapies. (30 marks)

2 (a) Describe one or more therapies based on classical conditioning, and one or more therapies based on operant conditioning. (15 marks)

(b) Evaluate the behavioural therapies described in (a) in terms of the issues surrounding their use. (15 marks)

3 Discuss issues surrounding the use of any two behavioural therapies (e.g. effectiveness and appropriateness). (30 marks)

4 Compare and contrast biological and behavioural therapies. (30 marks)

ALTERNATIVES TO BIOLOGICAL AND BEHAVIOURAL THERAPIES (I)

PSYCHODYNAMIC THERAPIES

Free association
• Client is asked to allow the free flow of feelings, thoughts and images without censorship.
• Reasoning is that associations should arise from (and reflect) internal dynamic conflict.
• Assumes that all memories are arranged in an associative network, and that eventually the client would stumble across the crucial memory.

Word association
• Client is read a list of words one at a time and asked to reply with whatever comes to mind.
• This allows unconscious thoughts to enter the conscious mind.
• Assumes that unusual responses or hesitations may indicate that repression is operating.

PSYCHOANALYSIS
• The purpose of psychoanalysis is to uncover unconscious conflicts and anxieties that have their origins in the past, in order to gain insight into the causes of psychological disturbance. A variety of techniques are used to achieve this.

Dream analysis
• Unconscious drives are expressed through dreams although they are disguised in symbolic form.
• Analyst tries to help the client interpret their dreams.
• Dreams are interpreted as wish fulfilment, usually of a sexual or aggressive nature.

Transference
• Occurs when client redirects feelings towards the therapist that were unconsciously directed towards a significant person in their life.
• Indicates that repressed conflict is coming close to conscious awareness.
• Aim is to identify the source of the transference and circumstances surrounding the repression.

Projective tests
• The client is shown a series of abstract ink blots (e.g. Rorschach ink blot test).
• They are then asked to explain what they see or create a story based on the images.
• This uncovers recurrent themes that reveal unconscious needs and motives.

PSYCHODRAMA
The essence of psychodrama is that problems and anxieties can be expressed or 'acted out' in a role-play situation within the safety of an understanding and supportive therapy group.

The principles of psychodrama
• Every human being is an actor, performing their own personal drama (e.g. a woman must play many roles).
• A psychologically healthy person can switch roles easily, but problems emerge when people are rigidly fixed within a specific role or when one role dominates the person.
• Everyone is capable of being their own saviour.

Psychodrama in action
Psychodrama takes place within a group setting, with usually 10–15 people, each one being assigned a role. One member of the group elects to play out a chosen scenario from a problem area in their life. The roles are:
• **Director:** therapist trained in the use of psychodrama who monitors the drama as it unfolds, and changes direction if necessary.
• **Protagonist:** volunteer who has elected to play out their drama.
• **Auxiliary egos:** significant people within the drama such as parent or spouse.
• **Double:** someone who mirrors the actions and words of the protagonist who can then observe aspects of themselves of which they were previously unaware.
• **Audience:** other people in the group who give their feedback at the end.

ISSUES SURROUNDING THE USE OF PSYCHODYNAMIC THERAPIES

APPROPRIATENESS OF PSYCHOANALYSIS

- Psychoanalysis is most **appropriate** for anxiety disorders and eating disorders, although **effectiveness** is thought to be limited with depression (Comer, 1995).

- APA warns against danger of transference in depressive patients because of tendency to be overly dependent on important people (i.e. psychoanalysis inappropriate for depressives).

DANGER OF EMOTIONAL HARM

- Psychodynamic therapies are inappropriate because they may cause emotional harm – i.e. they may guide the client towards an insight that is more distressing than the current problem.

- Recovered memories of child abuse in therapy are criticised because therapists are not helping patients recover *real* memories that have been repressed, but are unwittingly planting 'false memories' of sexual abuse.

RESEARCH SUPPORT

- Thase et al. (1997) – meta-analysis of studies of treatment of people with major depressive disorder. Evaluated **effectiveness** of psychotherapy with or without medication. With less severe patients, improvement was due to psychotherapy alone, but with more severely depressed patients, therapy plus medication group did much better.

- Mufson et al. (1999) – 12 weeks of psychotherapy decreased depressive symptoms in adolescents more than in control group.

This suggests that...

- If depression is more severe, psychotherapy alone is **ineffective**, and must be combined with drug medication.

- Both studies were conducted over a relatively short period (12 weeks). It may not be possible to test the **effectiveness** of psychotherapy over such a short period.

RESEARCH AGAINST

- Eysenck (1952) examined 10,000 patient histories – found that only 44% of patients who had undergone psychoanalysis had actually improved.

- Smith et al. (1980) – meta-analysis of 475 studies. **Effectiveness** of psychodynamic therapies significantly lower than cognitive–behavioural and only just better than placebo.

However...

- Bergin (1971) re-analysed Eysenck's data, selecting different outcome criteria and found over 80% success for psychoanalysis and 30% for control groups.

- Eysenck (1965) argued that therapy *delayed* recovery in many individuals, and even if it was **effective** it is only **appropriate** for certain disorders and certain types of individual.

EFFECTIVENESS OF PSYCHODRAMA

- Kellermann (1987) examined outcome of psychodrama in a classroom setting in 23 studies. Concluded that psychodrama was an **effective** alternative to other therapeutic approaches in promoting behaviour change in adjustment and antisocial disorders.

- Rezaeian et al. (1997) found that psychodrama group therapy was an **effective** psychotherapeutic method for reducing the depression level of depressed individuals.

However...

- The majority of subjects included in psychodrama research tend to be volunteer participants. This makes it difficult to generalise its **effectiveness** from these non-clinical groups to patient groups (Kellermann, 1987).

- A problem for research in psychodrama is whether there is sufficient length for each person to get involved. The therapeutic use of psychodramatic methods requires more time than other approaches, but many studies have failed to address this when assessing **effectiveness**.

APPROPRIATENESS OF PSYCHODRAMA

- Scheiffele and Kaye (2002) investigated the value of psychodrama in social issues – intolerance towards homosexuality. Through psychodrama students were able to develop new ways of relating to the people in their lives.

- Loughlin (1992) – used psychodrama on a group of six women with alcohol problems. Found that psychodrama was perceived as useful by the four women who were better educated, more verbally expressive and extroverted. This suggests that psychodrama is most **appropriate** for people who are better able to make use of the opportunities it offers.

IS IT VALUABLE FOR EVERYONE?

- The value of working through problems within a supportive group is widely recognised. Working with those who share the same experience helps the individual to feel less alone or 'different', and enables them to address their problems more openly.

- There are some people who appear to find it hard to engage in role-play with an audience, and wouldn't wish to explore their problems in such a public way.

- Davies (1993) claims that psychodrama requires a great deal of risk-taking, and many people prefer the safer, more traditional one-to-one therapies.

ALTERNATIVES TO BIOLOGICAL AND BEHAVIOURAL THERAPIES (2)

COGNITIVE–BEHAVIOURAL THERAPIES (CBT)

REBT = Rational–emotive behavioural therapy. Used where therapist believes problem is the unrealistic beliefs that individuals have about themselves and their behaviours.

MUST REMEMBER...
Don't have to cover this **and** psychodynamic therapy; just one or the other.

REBT (ELLIS, 1962)

Underlying assumptions of REBT are that:
- People are responsible for their own emotions and actions.
- Dysfunctional emotions and maladaptive behaviours are the product of a person's irrational thinking.
- People are able to learn more realistic views of the world and make these a part of thinking processes.
- People can experience a better acceptance of themselves by developing a more realistic view of the world.

- Rationale for CBT is that **thoughts have an enormous influence** on emotions and behaviour.
- When thoughts are persistently negative and irrational, they result in **maladaptive behaviour**.
- Client is encouraged to become aware of beliefs that contribute to maladaptive behaviour.
- Client is encouraged to recognise consequences of their faulty cognitions.
- **More realistic and rational beliefs** are then incorporated into ways of thinking.

The ABC model of REBT
- A – Activating Events are things that happen in a person's life.
- B – Beliefs are explanations of the event. They may be rational or irrational, and self-defeating.
- C – Consequences may be desirable (i.e. productive) or undesirable (i.e. unproductive) dependent on the beliefs an individual has about the activating event.

Irrational beliefs
- Irrational beliefs are experienced as self-defeating thoughts.
- These are disruptive and lead to unproductive outcomes.
- Ellis called this mental process 'catastrophising'.

Disputing self-defeating beliefs
- REBT focuses on the self-defeating beliefs that accompany activating events.
- The client is encouraged to dispute these beliefs.
- Effective disputing changes self-defeating beliefs into more rational beliefs.
- Client can then move from catastrophising to more rational interpretations of events.

STRESS-INOCULATION MODEL (MEICHENBAUM, 1972)

The nature of stress-inoculation
- Individual is helped to develop effective coping before a problem arises.
- People are able to 'inoculate' themselves against stress in the same way that they might receive inoculations against infectious diseases.
- Stress-inoculation has been applied in a number of stress-related behaviours, e.g. anger management and treatment of avoidance behaviour in rape victims.
- For example, in anger management, stress-inoculation may prevent anger from occurring in situations when it would be maladaptive, and regulate the arousal and expression of anger in those situations (Novaco, 1975).

Stress-inoculation was also covered at AS level, so could use some of that material again here!

Three main phases:
1 Identifying the problem: aim is to identify and examine faulty thought processes that lead to maladaptive behaviour.
2 Acquiring coping skills: coping skills are taught and practised. Therapist attempts to restructure thinking by converting negative thoughts into positive self-statements.
3 Practising coping responses: clients given opportunities to apply their newly learned coping skills in different situations, which become increasingly stressful.

MUST TAKE CARE...
To cover at least two types of CBT, although no need to cover **more** than two.

MUST TAKE CARE...
Not to confuse CBT with **behavioural** therapies.

ISSUES SURROUNDING THE USE OF COGNITIVE–BEHAVIOURAL THERAPIES

APPROPRIATENESS OF REBT
- Ellis (1980) claims that REBT is appropriate for any kind of psychological problem, e.g. anxiety disorders, depression, etc., but *not* for severe mental disorders.
- David and Avellino (2003) claim REBT is not only appropriate for clinical populations, but also for sub-clinical populations (e.g. lack of assertiveness).

However...
- Rosenhan and Seligman (1989) claim REBT is one of the most aggressive and judgemental forms of CBT, raising ethical concerns about its appropriateness.
- Although irrational beliefs may be maladaptive, there is evidence that they are frequently more realistic, e.g. Alloy and Abrahamson (1979) found depressed people gave more accurate estimates of the likelihood of a disaster than non-depressed controls.

EFFECTIVENESS OF REBT
- Smith and Glass (1977) – meta-analysis of the effectiveness of different psychotherapies showed REBT having second highest success rate to SD.
- Haaga and Davison (1989) found REBT effective for treatments of anger, aggression and depression, although not as effective as SD for treatment of anxiety.
- Engels et al. (1993) examined data from 28 studies where REBT was compared to other therapies. Found REBT was superior to placebo or no treatment, but only equally effective when compared to SD.

However...
- A problem with assessing the effectiveness of REBT concerns the consistency of the methods used. Only half of REBT therapists use variations of Ellis' method, making accurate assessments of effectiveness difficult.
- The effectiveness of CBT is not restricted to the treatment of mental disorders. They can also reduce the patterns of thinking and behaviour associated with cancer and heart attack and so increase patient lifespan (Eysenck and Grossarth-Maticek, 1991).

APPROPRIATENESS OF STRESS-INOCULATION THERAPY
- SIT has been used in a wide range of therapeutic settings, including preparation for examinations (Jay and Elliot, 1990); surgery (Ross et al., 1996); prolonged occupational stress such as police work (Meichenbaum, 1993); and with rape victims (Vernon and Best, 1983).
- With SIT treatment of rape victims, SIT produced a significant improvement on PTSD symptoms immediately after treatment and at follow-up.
- CBTs such as SIT are appropriate for clients who find insight therapies (such as psychoanalysis) threatening.

This model has been successfully applied to...
- Attempts to improve early care for victims of traumatic stress, particularly that resulting from military combat. Project DE-STRESS (Engel et al., 2005) has compared stress inoculation and traditional post-trauma care to discover best way to reduce long-term consequences of exposure to military trauma.
- Sports professionals, where individual is gradually exposed to more threatening situations while self-control is acquired as a means to combat learned helplessness (Weinberg and Gould, 1995).

EFFECTIVENESS OF STRESS-INOCULATION THERAPY (SIT)
- Meichenbaum (1977) compared SIT and SD in the treatment of snake phobia. Both were effective in reducing fear of snakes, but only SIT generalised to help clients deal with another, non-related phobia.
- SIT has produced effective results in the treatment of adolescents and adults who have problems with anger control (Deffenbacher et al., 1988).
- Kiselica et al. (1994) used SIT in the treatment of adolescents with raised self-reported anxiety. By training participants in coping skills and assertiveness training, researchers were able to reduce anxiety and stress levels.

However...
- SIT is effective because it teaches the individual many new skills that help them to deal effectively with stressful events in the future.
- It is unnecessarily complex, and so the range of activities could be reduced without losing much of its effectiveness.

TYPICAL QUESTIONS...

1 Describe and evaluate two or more therapies derived from either the psychodynamic or cognitive–behavioural models of abnormality. (30 marks)

2 Critically consider issues surrounding the use of two or more therapies derived from either the psychodynamic or cognitive–behavioural models of abnormality. (30 marks)

3 Compare and contrast biological therapies with **either** psychodynamic **or** cognitive–behavioural therapies. (30 marks)

GENDER BIAS IN PSYCHOLOGICAL THEORIES AND STUDIES

GENDER BIAS IN PSYCHOLOGICAL THEORIES

Stereotypes (social constructions) of gender produce types of gender bias in research (Hare-Mustin and Maracek, 1988):

- **Alpha bias:** assumes real and enduring differences. May heighten or devalue women or men.

- **Beta bias:** ignores or **minimises differences**, e.g. because male-based research applied to women (or vice versa). Results in:
  - **androcentrism:** based on and concerning males
  - **estrocentrism:** bias towards females.

ALPHA-BIASED THEORIES

ANDROCENTRISM: FREUD'S THEORY OF PSYCHOANALYSIS

- Took male behaviour as **the standard**.
- Female behaviour described as a **deviation** from that standard.
- e.g. Oedipus complex versus penis envy.

- Freud *actually* said that the differences are not innate; **social context** creates differences. Women envy male penis because it represents **dominance**.

- **Supported by:** Gilligan and Attanucci (1988).
- **Challenged by:** Walker (1984) – meta-analysis of over 100 studies found no gender differences.

ESTROCENTRISM: GILLIGAN'S (1982) THEORY OF MORAL DEVELOPMENT

- Women have a 'different moral voice'; **interpersonal concerns** rather than justice.

POSITIVE CONSEQUENCES OF ALPHA BIAS
- Estrocentric theories counter the devaluation of women.
- Has led to healthy criticism of cultural values that extol male qualities, e.g. individualism.

BETA-BIASED THEORIES

UNISEX: BEM'S (1976) THEORY OF PSYCHOLOGICAL ANDROGENY

- 'Healthiest' psychological state is androgyny – men and women are free to choose masculine and feminine traits as appropriate to their temperament.

- Theory of androgeny **overlooks social context** because masculine and feminine qualities are not equivalent – masculine qualities more valued.

- When used to assess female morality, lead inevitably to finding women to be inferior.

UNIVERSAL: KOHLBERG'S (1963) THEORY OF MORAL DEVELOPMENT

- Stage theory developed from **moral dilemmas** based on justice-orientation (male perspective) and **sample of all boys**.

POSITIVE CONSEQUENCES OF BETA BIAS
- Leads to equal treatment and equal access to e.g. employment.

NEGATIVE CONSEQUENCES OF BETA BIAS
- Draws attention away from women's special needs.

BIAS-FREE THEORIES

WORRELL AND REMER (1992)
Theories should be:
- **flexible** – within- and between-sex differences
- **interactionist** – recognise multiple influences rather than focus on gender.

FEMINIST PSYCHOLOGY
Aims to challenge:
- androcentric generalisations
- pathologisation of female behaviour
- biological explanations that perpetuate view of inevitability and ignore social construction.

REAL DIFFERENCES
- Real psychological and physiological differences, e.g. **Maccoby and Jacklin (1974)** – boys better at spatial tasks and girls have superior verbal ability; also hormonal differences cause different behaviours.
- But differences may be due to expectations and because findings are from biased studies.

GENDER BIAS IN PSYCHOLOGICAL STUDIES

Research design
Experimental approach is 'masculine' (logical and rational).

Question formation
Choice of topics for study reflect prevalent gender stereotypes, e.g. leadership defined in terms of dominance.

Research methods
Researchers more friendly and encouraging with female participants (Rosenthal, 1966) – acts as an extraneous variable.

GENDER BIAS FOUND AT ALL STAGES OF RESEARCH PROCESS (DENMARK ET AL., 1988)

Publication bias
Trend to publish studies with positive findings, therefore more likely to publish those that find gender differences than not, producing an alpha bias (Tavris, 1993).

Inappropriate conclusions
Findings based on one sex applied to both sexes.

Selection of participants
Most research conducted with white, male, undergraduates and findings taken to represent human behaviour (Fine and Gordon, 1989).

Can use research studies as AO2 if used effectively.

ALPHA-BIASED STUDIES (assume real differences)

- Studies of the evolution of human behaviour, e.g. Dunbar (1995).
- Evolutionary theory predicts men look for attractiveness and advertise resources.
- Gender bias in the way the research question is asked and how the study is designed.

BETA-BIASED STUDIES (ignore differences)

- Studies of social influence, e.g. Asch, Zimbardo, Milgram, all used male participants – assumed that studies conducted with men could be generalised to human behaviour.
- Evidence that men and women behave differently on obedience tasks – Kilham and Mann (1974) found that women less obedient than men (16% and 40% respectively).

- Have exaggerated male–female differences.
- At least estrocentric theories counter the devaluation of women.
- Has led to healthy criticism of cultural values that extol male qualities, e.g. individualism.

- Have tended to misrepresent women and present their behaviour as inferior and pathological (disordered).
- May draw attention away from women's special needs.
- May sustain prejudices by misrepresenting one or both genders.
- However, minimising differences also leads to equal treatment and equal access to e.g. employment.

GENERAL COMMENTARY

- It may not be possible to extricate the 'true' effects of sex (based on biological factors) but we can be aware of the biases that distort our thinking.

MUST REMEMBER...
Not to evaluate the study/research process, but to evaluate the gender bias.

TYPICAL QUESTIONS...

1 Discuss gender bias in psychological research (theories and/or studies). (30 marks)

2 Discuss gender bias in **two or more** psychological theories. (30 marks)

3 (a) Outline **two** types of gender bias in Psychology. (5 marks)

(b) Discuss gender bias in **two or more** psychological studies. (25 marks)

CULTURAL BIAS IN PSYCHOLOGICAL THEORIES AND STUDIES

DEFINITION
Culture refers to the rules, customs, etc. that bind a group of people together.

CULTURAL BIAS IN PSYCHOLOGICAL THEORIES

TYPES OF CULTURAL BIAS

CULTURAL BIAS IN THEORIES

ALPHA AND BETA BIAS
- Alpha: real differences.
- Beta: minimise differences.

e.g. Kohlberg's (1963) theory of moral reasoning:
- Beta bias – developmental stages related to maturation therefore should be universal.

- Cross-cultural support: Snarey et al. (1985) found similar progression in 44 countries.
- However, stages 5 and 6 not universal possibly because they are more typical of urban, industrialised societies but not rural ones (Snarey and Keljo, 1991).
- May be that complexity of urban life creates greater moral sophistication. Urban is not superior, just

INDIVIDUALISM–COLLECTIVISM
- Individualism: personal achievement, independence and individual identity valued.
- Collectivism: sharing, interdependence and group identity.

e.g. Piaget's theory of cognitive development:
- May not be universal but appropriate for individualist cultures, whereas Vygotsky's theory is more appropriate for collectivist societies.

- However, individualism–collectivism dimension masks differences within cultures.
- Individualism–collectivism tends to co-vary with urban/industrialised and rural/non-industrialised dimension.

ETHNOCENTRISM AND EUROCENTRISM
- One's own cultural perspective is the standard.
- Own culture seen as superior.

e.g. 'Economic theories' of relationship formation (e.g. equity theory):
- Western relationships – based on individualism and self-interest.
- Non-Western relationships – based on collectivism and sharing.

- These theories are Eurocentric because they are written from one cultural perspective.
- Suggests that being able to make own choice is superior.

EMIC–ETIC DIMENSION
- Etic analyses: focus on universals, e.g. using tests and procedures developed in one culture to assess all cultural groups.
- Emic analyses: study culture using own rules and systems.

e.g. DSM and ICD:
- Standard measure used to diagnose mental illness based on dominant white culture.

- Can explain why seven times more African-Caribbean immigrants diagnosed with mental illness (Cochrane and Sashidharan, 1995).
- However, cultural differences may be due to more stressful lives for immigrants.
- Not supported by Cochrane (1983) – immigrants from South Asia not diagnosed more than norm.

HISTORICAL BIAS
- Culture of 1950s Britain was different to 21st century.

e.g. Freud's theory of personality:
- Overemphasis on sex appropriate for Victorian times.

- Neo-Freudians involved social factors but even those theories out of date, e.g. Erikson's notion of a 'job for life'.

GENERAL COMMENTARY
- Operationalising culture often results in cross-country comparisons; presumes that each country has one culture.

CULTURAL BIAS IN PSYCHOLOGICAL STUDIES

Cross-cultural research
- Psychologists repeat studies in different countries/cultures to see if a theory is universal (e.g. testing Kohlberg's theory of moral development).
- Differences may be due to cultural differences or they may be due to other problems (Smith and Bond, 1998).

EXPANSION
- Instructions to participants and their responses may have to be translated and **may be inaccurate**.
- The impact of any variable may have **a different impact in a different setting**, e.g. an insult.
- Participants, even if from same social group (e.g. students), may have **a different social background** in a different country (e.g. university requirements are different).

BIAS IN THE RESEARCH PROCESS

Sampling
- Large portion of Psychology based on middle-class, academic, young adults, often male.
- Sears (1986) – 82% of studies used undergraduates as participants and 51% were Psychology students.
- Smith and Bond (1993) – found that 94% of studies cited in US textbook were US, and 68% were US in one UK textbook.

- **Example:** Asch's (1956) study of conformity used male US students, and influenced psychological explanations of conformity. Moscovici et al.'s (1969) study of minority influence used women and represented a more eurocentric view.

Imposed etic
- If research is conducted with wider sampling, researchers still use Western tests and procedures, e.g. American IQ test = an imposed etic.
- Imposed etics assume that the research tool is universally valid, which is unlikely.

- **Example:** Takahashi (1990) – Japanese infants responded quite differently in the Strange Situation to US infants (more disturbed after being left alone). Japanese infants are almost never left alone which means that the Strange Situation was more than mildly stressful. Using the Strange Situation (an imposed etic) with Japanese infants was not comparable to using it with US infants.

COMMENTARY
- Problems conducting cross-cultural research mean that such research may lack validity – the researchers were not testing what they intended to test.
- Biases in sampling mean that much psychological research is unrepresentative globally and also unrepresentative within our own culture.

POSSIBLE SOLUTIONS
- A derived etic approach – Berry (1969) suggested participants should be observed in natural environment before study conducted. Would be a more *emic* approach.
- Indigenous psychologies – psychological research conducted in non-Western cultures by non-Westerners. Yamagishi (2002) reports there are more psychologists working in Asia than Europe.

MUST REMEMBER...
Not to evaluate the study/research process, but to evaluate the cultural bias.

TYPICAL QUESTIONS...

1 Discuss cultural bias in psychological research (theories **and/or** studies). (30 marks)

2 Discuss cultural bias in **two or more** psychological theories. (30 marks)

3 (a) Outline **two** types of cultural bias in Psychology. (5 marks)

(b) Discuss cultural bias in **two or more** psychological studies. (25 marks)

ETHICAL ISSUES AND SOCIALLY SENSITIVE RESEARCH

ETHICAL ISSUES

DEFINITION

An ethical issue arises when there are conflicts between the rights of participants and the needs of researchers.

MUST KNOW...
- Ethical issues involved in psychological investigations using human participants.
- The ethics of socially sensitive research.

ETHICAL ISSUE

INVESTIGATION

DECEPTION
- Rights of participants – to be given informed consent and chance to withdraw; can't do this if deceived.
- Needs of researchers – lack of validity if participants know aims because their expectations will change their behaviour.

MILGRAM'S OBEDIENCE RESEARCH
- Deception necessary because participants would have behaved differently.
- Demonstrated by survey beforehand – estimated that 3% would go to highest shock level.

- Participants may not believe the deception – Orne and Holland (1968). Participants knew shocks weren't real (deception didn't work).
- Deception justified because:
  – effects not anticipated thus potential for harm was minimal
  – study was non-trivial – Elms (1972) cites it as the 'most morally significant piece of research'
  – adequate debriefing.

INFORMED CONSENT
- Rights of participants – to be able to decide to take part based on comprehensive information.
- Should be able to withdraw at any time.

PILIAVIN ET AL. BYSTANDER BEHAVIOUR
- Participants didn't know they were in a study – no informed consent and no opportunity to debrief.
- Findings also raise issues – may lead people to rationalise their anti-social behaviour (Baumrind, 1977).

- Not possible in most field studies which are necessary to conduct more natural research.
- Research details may not be comprehensible – Epstein and Lasagna (1969) found two thirds of participants didn't understand what was involved in a study. Therefore researcher must point out likely risks.

PSYCHOLOGICAL HARM
- Acceptable if risk no greater than normal life.

ZIMBARDO PRISON STUDY
- Prisoners became very distressed.

- May not be able to anticipate harm beforehand.
- Could have stopped the study earlier.

PRIVACY
- Observation acceptable:
  – in public settings
  – with public personalities
  – if anonymity protected

KITTY GENOVESE – BYSTANDER APATHY
- The events of her death have been immortalised which may be distressing for her family.
- Same true of other case studies, e.g. Genie, HM.

- This case was in the public domain.
- Used to improve human lives.

GENERAL COMMENTARY
- Using cost-benefit analysis may create as many problems as it resolves.
- Debriefing may not be an adequate solution because harm already done.
- Guidelines absolve researchers of sense of responsibility.

Alternatives
- Can use presumptive consent – ask similar people if they would give informed consent.

SOCIALLY SENSITIVE RESEARCH (SSR)

DEFINITION

Socially sensitive research:

- Research which potentially has social consequences for participants or class of individuals represented by research (Sieber and Stanley, 1988).
- Research that has social impact which may attract media interest and lead people to form sometimes ill-informed views.

GENERAL ISSUES

- Avoiding such research raises ethical issues because prejudice may continue and researchers have social responsibilities.
- Special ethical issues because of conflict between long-term wider interests of groups represented and short-term effects on individual participants.
- Ethical guidelines inadequate because focused on short-term needs of individual participants.

Privacy

- Skilled interviewer may extract unintended information from participant.
- May lead to social policies which invade people's lives.

Equitable treatment

- No resources should be withheld from any group.
- Findings should not lead to devaluation or prejudicial treatment of any group.

Scientific freedom

- Freedom to conduct research balanced against obligations to protect participants and the sectors of society they represent.

SPECIAL ETHICAL ISSUES

Methodology

- Findings from poorly designed studies may still get taken up by the media and shape social policy.

Confidentiality

- Data collected may be sensitive.
- Lack of confidentiality may affect subsequent willingness to take part.

Gay and lesbian relationships

- Early research beta-biased (differences minimised) – homosexual relationships seen as same as heterosexual ones = liberal humanism (Kitzinger and Coyle, 1995).
- Recent research alpha-biased – recognises differences, e.g. Nardi (1992) – ex-homosexual partners more likely to remain friends than heterosexual ones.

- Alpha-biased approach ignores differences *within* homosexuals, e.g. differences between gay and lesbian relationships found in personal ads (Davidson, 1991).
- Research signals greater acceptance of and places greater value on homosexuals, reducing prejudice.

EXAMPLES OF SSR

Intelligence and race

- Jensen (1969) claimed that 15 point IQ difference between blacks and whites was inherited.

- Implies that disadvantaged children won't benefit from enrichment programmes.
- Important environmental influences on IQ despite large genetic component.

Eating disorders

- People with eating disorders may be distressed by being interviewed and may reveal more than they intended.

- Research is important in educating the general public and policy-making groups about prevalence and causes.

Drug abuse

- Research relies on making contact through trusted gatekeepers, e.g. clinic, so confidentiality important.

- Can benefit abuse clinics by sharing the findings.

Domestic violence

- Abuser may find out about research and harm the participant or researcher.

- Therefore, must put protection in place.

TYPICAL QUESTIONS...

1 Discuss ethical issues involved in psychological investigations using human participants. (30 marks)

2 Critically consider the ethics of socially sensitive research. (24 marks)

NON-HUMAN ANIMALS IN PSYCHOLOGICAL RESEARCH

THE USE OF ANIMALS

LAB EXPERIMENTS

- Harlow (1960) raised young monkeys with wire or cloth-covered 'mother' to observe effects on attachment.
- Skinner (1938) demonstrated operant conditioning using the Skinner box where food pellets delivered as reinforcement.

FIELD EXPERIMENTS AND STUDIES

- Seyfarth and Cheney (1992) played alarm signals to monkeys to test understanding of meaning.
- Gardner and Gardner (1969) taught Washoe to use sign language.

NATURALISTIC OBSERVATION

- Kawai (1965) observed imitative learning in Japanese macaque monkeys washing sweet potatoes.
- Von Frisch (1967) recorded dance of the honey bees.

- Not all lab experiments involve harm, though it could be argued that Skinner's experiments led to lasting change which might count as 'harm'.
- Field experiments may be just as harmful – Seyfarth and Cheney used signals that would alarm the monkeys and might lead them in future to ignore alarm signals.
- Cost-benefit – Harlow's research contributed much to understanding behaviour; findings were unexpected.

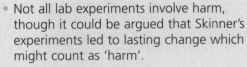

MUST TAKE CARE...
To beware of questions that mention 'investigations'; these require mention of actual studies and not just the theoretical debate.

CONSTRAINTS ON THE USE OF ANIMALS

LEGISLATION

- Animals (Scientific Procedures) Act (1986): mainly for commercial research; psychological research relatively minor. Main points:
  - **law:** must obtain a licence
  - **ethics:** consider alternatives
  - **species:** special needs and suitability
  - **number:** reduce number used
  - **caging:** ensure it is adequate
  - **motivation:** where rewards used these should be related to species' needs.

HOME OFFICE ENDORSES 3 R'S (RUSSELL AND BIRCH, 1959)

- Refine, reduce, replace.

CODE OF CONDUCT

- BPS and APA issue guidelines for psychological research, e.g.:
  - legislation, e.g. Animals Act
  - choice of species
  - number of species
  - procedures – avoid those that cause pain.

- Effective – number of live experiments in Britain has halved.
- Not effective – BUAV (2003) claims it needs reviewing.
- Unavoidable – British law requires that any new drug (e.g. anti-depressants) must be tested on at least two different species of live mammal. One must be a large non-rodent.

BATESON'S DECISION CUBE

- Can be used to decide on costs-benefits:
  - quality of research
  - certainty of benefit
  - animal suffering.

- Difficulties measuring suffering – Dawkins (1985) suggests three factors: animal's physical state of health, signs of stress and animal's behaviour.
- Most difficult to assess potential benefits – should seek real understanding.

ARGUMENTS **FOR** THE USE OF NON-HUMAN ANIMALS

ETHICAL ARGUMENTS	COUNTERARGUMENTS
• Morally obliged to use animals to ease human suffering.	• 'Naturalistic fallacy' – it is possible to overcome innate predispositions.
• Animals don't have rights because they have no responsibilities.	• Infants and the mentally ill don't have responsibilities, but they do have rights.
• Animals don't have feelings.	• There is evidence that animals *do* feel pain, e.g. Sneddon et al. (2003) – research on fish. However, response to noxious stimuli may not include awareness.
• Animals are protected by legislation (1986 Animals Act) and also by code of conduct (e.g. BPS).	• Based on costs-benefits model – costs to animals and benefits to humans, which ignore animal rights.
• Can use less invasive methods to minimise suffering.	• If animal research stopped it would lead to development of other techniques, but some of these aren't true substitutes, e.g. computer modelling isn't the same.

SCIENTIFIC ARGUMENTS	COUNTERARGUMENTS
• Usefulness of the research, e.g. cure for Alzheimer's.	• But at cost to animals, benefits calculated in human not animal terms, committing 'speciesism'.
• Studying animals in their own right, e.g. ethological research.	• Even field studies have ethical concerns, e.g. Seyfarth and Cheney (1992).
• Greater control and objectivity.	• It is true that behaviourist research raises fewer ethical objections, though choice of rewards is a concern.
• When research on humans not possible.	• Is it any better to conduct research with animals which is ethically inappropriate with humans?

ARGUMENTS **AGAINST** THE USE OF NON-HUMAN ANIMALS

> **MUST REMEMBER...**
> That counterarguments are AO2 **only** if the material is presented as a direct counterpoint.

ETHICAL ARGUMENTS	COUNTERARGUMENTS
Animal rights (Regan, 1983)	
• Animals have inherent rights, e.g. to be treated with respect.	• Can't have rights without responsibilities.
• Cost-benefit considerations are not sufficient.	• Morally obliged to use animals to ease human suffering.
• No research should be tolerated ('not fewer cages but empty cages').	• Animals may have feelings but no awareness.
	• Can use less invasive procedures to minimise suffering.
Utilitarian argument: Speciesism (Singer, 1975)	
• What is acceptable is what produces greatest pleasure/value.	• However, animal research acceptable under some circumstances.
• Principle of equality, to discriminate on basis of species (speciesism) is wrong.	• There is legislation to protect animals.

SCIENTIFIC ARGUMENTS	COUNTERARGUMENTS
• Animals and humans are too dissimilar for useful insights, e.g. human behaviour affected by thinking.	• Basic physiology of the nervous systems is more similar than different.
	• Many behavioural processes (e.g. conditioning) are the same.

TYPICAL QUESTIONS...

1 Discuss the use of non-human animals in psychological investigations, including the constraints on their use. (30 marks)

2 (a) Describe constraints on the use of non-human animals in psychological investigations. (15 marks)

(b) To what extent have such constraints been successful? (15 marks)

3 Critically consider arguments **for** the use of non-human animals in psychological research. (30 marks)

4 Discuss arguments **against** the use of non-human animals in psychological research. (30 marks)

FREE WILL AND DETERMINISM

MUST KNOW...
- Definitions of free will and determinism.
- The debate in relation to psychological theories and studies.
- Arguments for and against free will and determinism in Psychology.

DEFINITIONS OF FREE WILL AND DETERMINISM

FREE WILL

- Individuals are capable of making own choices.
- Self-determining.
- Free from coercion.
- Fundamental to many theories of Psychology.

DETERMINISM

- Individual's behaviour shaped or controlled by forces other than one's will.
- Behaviour is predictable.
- May be due to external factors (environmental determinism).
- Or due to internal factors, e.g. the unconscious or genes (biological determinism).
- Part of the scientific perspective.

Reconciling free will and determinism

- **Soft determinism** (James, 19th C.) – separates behaviour into **mental realm** (free will) and **physical realm** (determined); this is a **dualist** approach.
- **Liberal determinism** (Heather, 1976) – behaviour is determined insofar as it is consistent within a person's character, i.e. choice (free will) within a range of options (determined).
- Free will is simply **free from coercion** – giving money at gun point is determined; putting money in a charity tin is free will – both are determined but latter is free from coercion.

THE DEBATE IN RELATION TO PSYCHOLOGICAL THEORIES

- Successful therapy (psychoanalysis) with certain people and disorders (Bergin, 1971).
- However, Eysenck (1952) reviewed therapies – only 44% success rate for psychoanalysis.
- Success of psychoanalysis may be due to therapist–patient interaction rather than unconscious factors.
- Theory lacks falsifiability, e.g. for Freud if an explanation denied, this indicates repression.

Psychodynamic approach

- Psychic determinism – behaviour is not by chance but controlled by unconscious processes.
- Perceived freedom of choice is an illusion.

Behaviourist approach

- Environmental determinism – behaviour determined by reinforcement history.
- Free will is an illusion.

- Successful therapies (e.g. systematic desensitisation, token economy).
- However, determinist approach raises ethical concerns about patient manipulation.
- Reductionist approach – simplified explanation may be suitable for animals that lack cognitive abilities of humans.
- Reciprocal determinism (Bandura) – individual is controlled by environment but also makes choices about what environments to be in.

PSYCHOLOGICAL THEORIES

- Successful cognitive-behavioural therapies (e.g. SIT) which are related to self-determination (free will) but are quite directive (deterministic).
- Schema theory suggests that previous experiences lead to expectations which *determine* our responses unconsciously.

Cognitive approach

- Behaviour controlled by how we think about a situation, related to free will.
- Irrational thinking (with full awareness) leads to maladaptive behaviour.

Humanistic approach

- Individuals free to plan own destiny.
- Each of us is responsible for own behaviour (Rogers, 1974).
- Individuals strive to self-actualise (Maslow, 1954).
- Mental health problems arise when we are prevented from self-actualising (Jahoda, 1958).

- Successful therapy (e.g. counselling) based on drive for each of us to be self-determining and self-righting.
- Culturally-biased approach appropriate for individualist societies that are concerned with self rather than group goals.

ARGUMENTS FOR AND AGAINST FREE WILL

ARGUMENTS **FOR** FREE WILL	COMMENTARY/COUNTERARGUMENTS
1 Psychological argument: most people think they have free will.	• Evidence to support the existence of free will from the fact that research is conducted on it, e.g. found to increase with age. • Feeling free doesn't mean you are free. Skinner and Freud claimed free will is an illusion – behaviour is determined by reinforcements or unconscious factors.
2 Ethical argument: free will is a pre-requisite of moral responsibility – the law assumes that individuals have free will.	• Can behave in a moral fashion without freely deciding this, e.g. behaviourists claim we learn moral behaviour through reinforcement. • Can resolve conflict by saying that we are free to make moral decisions from a limited range of choices.

ARGUMENTS **AGAINST** FREE WILL	COMMENTARY/COUNTERARGUMENTS
1 Difficulty specifying free will – what is doing the willing?	• Response to materialists – free will is equivalent to voluntary control which is absent in e.g. schizophrenia; such voluntary control may be located in the limbic system (if removed, animal can't initiate activity) (Ridley, 2003).
2 Inconsistency with science – scientific investigation is based on determinism.	• Modern science takes a probablistic rather than determinist approach, e.g. Heisenberg's Uncertainty Principle that subatomic particles don't always follow laws of physics.

ARGUMENTS FOR AND AGAINST DETERMINISM

ARGUMENTS **FOR** DETERMINISM	COMMENTARY/COUNTERARGUMENTS
1 The scientific approach has made important and valid discoveries in Psychology, e.g. research on stress and physical illness.	• Many research findings can't be applied in the real world, e.g. criticisms of Milgram's obedience studies. • Science is reductionist and oversimplifies complex behaviours, so findings are meaningless.
2 We have a subjective sense that people's behaviour is predictable, e.g. someone who is generous in one situation is always expected to behave like that.	• Situationalism (Mischel, 1968) – people appear predictable only because we tend to see them in the same situations; situation rather than personality determines behaviour – but this is still determinist.
3 One's 'will' is the outcome of brain activity, i.e. physical and determined.	• Volition (initiating activity) is not the same as free will – free will is more than having the power of choice.

ARGUMENTS **AGAINST** DETERMINISM	COMMENTARY/COUNTERARGUMENTS
1 Determinism isn't falsifiable – advocates claim that if we haven't found a cause yet this doesn't mean that we won't eventually find one. This position is not falsifiable.	• Determinism is falsifiable because it has been shown to be wrong, e.g. by the Uncertainty Principle (Valentine, 1982).
2 Ethical argument – free will is a pre-requisite of moral responsibility; embodied in law. Determinist position challenges this.	• Can behave in a moral fashion without freely deciding this, e.g. behaviourists claim we learn moral behaviour through reinforcement.

|| **MUST REMEMBER...** ||
• Can turn counter arguments (AO2) into AO1, and vice versa.

> If free will is seen as being free to make choices from a range of possibilities (liberal determinism), then we can have free will and determism.

- -

TYPICAL QUESTIONS...

1 (a) Explain what is meant by the terms 'free will' and 'determinism'. (5 marks)

(b) Discuss determinism in psychological theories. (25 marks)

2 Critically consider free will and determinism in psychological theories **and/or** studies. (30 marks)

3 Critically consider arguments **for** determinism in Psychology. (30 marks)

4 Discuss arguments **against** free will in psychological research. (30 marks)

REDUCTIONISM

REDUCTIONISM AS A FORM OF EXPLANATION

MUST KNOW...
- Reductionism as a form of explanation.
- Arguments for and against reductionist explanations in Psychology.
- Examples of reductionism in psychological theories and studies.

REDUCTIONISM IN EXPLANATIONS: MORGAN'S LAW OF PARSIMONY
- Simplest explanations are generally best – no need to explain behaviour in terms of complex processes if a simpler explanation is adequate.

REDUCTIONISM IN METHODOLOGY
- Researchers reduce behavioural phenomena to simple variables (IV and DV) which can be controlled and measured to demonstrate causal relationships.

REDUCTIONISM IN THEORIES
- Theories from different disciplines can be related to each other and reduced to one all-embracing explanation of the world.

ARGUMENTS FOR AND AGAINST REDUCTIONISM

ARGUMENTS **FOR** REDUCTIONISM	COMMENTARY/COUNTERARGUMENTS
1 The scientific approach has led to important discoveries which have enabled people to predict and control the world; scientific Psychology is desirable.	• Methodological reductionism may not be appropriate for research with humans who are more complex. • There are alternative approaches, e.g. Gestalt approach to perception; holism as in connectionist networks as representations of human mental processes. • The whole is not a simple sum of individual links.
2 Behaviours can be explained using different levels, some more reductionist than others, e.g. molecular (Physics), parts of individuals (Physiology), behaviour (Psychology) and groups (Sociology) (Rose, 1997).	• No one level is 'correct' – they all contribute to full understanding. • Difficult to select the right level – wrong level may prevent true understanding of behaviour, e.g. seeing depression as biochemical may lead one to miss psychological explanations.
3 Reductionist explanations are successful, e.g. drug therapies or behavioural therapies for mental illnesses.	• Such therapies are not 100% effective. • Relying on such therapies may mask other causes.

ARGUMENTS **AGAINST** REDUCTIONISM	COMMENTARY/COUNTERARGUMENTS
1 Methodological reductionism may oversimplify variables, e.g. testing memory with nonsense syllables as opposed to testing it with photographs of known people.	• Simplified studies shouldn't be dismissed because they are often confirmed by more 'real-world' studies. • Such research has a place in leading to greater understanding if limitations are recognised.
2 Reductionist goals aren't appropriate for Psychology – can't derive higher levels of explanation from lower ones, e.g. moving from chemical descriptions of schizophrenia to family dynamics (Laing, 1965).	• Holist approach might be more appropriate for Psychology. • The more holist approach is supported by relatively modest success of determinist drug therapies. • Psychological therapies, which are less reductionist, have also not proved wholly successful, so non-reductionist approaches may be no better than reductionist ones.
3 Limited to certain kinds of question –those that focus on structures rather than processes, e.g. understanding stress concerns structures, whereas stress management is concerned with process.	• Higher-level explanations lack predictive power – can't produce causal relationships which ultimately may mean we learn less about human behaviour.

EXAMPLES OF REDUCTIONISM IN PSYCHOLOGICAL THEORIES AND STUDIES

PHYSIOLOGICAL REDUCTIONISM

Physiological theories
- Complex behaviour reduced to neurophysiological components.
- Means that scientific research can be conducted, demonstrating causal relationships.

Biochemical theory of schizophrenia
- Excess dopamine causes schizophrenia.
- Antipsychotic drugs reduce dopamine levels and reduce symptoms of schizophrenia.
- De-emphasises importance of environmental factors.

- Theory leads to hope that schizophrenia might be controlled by such drugs.
- However, doesn't lead to a cure and is also not effective with all patients.
- Reductionist explanations may mask real cause (Laing, 1965).
- Thus reductionist theory has benefits and limitations.

EVOLUTIONARY REDUCTIONISM

Theory of evolution (Darwin)
- Principles of natural selection and Mendelian genetics explain how species change.
- Reduce to concept of adaptiveness – only those behaviours survive which increase reproductive success.

- Provides justification for comparative studies of non-human species.
- Brain and behaviour not simply determined by our biology, also affected by the environment, e.g. Haier et al. (1992) showed playing computer games over time changed brain processes.
- Evolutionary approach leads to assumption that genes determine behaviour, minimising important role of nurture.

ENVIRONMENTAL REDUCTIONISM

Behaviourism
- Behaviour can be explained by reinforcement.
- Behaviourist principles used in e.g. training animals, behaviour modification programmes.

- Considerable success, e.g. in training severely disturbed adults and those with severe learning difficulties to earn a living in the community.
- Behaviourist explanations are oversimplifications – human behaviour affected by other factors such as emotion and free will.
- Applying behaviourist explanations to the real world may mean indiscriminate use of reinforcers which ignores whether the behaviour being reinforced is worthwhile in the first place ('bribes in disguise') (Skinner, 1987).

MACHINE REDUCTIONISM

Cognitive theories
- e.g. Multi-store model of memory – memory as a series of inputs, outputs and processes.
- Suggests that human information processing works like a machine.

- Memory has more recently been explained in terms of connectionist networks which are holist – the network as a whole behaves differently from the individual parts.

For practice in answering A2 Psychology questions, why not use *Collins Do Brilliantly A2 Psychology*?

TYPICAL QUESTIONS...

1 Critically consider arguments **for** reductionism in Psychology. (30 marks)

2 Critically consider reductionism in psychological theories **and/or** studies. (30 marks)

3 (a) Explain the concept of reductionism in Psychology. (5 marks)

(b) Discuss arguments **against** reductionism in psychological theories and/or studies. (25 marks)

PSYCHOLOGY AS A SCIENCE

DEFINITIONS AND CHARACTERISTICS OF SCIENCE

WHAT IS SCIENCE?
- Science is:
  - concerned with what we know to be true rather than beliefs
  - a body of knowledge regarded as trustworthy.
- A scientific method is a means of obtaining such knowledge.

CYCLE OF SCIENTIFIC ENQUIRY
- Uses empirical methods, i.e. sensory (direct) methods, rather than thoughts.
- Direct observation leads to theory construction (induction).
- Theories lead to predictions which can be tested (deduction).
- Leads to validation of a theory (falsifying).

Scientific observation:
- is objective
- uses controlled conditions
- can be replicated.

- Culture-specific account from Western science of the 19th and 20th Century – past approaches and Eastern ones don't use same methods, e.g falsification.

VARIETIES OF SCIENCE

SCIENCE AS KNOWLEDGE
- Scientific knowledge rejects subjective explanations, e.g. magic.
- Scientific explanations stated as laws or general principles which enable us to predict and control our world.

SCIENCE AS METHOD
- Involves empirical observation.
- Leads to theory construction.
- Followed by testing in e.g. experiments.

HARD SCIENCES
- Physics and Chemistry.
- Lend themselves to more reductionist approaches and determinism.

SOFT SCIENCES
- Psychology and Sociology.
- Subject matter means that research is more subjective.

INDUCTION
- Reasoning from particular to general.
- Observed the world and produced general principles (natural laws).

DEDUCTION
- Karl Popper (1959) argued that induction can never demonstrate truth whereas falsification can, e.g. one black swan proves 'all swans are white' is false.
- General principles (theories) produce hypotheses which can be tested to accept or refine a theory.

COMMENTARY
- Soft sciences may still be scientific despite lack of rigour because they aim to be objective, replicable, etc.
- Hard sciences aren't as hard as they may appear.
- Science doesn't operate through induction and deduction according to Kuhn (1962) – it evolves through revolution or paradigm shift.
- Eventually dominant position overthrown by minority position.

e.g. Qualitative methods can be validated through triangulation.

e.g. Unofficial story of scientific research includes the effects of personal ambitions on supposedly objective data collection.

Kuhn's view in itself was a paradigm shift.

e.g. Copernician revolution in 16th Century when Copernicus argued that the sun doesn't revolve around the earth.

ARGUMENTS FOR AND AGAINST PSYCHOLOGY AS A SCIENCE

ARGUMENTS **FOR** PSYCHOLOGY AS A SCIENCE	COMMENTARY/COUNTERARGUMENTS
1 Science is the preferred method for most psychologists, using laboratory experiments in order to control variables and predict behaviour.	• Highly controlled research accused of lacking external validity, e.g. memory studies. • Demand characteristics or experimenter bias may lead to low internal validity, e.g. in Milgram's study.
2 Some levels of Psychology may not be scientific, but some levels (e.g. Physiological Psychology) are.	• Psychology hasn't got a paradigm, which (according to Kuhn (1962)) is a key feature of a science – having a shared set of assumptions and shared methodology. • On the other hand, Rose (1997) argued that even in Biology (regarded as a science), there are a number of mini-paradigms.

ARGUMENTS **AGAINST** PSYCHOLOGY AS A SCIENCE	COMMENTARY/COUNTERARGUMENTS
1 Science is a determinist approach and determinism denies free will which is important in many theories of Psychology and concept of moral responsibility.	• Free will can be incorporated within a determinist framework by, e.g. liberal determinism (selecting options from a limited range of possibilities). • In any case, even the physical sciences accept probablistic explanations rather than determinist explanations.
2 Science is reductionist; in order to investigate psychological phenomena we have to operationalise variables which may reduce them to humanly insignificant variables.	• This leads to conclusions related to phenomena that are divorced from reality – which is what researchers aim to be studying (i.e. lacks mundane realism). • However, simplified studies shouldn't be dismissed because they are often confirmed by more 'real-world' studies.
3 Objectivity may not be possible when humans study humans because of e.g. experimenter/observer/interviewer bias.	• Problems related to objectivity occur even in the physical sciences, e.g. Heisenberg's Uncertainty Principle states that the act of measuring a sub-atomic particle's behaviour may alter that behaviour so that objectivity is an impossible ideal.
4 Psychology has no paradigm – according to Kuhn (1962), Psychology has no characteristic way of thinking about phenomena and conducting research. Kuhn claims that Psychology is a pre-science.	• Psychology may not have one paradigm, but neither does Biology. There are mini-paradigms (e.g. behaviourism, psychoanalysis) each with characteristic assumptions and methodology. • There have been dominant paradigms throughout the history of Psychology, e.g. behaviourism in the early 20th Century, Cognitive Psychology in the 1950s. • Kuhn's view may be extreme – Lakatos (1970) suggests that a science consists of a succession of theories linked by a hard core of assumptions. Theories are continually tested and revised in a rational process.

TYPICAL QUESTIONS...

1 Critically consider arguments **for** Psychology as a science. (30 marks)

2 (a) Outline varieties of science. (5 marks)

   (b) Discuss arguments **against** Psychology as a science. (25 marks)

3 (a) Define the concept of science. (5 marks)

   (b) Discuss arguments **for** Psychology as a science. (25 marks)

NATURE–NURTURE

DEFINITIONS AND ASSUMPTIONS

NATURE

- Characteristics and abilities determined by genes.
- Not the same as the characteristics you are born with.
- Supported by: hereditarians (believing in the inheritance of characteristics) or nativists.

ASSUMPTIONS
Evolutionary theory
- Main assumption: behaviours evolve because they increase an individual's opportunities for passing on their genes. For example:
  – Bowlby (1969) suggested that attachment is adaptive – leads to perpetuation of the parents' genes
  – rank theory of depression explains depression as an adaptive response to defeat in power conflicts.

- Hard to test such explanations.
- Evolutionary explanations don't exclude environmental influences, e.g. Bowlby proposed that infants become most strongly attached to the caregiver who responds most sensitively to their needs.
- There are alternative psychological explanations such as Beck's theory.

NURTURE

- Influences of experience, i.e. what is learned.
- Includes interactions with both physical and social environment.
- Supported by: empiricists (all knowledge is gained through experience as in 'empirical research').

ASSUMPTIONS
Behaviourist theory
- Main assumption: all behaviour is the result of learning through classical or operant conditioning. Neo-behaviourists include social learning through observation, indirect reinforcement.
  For example:
  – explaining attachment in terms of secondary reinforcement
  – social learning explanations of gender and personality development and aggression (Bobo doll studies).

- Behaviourist explanations lend themselves to empirical investigation.
- Learning itself has a genetic basis because it relies on neural mechanisms.
- e.g. Mutant fruit flies who don't have a crucial gene can't be conditioned (Quinn et al., 1979).

NATURE AND NURTURE

- Hebb compared it to the relative contributions of length and width to the area of a rectangle.

ASSUMPTIONS
Explaining perceptual development
- Innate biological system (e.g. orientation cells in visual cortex) affected by experience in experiment with kittens (Blakemore and Cooper, 1970) – kittens raised in vertical strip cylinder were blind to horizontal lines.
Piaget's theory of cognitive development
- Biological structures unfold when placed in a nurturing environment.
Intelligence
- Traditional view was that intelligence was a fixed, inherited ability.
- More recent projects like Head Start emphasised environmental component.

- The neural plasticity shown by Blakemore and Cooper's experiment makes good sense – it is advantageous for the brain to adapt to environmental conditions.
- Vygotsky's theory of cognitive development placed greater emphasis on nurture (cultural influences) but also recognised innate elementary functions (e.g. attention and sensation).

DIFFERENT VIEWS REGARDING THE RELATIONSHIP BETWEEN NATURE AND NURTURE

MUST REMEMBER...
- To focus on the **relationship** between nature and nurture.

GENE-ENVIRONMENT INTERACTIONS

- Genes may directly influence the environment, for example:
  - an attractive baby is smiled at more frequently which makes the baby more friendly – attractiveness is innate, changes the environment (people smile more) which affects behaviour;
  - we may choose certain experiences because they fit best with our innate preferences.

- Three types of gene-environment relationships (Azar, 1997):
  - passive relationship: parent's genetic characteristics determine a child's environment
  - evocative relationship: genetically distinct individuals evoke different reactions in those around them
  - active relationship: individuals actively seek experiences that fit their innate preferences.

- Thus correlation between parent and child due to direct and indirect influences (e.g. for IQ).
- Supported by: Braungart et al. (1992) who found a higher correlation between HOME (measure of home environment) scores and IQ for children and their biological parents than children and their adopted parents.

- Scarr and McCartney (1983) call this **niche picking** – explains findings from Texas Adoption Project (Horn, 1983) that adoptive children's IQ become closer to biological relatives as they get older and less close to adoptive families.

REACTION RANGE

GOTTESMAN (1963)

- Experience affects the development of any skill, e.g. your height is affected by your diet.
- But this development is limited by our biological endowment.
- The same genotype can lead to phenotypes depending on life experiences.

- The description of gene-environment interactions may fail to go far enough in expressing the relationship between nature and nurture – it isn't just nature that is affected by experience but genes themselves are affected by nurture, as expressed by Ridley.
- Scarr and McCartney (1983) call this niche picking. As children grow older, they seek out experiences and environments that suit their genes. This explains why the influence of genes increases and the influence of shared environment gradually disappears with age.

Can use material on nature and nurture.

NATURE VIA NURTURE

RIDLEY (2003)

- Genes don't simply interact with the environment but they are activated by experience.
- Switching is performed by tiny stretches of DNA called promoters.
- Some of these promoters are affected by our environments.
- This explains how nurture has such a profound impact on the individual, because it influences living organisms via their genes.

- An interesting extension of this new understanding is that genetic explanations can now be reframed as examples of free will rather than being determinist. Genes do not hardwire our behaviours but provide a means of responding to the demands of the environment.
- Evidence from Mirnics et al. (2001) – the gene RSG4 is low in schizophrenics but its activity is lowered further when individuals experience acute stress. This is an explanation of the diathesis-stress model at the level of genes.

TYPICAL QUESTIONS...

1 (a) Explain what is meant by nature and nurture in Psychology. (5 marks)

  (b) Discuss assumptions made about nature **and/or** nurture in **two** psychological theories. (25 marks)

2 Critically consider assumptions made about nature and nurture in psychological theories **and/or** studies. (30 marks)

3 Discuss different views regarding the relationship between nature and nurture. (30 marks)

THE BEHAVIOURAL APPROACH

KEY CONCEPTS OF THE BEVAVIOURAL APPROACH

LEARNING THEORY

- All behaviour can be explained through observable stimuli and responses.
- Behaviour change occurs without thought.

SOCIAL LEARNING THEORY

- Observational learning – vicarious (indirect reinforcement leads to modelling) and then direct reinforcement.

Operant conditioning

- Learning through reinforcement/consequences.
- An animal operates in its environment.
- A particular behaviour may be rewarded or punished which increases or decreases the likelihood that it will be repeated.
- Rewards are also called reinforcers.
- Positive reinforcement occurs when the reward is pleasant.
- Negative reinforcement is also pleasant but is a consequence of escaping from something that was unpleasant!
- Continuous schedules induce rapid initial learning and rapid extinction whereas the opposite is true of partial reinforcement.

Classical conditioning

- Learning through association.
- Unconditioned stimulus (UCS) produces unconditioned response (UCR).
- UCS associated with neutral stimulus (NS) which acquires the properties of the UCS.
- NS becomes a conditioned stimulus (CS) and produces conditioned response (CR).

Shaping

- Organism is initially rewarded for quite simple behaviours.
- Gradually the rewards are reserved for behaviours that are closer and closer to the target behaviour.

KEY CONCEPTS OF LEARNING THEORY

Generalisation, discrimination and extinction

- Things that are learned are generalised to similar situations.
- If subsequent experience produces no further association or reinforcement, then the learned response will become extinguished.
- An organism learns to discriminate between different stimuli.

Indirect reinforcement and modelling

- Behaviour is imitated (modelled) if there is an expectation of success due to vicarious reinforcement.

Observational learning

- Organisms learn indirectly by observing the behaviours of others.
- Organisms store representations of behaviour and expectancies of future outcomes.

Direct reinforcement

- If a behaviour is imitated, then it may or may not receive direct reinforcement.

KEY CONCEPTS OF SOCIAL LEARNING THEORY

Self-efficacy

- A person's sense of their own effectiveness.
- Self-efficacy is derived from both direct and indirect experience.

Reciprocal determinism

- As an individual acts, this changes their environment, thus affecting subsequent behaviour.
- Individuals are capable of making their own choices and this ultimately affects what they imitate.

STRENGTHS AND LIMITATIONS OF THE BEHAVIOURAL APPROACH

STRENGTHS

- It is a scientific approach. Reductionism can be a strength because it permits variables to be operationalised and experiments conducted to test explanations.

- Can explain individual differences – due to different reinforcement experiences.

- Social learning theory has the additional advantage of including social influences and thus explaining cultural as well as individual differences.

LIMITATIONS

- Determinist, which has implications for moral responsibility and self-responsibility.

- Reductionist – reduces all behaviour to stimulus–response units:
  - complex human behaviours often have multiple influences, such as emotion and thought
  - complex systems may not behave predictably, i.e. as a simple summation of the constituent parts.

- Based on research with non-human animals, findings may not apply to human behaviour.

- Research in contrived laboratory environments which do not represent the complexities of real life. Such studies also focus on short-term effects and may not demonstrate how longer-term behaviours are learned.

METHODOLOGY

MUST REMEMBER...
To present a plausible method.

LAB EXPERIMENT

- With human or animal participants:
  - identify IV and DV
  - operationalise these variables
  - write a hypothesis
  - select experimental design (e.g. repeated measures or independent groups)
  - identify and control any possible extraneous variables
  - decide on sampling technique to use
  - decide how to deal with any ethical issues
  - decide how to analyse the data.

STRENGTHS

- Objective and controlled so that we can make statements about cause-and-effect relationships.

- Experiments can also be replicated as a way of verifying the findings.

LIMITATIONS

- Low internal validity may be due to:
  - experimenter bias or demand characteristics
  - confounding variables that were not controlled
  - operationalisation: results in studying something that may be different to the thing originally interested in.

- Low external validity – findings may not generalise to situations and/or participants outside the experiment.

- Studies of non-human animal behaviour may not generalise to human behaviour.

- Ethical issues with human participants, reinforcing new behaviours means that participants don't leave experiment in the same condition as when they started.

THE PSYCHODYNAMIC APPROACH

THE KEY CONCEPTS OF THE PSYCHODYNAMIC APPROACH

THE PSYCHODYNAMIC METAPHOR
- The working of the mind is explained in terms of:
  - an analogy with an iceberg: a large part of the mind (the unconscious) is under the surface
  - a dramatic conflict between different forces struggling for control.

THE STRUCTURE OF THE MIND

Id	Unconscious, primitive, instinctive, wants immediate satisfaction, not concerned with social rules.	From birth.	**Pleasure principle:** seeks gratification, avoids pain.
Ego	Conscious, rational mind; considers consequences of an action; modifies demands of id.	During first two years.	**Reality principle:** accommodates to demands of the environment.
Superego	Conscience and sense of right and wrong.	Around age of five.	**Sexual conflicts** (e.g. Oedipus) reconciled through identification with same-sex parent.

DYNAMICS OF THE PERSONALITY
- Pleasure and reality principles.
- Drives.
- Libido.

LIBIDO AND PSYCHOSEXUAL STAGES
- Each stage characterised by a focus on a different region of the body.
- An individual's sexual drive or libido is focused on that part of the body during the particular period and requires gratification.
- If right amount of gratification not received (too much or too little), we become fixated in a particular stage.

STAGE	Pleasure from...	Frustration leads to...	Overindulgence leads to...
Oral (0–18 months)	Mouth.	**Oral aggressive:** dominating.	**Oral receptive:** gullible, dependent.
Anal (18–36 months)	Expelling/ withholding faeces.	**Anal-retentive:** rigid, possessive.	**Anal-explusive:** reckless, disorganised.
Phallic (3–6 months)	Own and parents' genitals.	**Phallic personality:** vain, impulsive.	**Conflict** may lead to homosexuality, authority problems.
Genital (puberty)	Genitals.	Unresolved issues restrict development of **independence**.	

DRIVES
- Two drives (instincts) motivate all behaviour:
  - sex (Eros, the Life force) represents drive to live, prosper and reproduce
  - aggression (Thanatos, Death force) represents need to stay alive and stave off threats to our existence.
- When sexual instinct is high, id demands gratification.
- But superego may oppose demands for sexual gratification because of conflict with social morality.
- Ego is caught between conflicting demands from id (immediate gratification) and superego (conform to moral conventions).
- Helped by ego defences.

EGO DEFENCES
- Ego defences unconsciously reduce anxiety.
- May cause abnormal personality development.

For example:
- Repression places anxieties into the unconscious.
- Regression deals with anxiety by returning to an earlier, safer stage of development.
- Displacement of unacceptable feelings onto someone/something else.

STRENGTHS AND LIMITATIONS OF THE PSYCHODYNAMIC APPROACH

STRENGTHS

- There is support for some of the concepts, such as:
  - repression studied by Myers and Brewin (1994) – found link between personality type and tendency to repress anxiety-provoking childhood memories
  - Oedipus complex demonstrated in study of Little Hans (Freud, 1909)
  - importance of early childhood experiences to later development shown in Love Quiz (Hazan and Shaver, 1987).
- Reductionist explanations may help us to understand certain basic processes in behaviour.
- Subsequent psychodynamic theories (such as Erikson's) gave more weight to social influences.
- Recognises unconscious motivation which permits us to explain how someone can be both rational and irrational, e.g. when people predict they will behave in one way and actually do something quite different.

LIMITATIONS

- Lacks empirical support largely because the concepts are not falsifiable (i.e. cannot be demonstrated to be wrong – they can be made to fit).
- Research that was conducted used biased sample (white, middle-class, female Europeans) and normal personality development based on abnormal individuals.
- Reductionist, which tends to oversimplify complex behaviours and may prevent us from investigating more complex and possibly more useful explanations.
- Overemphasises sexual influences, which may have been important in 19th C. society, but are less applicable today.
- Determinist account – denies individual's ability to self-determine despite evidence for free will, e.g. people do make choices from a limited repertoire.

METHODOLOGY

CASE HISTORY

Aim

To see if psychodynamic explanations can account for an individual's behaviour by looking at their early experiences. Techniques used to enable unconscious thoughts to be revealed.

EXPERIMENTS

- See page 130.

Free association

- Client expresses free flow of feelings, thoughts and images without censorship.
- Therapist may ask for more elaboration or for comment on the personal significance of any associations.

Dream analysis

- Discussions of dream content may be a way to access the unconscious mind.
- Therapist has to attempt to understand the symbolic form (manifest content) of the dream.

STRENGTHS

- Interviewer can adjust questions as a response to previous answers and thus build up a complex picture of human behaviour and experience which provides rich data and may better represent real life.

LIMITATIONS

- Low internal validity due to the affect of interviewer's expectations on participant's recollections.
- Low external validity – hard to generalise from case histories which concern unique experiences of only a few individuals.

THE BIOLOGICAL APPROACH

KEY CONCEPTS OF THE BIOLOGICAL APPROACH

PHYSIOLOGICAL METAPHOR
- Looking at people as if they are biological machines.
- Concerned with the structure and biochemistry of the nervous system.

EVOLUTIONARY METAPHOR
- Behaviour has developed in the same way our bodies have.
- Features that are adaptive to the environment are passed on.

Brain organisation
- Two hemispheres – each have different characteristics.
- Left is verbal processing, analytic/logical (Sperry, 1985).
- Right is visuo-spatial processing and emotion, holistic.
- Areas of the brain:
  - prefrontal cortex for forward planning
  - limbic system for emotions
  - hypothalamus contains the pleasure centre which can explain reinforcement.
- Brain damage may lead to characteristic behaviours.

Brain chemistry: neurotransmitters
- Effects vary depending on neuron acted on.
- Morphine mimics body's natural pain relievers (endorphins).
- Adrenaline for arousal, and fight or flight.
- Serotonin – low levels lead to depression, impulsive aggression; slightly increased levels lead to happiness; too much leads to fearfulness and shyness.
- Dopamine creates intense feelings from any enjoyable activity.

Hormones
- Biochemical substances that have a profound effect on behaviour; quickly disappear if not secreted continuously.
- Testosterone (testicles) influences aggressiveness.
- Oxytocin (pituitary) reduces stress; tend and befriend.
- Pheromones, released by one individual and affect the behaviour of another of the same species.

KEY CONCEPTS OF THE PHYSIOLOGICAL APPROACH

Autonomic nervous system
- Parasympathetic division governs the resting state.
- Sympathetic division linked to adrenaline and bodily arousal – fight or flight.

Natural selection
- Characteristics that promote survival and reproduction are naturally selected.
- Only applies to genetically-determined behaviours.
- Genetic characteristics of those who do not breed are lost.
- Selective pressure exerted by social and physical environment.
- It is the characteristics that are selected, not the individuals or the species.

Sexual selection
- Traits solely concerned with increasing reproductive success are naturally selected and retained.
- Leads to more successful reproduction.
- Males tend to compete and females are selectors because of egg–sperm differences.

KEY CONCEPTS OF THE EVOLUTIONARY APPROACH

Mental modules
- Underlying psychological mechanisms (mental modules), not behaviours, are selected.
- Genetically-determined modules selected in the EEA.
- These are ultimate rather than proximate explanations of behaviour.

Kin selection
- An individual may pass on their genes to future generations not just by means of their own reproductive success but also by facilitating the reproductive success of genetic relatives.
- Inclusive fitness describes an individual's own fitness plus his or her effect on the fitness of any relative.

STRENGTHS AND LIMITATIONS OF THE BIOLOGICAL APPROACH

STRENGTHS

- It is a **scientific approach**. Describes causal relationships. Determinism/reductionism can be a strength because it leads to experimental research to test explanations.

- Theoretical reductionism can be good because one way to understand complex behaviours is to break them down into smaller units.

- Can explain some individual differences, e.g. gender differences and differences due to abnormal development.

- Physiological explanations have **useful applications**, e.g. drug therapies for mental illness (though, arguably, such treatments have not been that successful).

- Evolutionary explanations consider ultimate rather than proximate causes, and thus may lead to more valid ways of treating apparently maladaptive behaviours.

LIMITATIONS

- **Determinist approach** that suggests our behaviour is not subject to free will.

- Reductionist explanations may be undesirable because selecting the wrong level may prevent a truer understanding of a behaviour.

- Biological explanations can't explain cultural differences nor some individual differences, e.g. why people respond differently to the same drugs, nor why they react differently to stress situations.

- Based on research with non-human animals, physiological and evolutionary explanations may apply less to more complex human behaviour which is affected by many other factors such as emotion and thought.

- Evolutionary theory is difficult to falsify; the arguments can be made to fit the facts.

- Human behaviour must be subject to continuing selective pressures and not just governed by the EEA.

MUST REMEMBER...

To present an appropriate method for the named approach.

METHODOLOGY

PHYSIOLOGICAL APPROACH

- Experiments (see page 130) using techniques such as:
  - **electrical stimulation** to observe behavioural effects
  - **chemical stimulation** to test effects of neurotransmitters and hormones
  - **ablation/lesioning in animals** and extrapolate to humans
  - studying brain damage, brain tumours, etc.
  - EEG to assess patterns of electrical activity
  - MRI scan to build up 3D picture of brain and fMRI
  - PET scan: radioactive glucose used to detect active areas of the brain.

STRENGTHS

- Well-controlled studies; high internal validity.

LIMITATIONS

- Can't assume that you have found the ultimate cause, e.g. studies mistakenly assume that effects of brain damage due to the area of brain damaged.

- Low external validity – may not be able to generalise from animal studies or brain-damaged individuals.

EVOLUTIONARY APPROACH

- With **human** or **animal** participants:
  - **gene mapping** studies can be used to demonstrate genetic basis of a behaviour
  - **family studies** (twins, adoptees, etc.) can be used to demonstrate genetic basis
  - **experiments** or **surveys** may be used to test some hypotheses, e.g. male/female preferences for mate selection
  - **cross-cultural studies** can show what behaviours are universal and thus presumably genetic/adaptive.

LIMITATIONS

- Family studies don't demonstrate causal relationships because quasi-experiments.

- Experiments operationalise behaviours leading to oversimplification.

- Surveys affected by social desirability bias or interviewer bias.

INDEX

ACE model 12
action slips 46
activation-synthesis model 35
active learning 63
adolescence
    behaviour and culture 80
    identity formation 77–8, 80
    relationship and culture 78–9
adoption studies 65, 97, 99
aggression 13–14, 15, 23
alpha bias 69, 70, 113, 114, 115
altruism 17, 18, 70
    in animal behaviour 81, 82
androcentrism 113
androgeny, psychological 113
animal behaviour
    classical conditioning 83–4
    and evolution 81–2
    intelligence 88
    operant conditioning 85–6
    in psychological research 119–20
    and social learning 87
anti-social behaviour
    aggression 13–14
    stressors 15–16
    media influences 23–4
anxiety disorders 92, 96, 101–4
approval oriented behaviour 67
attention 43–6
    and recognition 47–8
attentional slips 46
attraction, interpersonal 1–2
automatic nervous system 133
automatic processing 46
autonomy 77, 79, 80

Bandura 21, 23, 108
Bandura's theory 73, 74
basic rest activity cycle (BRAC) 25, 26
behaviour
    aggression 13–14
    altruism/bystanders 17–18
    cultural differences 19–20
    stressors 15–16
    and evolution 89–94
    media influences on 21–4
    and moral understanding 67
    see also animal behaviour
behavioural approach 129–30, 133
behavioural explanations
    free will/determinism 121
    mental disorders 99, 100, 102, 104
    nature–nurture debate 127
    reductionism 124
behavioural specificity 73
behavioural therapies 107–8
Bergin 110, 121
beta bias 69, 113, 114, 115

bias
    cultural 115–16
    gender 113–14, 121
Binkley 25, 27
binocular visual perception 53
biochemical explanations, mental
    disorders 101, 103
biological approach 133–4
biological explanations
    animal behaviour 82, 84
    mental disorders 97, 101, 103
biological mechanisms, recognition
    47
biological rhythms 25–36
biological therapies 105–6
Blos 77, 79
body-weight set-point 37
Bower 55, 57
BRAC 25, 26
brain
    biological approach 133
    size of 94
    structures 37–8, 41
breakdown, of relationships 7–8
Broadbent 43, 44
bystander behaviour 17, 18, 117

Cannon-Bard theory 41
capacity/resource allocation model 45
carpentered world hypothesis 51, 56
chemotherapy 105, 106
Cherry 43, 44
child-centred cognitive theories
    59–60, 63, 75–6
child-centred families 9
circadian rhythms 25, 26
circannual rhythms 25
classical conditioning (CC) 2, 83–4,
    129
    therapies based on 107, 108
CLT 42
CMC 12
cognitive behavioural therapies
    111–12
cognitive development
    intelligence tests 65–6
    moral understanding 67–70
    Piaget's theory 59–60, 63, 115, 127
    Vygotsky's theory 61–2, 64, 115
cognitive explanations
    free will/determinism 121
    mental disorders 98, 100
    reductionism 124
cognitive labelling theory 42
cognitive models
    anti-social behaviour 23
    bystander behaviour 17, 18
cognitive-behavioural explanations of
    mental disorders 100, 104

cognitive-developmental theory of
    gender development 76
    see also social cognitive theory
Coleman 77, 79
collaborative learning 64
collectivist cultures 9, 19, 70, 80, 115
colour processing 50
combined approaches
    to emotion 42
    to learning 64
    to motivation 39
competence 1
complementarity 1
computer mediated communication
    12
concept formation 61
concrete operational development
    59, 60
confidentiality 118
conflicting cues theory 51
constancies, visual 54
constructivist theories of visual
    perception 51, 52, 54, 57
contrast processing 50
controlled processing 46
Cooper et al. 77, 79
core sleep theory 31, 32
creativity, and dreams 33
cross-cultural studies 56, 115, 116
crowding, as stressor 16
crowds, football violence 14
cultural bias 115–16
cultural differences
    adolescent behaviour 80
    moral understanding 70
    and nightmares 34
    pro-social behaviour 19–20
    relationships 9–10, 19
cultural influences
    cognitive development 61, 62, 66
    emotional experience 5
    perceptual processes 56, 58
    phobias 102
Czeisler et al. 26, 28

Davidson 86, 118
daylight, as zeitgeber 27
deception 117
deindividuation theory 13
depression 92, 95, 99–100
deprivation studies 58
depth perception 53, 55, 56
desensitisation 23
determinism 121, 122, 130, 132, 134
developmental trends 21
    see also cognitive development;
        perceptual processes; social and
        personal development
differentiation theory 57

direct theories of visual perception 52, 54, 57
discovery learning 63, 64
discrimination 129
distress 67
divided attention 45
divorce rates 10
dopamine hypothesis 97
dreams/dreaming 33–6
drive-reduction theory 39
drives 131
drugs, therapeutic 105, 106
dual-centre hypothalmic model of hunger 37
Duck's model of relationship dissolution 7

ecological theories
   of intelligence 93
   of sleep 29–30
ECT 105, 106
ego 71, 131
eight stages of man 71, 77
Eisenberg's theory 67, 68
Ellis 111, 112
EMIC–ETIC dimension 115
emotion 41–2
   as content of dreams 33
   see also love; motivation
emotional harm 110
emotional intimacy 11
empathetic (transitional) behaviour 67
empathy, and moral understanding 67
empathy–altruism model 17
empiricist explanations 57, 127
enactive experience 75
endogenous pacemakers 27
endothermy, and sleep 30
energy conservation, and sleep 29, 30
enrichment theory of visual development 57
environment, and intelligence tests 66
environmental reductionism 124
environmental stressors 15–16
equitable treatment 118
Erikson's theory 71, 72, 77
estrocentrism 113
ethical issues 117–18, 122
ethnic minorities 80
evolutionary approach
   animal behaviour 81–2
   human behaviour 89–94
   methodology 134
   nature–nurture debate 127
evolutionary metaphor 133
evolutionary reductionism 124
exogenous zeitgebers 27
expectancy theory 40
expressed emotion (EE) 98

extinction 129
eye 49

face recognition 48, 55
facial features 89
families
   adolescent relations with 79
   child-centred 9
   and depression 99
   mental disorders in 97, 98, 101, 103
feature detection/processing 47, 50
females see women
feminist psychology 113
filter model 1, 2
Flynn effect 66
focal theory 77
focused attention 43–4
football crowd violence 14
formal operational development 59, 60
free will 121, 122
Freud 77, 100, 102, 104, 113, 132
Freudian theories
   of dreaming 36
   of personality 71, 72
friendship 9

GABA 101
gay relationships 11
gender
   behavioural differences 20
   brain size differences 94
   differences and relationships 9
   and moral understanding 69
   and nightmares 34
   same-sex relationships 11
   social development 75–6
gender bias 113–14, 121
gene-environment interactions 128
generalisation 129
genetics 65
   and mental disorders 97, 101, 103
Gibson 33, 47, 52, 53, 57
Gilligan's theories
   of moral development 113
   stage theory 69
glucostat hypothesis of hunger 37
Gregory 51, 52, 57
guanxixue 19

hedonistic behaviour 67
help-seeking 20
heterosexual/non-heterosexual relations 11
hierarchy of needs (Maslow) 40
Hill and Kaplan 89, 93
Hobson and McCarley 35, 36
homeostatic drives 39
hormones 99, 133
Horn 16, 65, 128
Horne 31, 32

human behaviour see behaviour
humanistic approach 121
hunger, and motivation 37
hypnopompic/hypnogogic dreams 34
hypothalmic model of hunger 37
hypovolemic thirst 38

id 71, 131
identity, adolescent 77–8, 80
illusions, visual 51, 54, 56
imitation 87
imposed etic 19, 116
individual planes 61, 62
individualist cultures 9, 19, 70, 80, 115
individuated behaviour 13
infants' perceptual development 55, 58
   see also cognitive development
information
   invariant 52
   visual processing of 50
information overload 20
informed consent 117
infradian rhythms 25, 26
instinctive behaviour 86, 131
intelligence
   in animals 88
   in humans 93–4, 127
intelligence tests 65–6
internalised moral behaviour 67
interpersonal attraction 1–2
invariant information 52
involuntary relationships 10
IQ scores 65, 66, 128

James–Lange theory 41
Jensen 80, 118
jet lag 28
justification 23

Kendler et al. 97, 99, 101
kin selection 81, 82, 133
Kohlberg's theories
   of gender consistency 76
   of moral reasoning 67, 68, 69, 113, 115
Kuhn 125, 126

language 61, 62
learning theory 64, 129
   see also social learning theory
legislation 119
lesbian relationships 11
Lewis 43, 44
light, as zeitgeber 27
limbic system 41
love
   cultural differences 10
   psychological explanations 5–6
   see also emotion
lucid dreaming 33, 34

machine reductionism 124
maintenance difficulties 7, 8
males see men
Marcia's theory 78
marriages 9, 10
Martin and Halverson's theory of
    gender schema 76
Maslow's hierarchy of needs 40
matching hypothesis 1, 2
mate choice 89
McNaughten and Leyland 58, 64
Mead 77, 80
Meddis' theory of sleep 30
media
    and aggression 13, 23
    influences on behaviour 21–4
mediated relationships 12
Meichenbaum 111, 112
melatonin 27, 28
men
    gender roles 20
    husbands 9
    parental investment 90
menstrual cycle 25, 26, 89
mental disorders 95–104
    and evolution 91–2
    treatment of 105–12
mental modules 133
methodologies 118, 130, 132, 134
Milgram 20, 117
Miller 19, 94, 102
mind, theory of 88, 131
Mischel's theory 73, 74
modelling 73, 75, 129
modular theories, divided attention
    45
monocular visual perception 53
mood regulation hypothesis 36
moral development theory 113, 115
moral understanding 67–70
moral universalism 70
morality, stages of 67
Morgan's law of parsimony 123
motivation 37–40
    in cognitive development 63, 64
    see also emotion
movement, perception of 53, 56
Müller-Lyer illusion 51
Myers and Brewin 72, 132

nativist explanations 57
natural selection 81, 133
nature–nurture debate 127–8
    in animal behaviour 81
    in perception 58
needs oriented behaviour 3, 67
negative thinking 100
networking 19
neuroanatomical explanations of
mental disorders 103
neurobiological theories of
    dreaming 35

neurotransmitter theories 99, 133
nightmares 33, 34
non-human animals see animal
behaviour
NREM sleep 29, 30
    and dreaming 33
nurture see nature–nurture debate

observational learning 23, 73, 129
OCD 92, 96, 103–4
operant conditioning 2, 85–6, 129
    therapies based on 107
optic array 52
optimal arousal theory 40
osmotic thirst 38
Oswald's restoration theory 31–2

Palmer 47, 51
parental investment 90
parents, adolescents' relations with
    79
pattern recognition 47
peer relationships 79
peer tutoring 64
perceptual development 55–7, 127
perceptual processes 49–58
permanent/impermanent relationships
    10
person variables 73
personality development 71–4
    psychodynamic explanations 71–2,
    131
    social learning explanations 73–4
phobias 92, 96, 101–2
physical attractiveness 1, 2
physiological approach
    methodology 134
    and reductionism 124
    to emotion 5, 41–2
    to motivation 39
physiological metaphor 133
Piaget's theory 59–60, 63, 115, 127
pictorial cues 51, 55, 56
pineal gland 27
pleasure centres 38
pre-operational development 59, 60
precognitive dreams 34
predator avoidance 30
preparedness 84, 86, 92, 102
primate life style 94
privacy 117, 118
private self-awareness 13
pro-social behaviour
    and altruism 17, 18
    cultural differences in 19–20
    media influences on 21–2
    and moral understanding 70
pro-social messages 21
pro-social reasoning 67–70
processing, controlled/automatic 46
prototype theory 47
proximity 1, 2

psychoanalysis 109, 110, 113
psychodrama 109, 110
psychodynamic approach 131–2
psychodynamic explanations
    free will/determinism 121
    mental disorders 100, 102, 104
    personality development 71–2
psychodynamic therapies 109–10
psychological approaches
    dreaming 36
    emotion 42
    free will 122
    mental disorders 98, 100, 104
    motivation 40
psychological harm 117
psychology as a science 125–6
psychopathology 95–104
psychosexual development 71
psychosurgery 105, 106
public self-awareness 13

racial differences
    in brain size 94
    and intelligence tests 66
reasoning
    pro-social 67–70
    theory of moral 113, 115
REBT 111, 112
reciprocal determinism 73, 129
recognition 47–8
    and attention 43–6
    and perception 55
reduced cues theory 12
reductionism 123–4, 130, 132, 134
reinforcement
    of aggression 13
    direct and indirect 73, 129
    in operant conditioning 85
reinforcement-affect theory 3
relationships 1–12
    in different cultures 9–10, 19, 78
relativism, moral 70
REM sleep 29, 31
    and dreaming 33, 34, 35
reproductive behaviour 89
responsibility, diffusion of 20
rest, and sleep 29
restoration theory of sleep 31–2
retina 49
reverse learning model 35
romantic love 6
rural see urban–rural differences

SAD (seasonal affective disorder) 26
same-sex relationships 11
scaffolding 62, 64
Scarr and McCartney 65, 128
Scarr and Weinberg 65, 66
schema theory, of attentional slips 46
schizophrenia 95, 97–8
science 125–6
scientific freedom 118, 120

SCN 27
selection, natural/sexual 81, 89, 133
selective attention 43
self-awareness
   in animals 88
   public and private 13
self-centred behaviour 67
self-efficacy 73, 129
Seligman 100, 102
semiotic mediation 61
sensorimotor development 59, 60
sensory adaptation 50
sexual love 6
sexual selection 81, 89, 133
shape constancy 54, 56, 129
shift work 28
SIDE model 12
similarity 1, 2
situationism 73
size constancy 54, 55, 56
Skinner 119, 124
sleep 29–32
   and dreaming 33, 34, 35
sleep stages 25
sleep-wake cycle 25, 26
slips, automatic and attentional 46
SLT 13, 14, 21, 129
SMS-based relationships 12
Snarey et al. 68, 70
social and personal development
   71–80
social cognitive theory of gender
   development 75
   see also cognitive-developmental
      theory
social competition hypothesis 91
social cues, as zeitgebers 27
social density 16
social exchange theory 4

social intelligence
   in animals 88
   in humans 93
social learning explanations 73–4, 87,
   94
social learning theory 13, 14, 21, 129
social navigation hypothesis 91
social planes 61, 62
socially sensitive research 118
spatial density 16
SSR 118
stereotypes, gender 20, 76
stress
   environmental stressors 15–16
   storm and stress 77, 80
   and ultradian rhythms 26
stress-inoculation model 111, 112
superego 71, 131
suprachiasmatic nucleus 27
survival of the fittest 81
SWS, and bodily restoration 31

taste-aversion conditioning 84
teacher-centred cognitive theories
   61–2, 64
temperature
   and circadian rhythm 25, 26
   as stressor 15
template theory 47
texting 12
theory of mind 88
therapies 105–10
thinking
   development of 61
   and moral understanding 67
   negative 100
thirst, and motivation 38
three-factor theory 5, 6
time, in dreaming 33

treatment of mental disorders
   105–12
Treisman 43, 44
triangular theory of love 5, 6
Trivers 81, 82, 90
twin studies 65, 97, 101

ultradian rhythms 25, 26
unilateral sleep 29
urban–rural differences
   behavioural 20, 80
   crowding in cities 16
   in moral understanding 70

violent crime 15
visual constancies/illusions 54, 56
visual pathways 49
visual perception 49–58
visual system 49
voluntary relationships 10
Vygotsky's theory 61–2, 64, 115

Webb's theory, of sleep 30
women
   gender roles 20, 69
   parental investment 90
wives 9

ZDP 61, 62
zeitgebers 27
zone of proximal development 61, 62